# THE IMPORTANCE
# OF BEING EARNEST

## AND

## OTHER PLAYS

D1102256

OSCAR WILDE

# THE
# IMPORTANCE OF
# BEING EARNEST

AND

# OTHER PLAYS

*Introduction by Terrence McNally*

*Notes by Michael F. Davis*
LEMOYNE COLLEGE

THE MODERN LIBRARY

NEW YORK

Library of Congress Cataloging-in-Publication Data

Wilde, Oscar, 1854–1900.
The importance of being earnest and other plays / Oscar Wilde ;
introduction by Terrence McNally ; notes by Michael F. Davis.—2003
Modern Library paperback ed.
p.   cm.
Includes bibliographical references.
Contents: Lady Windermere's fan—An ideal husband—
The importance of being earnest.
ISBN 0-8129-6714-3
I. Title.

PR5815 2003
822'.8—dc21       2003044566

# OSCAR WILDE

Oscar Wilde was born in Dublin in 1854. His father was a celebrated surgeon, his mother a supporter of Irish independence who presided over literary salons in Ireland and England. Although his brilliance as a classicist at Dublin's Trinity College won him a scholarship to Magdalen College, Oxford, Wilde failed in his attempts at an academic career. Instead he set his sights on the literary and artistic worlds of London. Fusing the influences of Ruskin, the Pre-Raphaelites, Walter Pater, and Gautier's *l'art pour l'art*, he made himself the most visible manifestation of the Aesthetic movement; by 1881 a burlesque of Wilde provided the protagonist for the Gilbert and Sullivan operetta *Patience*. It was to exploit the popularity of the operetta, in fact, that the producer D'Oyly Carte underwrote Wilde's immensely successful lecture tour of America. Married in 1884 to Constance Lloyd, Wilde worked briefly as a magazine editor while publishing poetry, plays, fairy tales, and essays.

*The Picture of Dorian Gray* was commissioned by J.M. Stoddardt, the Philadelphia publisher of *Lippincott's Monthly Magazine*. It appeared in the July 1890 issue and immediately gained a certain notoriety for being "mawkish and nauseous," "unclean," "effeminate," and "contaminating." When it was published as a book the following year, Wilde greatly revised and expanded the text, filling it out with a melodramatic subplot and adding a preface that defended his aesthetic philosophy. As for the book's value as autobiography, Wilde noted in a letter that the main characters are in different ways reflections of him: "Basil Hallward is what I think I am; Lord Henry what the world thinks me; Dorian what I would like to be—in other ages, perhaps."

In the early nineties, Wilde was at the center of an artistic milieu characterized by *The Yellow Book,* the Rhymers' Club, and the art of Aubrey Beardsley. He wrote a poetic drama, *Salomé,* in French (1892), but it was banned in England; the play was published in book form with illustrations by Beardsley in 1894. *Salomé* was produced in Paris in 1896.

However, Wilde did achieve success as a popular playwright, writing in rapid succession *Lady Windermere's Fan, A Woman of No Importance, An Ideal Husband,* and *The Importance of Being Earnest.* In 1895, two of his plays were on the London stage simultaneously, and he was acknowledged as a pivotal figure in English literary life, admired for his wit and eloquence.

Since at least the mid-1880s, Wilde had lived a sexual double life, and in 1893 he distanced himself from his family by taking rooms at the Savoy Hotel. He had by then embarked on a passionate relationship with the considerably younger Lord Alfred Douglas, the English translator of *Salomé* whom he had met the year after he wrote *The Picture of Dorian Gray.* In March 1895, Wilde undertook a libel action against the Marquess of Queensberry, Lord Alfred's father, who had denounced Wilde as a "somdomite" [sic]. Wilde withdrew the suit following damaging cross-examination by the marquess's defense attorney, a former classmate of Wilde's. (Question: "Have you ever adored a young man madly?" Answer: "I have never given adoration to anybody except myself.") Shortly thereafter, Wilde was arrested for homosexual offenses and underwent two trials before being sentenced to hard labor at Wandsworth Prison and Reading Gaol. A long recriminatory letter to Douglas written while in prison was eventually published as *De Profundis.*

Released in 1897, Wilde left for France, calling himself Sebastian Melmoth, a name taken from the gothic novel *Melmoth the Wanderer*, written by Wilde's great-uncle. A poem based on his prison experience, *The Ballad of Reading Gaol*, was published in 1898.

His health destroyed, and bankrupted by legal expenses, Wilde lived in Paris for three years, making a conversion to Roman Catholicism just before his death in November 1900. He is buried in the cemetery of Père Lachaise.

# Contents

# INTRODUCTION

*Terrence McNally*

You are holding in your hand a volume of plays by Oscar Wilde, including the funniest, most subversive play in the English language, *The Importance of Being Earnest*. More than a century after its first performance in London at St. James's Theatre on February 14, 1895, it is fresh, pertinent, and very, very rude. It is a play that calls society's bluff by naming each and every one of us a hypocrite. If it weren't so funny, we would shun its bleak view of human society. No one likes to be made a fool of for a full evening in the theatre. And yet it is precisely because it *is* so spectacularly uproarious that we console ourselves that surely the playwright can't be that serious. Society is not that morally bankrupt, is it? Is it?

The answer to that question is not to be found in Wilde's plays but in his life itself. Wilde's opinions on this and that subject are everywhere in his plays. They are, in fact, the entire fabric of his theatre work. Wilde the man is somewhere else. I think we glimpse him occasionally in a poem or two, but it is not until after the catastrophe of his trial on charges of "gross indecency"—a sorry and ultimately fatal episode in his short, brilliant life that was instigated by Wilde's literally thumbing his nose at his titled male lover's outraged father—and subsequent imprisonment that we meet a recognizable fellow human being. The ravaged man in Reading Gaol who gives us *De Profundis,* with its bleak indictment of the human condition, would more than likely have left *Importance,* a work of infectious and deliberate shallowness, after the first interval.

Being a great "character" came naturally to Oscar. He was a journalist's delight: he was eccentric in dress and behavior, he spoke in exquisite bon mots, he was famous for simply being Oscar Wilde before he had written anything worth reading. He had a flair for being famous. It became him and he possessed it naturally. He even seemed to welcome the trial that would bring about his downfall, never doubting that he would emerge from his tribulations in the dock even more famous, notorious, and adored than before.

Being a great man came with more difficulty. It came of physical suffering, public humiliation, and almost total abandonment by those who should have cared for him most. His exile in France in the final few years of his life is one of the most painful third acts in English letters.

Not surprisingly, Wilde is still more interesting as a personality than any of the characters in his plays. Many a great actress has delighted audiences with her Lady Bracknell, but no matter who the actress playing her is—Dame Maggie Smith or Edith Evans—she cannot trump the author himself. Wilde will always be the definitive Lady Bracknell—the one we take home with us when the play is over. You can be a great Wildean actor, but Oscar himself will always be the star of the evening. Chekhov and Shakespeare's plays are always about Uncle Vanya and Falstaff and never about the playwrights themselves. A volume entitled *The Philosophy of William Shakespeare* would be a very slender volume indeed. Wilde's plays, on the other hand, are about nothing *but* Oscar. This diminishes them, of course, in the pantheon of great plays (is Wilde's name ever mentioned in the same breath as the Heavyweights?), but still they burn, especially *Importance,* with a brilliant comic light that for sheer technique is unsurpassed. Line for line, there is no better example of comic writing than *Importance.*

One can soon grow weary of quoting Oscar's funniest or most pithy one-liners. There are that many of them. Indeed, there is an entire cottage industry in slender volumes calling themselves "The Wit" or "The Best" or "The Funniest" of Oscar Wilde. He is quoted almost as endlessly as Shakespeare or the King James Version of the Holy Bible. "I have nothing to declare but my genius," Wilde said when he visited the United States to lecture the rubes on Aesthetics in 1882. "A little sincerity is a dangerous thing," he writes in an essay, "and a great deal of it is absolutely fatal." Such wit is clever—and cruel. Cruel about the world around him and equally lacerating to himself: "Crying is the refuge of plain women, but the ruin of pretty ones."

One can admire Wilde's comic technique endlessly, but any attempt to emulate it is doomed to failure. Wilde is a *sui generis* genius. Only a very great fool would attempt to write like him. Verbal dexterity is the be-all and end-all of Wilde's comedy. It is the play of and with words that delights us. The situations are rather routine, in fact—no French-farce banging of doors or mistaken identities in Algernon's flat on Half-Moon Street, and the notion of physical comedy is positively alien to the Wildean spirit. Jerry Lewis or Jim Carrey would be a disaster as *Importance*'s two gay deceivers.

I use "gay" in the sense of charming, witty, keeping-it-light. Wilde was a gay man, but there is not much point or fun in reading his plays as encoded depictions of his sexuality. Wilde saved that part of himself for his unflinching final pieces, written when he was imprisoned and punished by the same society he had made such a brilliant career of ridiculing.

Today, Wilde's escapades as a dandy, an aesthete, or a homosexual would still draw much media attention, but he would not end up in Reading Gaol for them. Instead, one can imagine Oscar being knighted by Her Majesty, the Queen, and certainly he would have been one of Princess Diana's favorites. Think Boy George and Elton John. This absolute turnabout in society's attitudes toward the sexual outlaw from outsider to *insider* is no small part of the legacy of Wilde's public flamboyant life.

After the disgrace of his trial and imprisonment, the producer of *Importance* took Wilde's name off billboards and out of the program.

Suddenly, Wilde's brilliant West End success was an anonymously authored one. I don't know exactly when the restoration of Wilde's reputation began (it surely must have started with a producer brave enough to restore Wilde's billing in the playbill), but I do remember that his name was never once mentioned in my high school English literature course. This was in Texas in the late 1950s.

As a very young man dealing with my own sexuality, I had certainly heard rumors about this Oscar Wilde fella. There was a "reason" he wasn't read in our classroom. His name conjured up the evil of the Marquis de Sade and his scandal was the stuff wild adolescent myths are made on. When our drama club put on *Importance* I could get none of my teachers to tell me anything I wanted to know about its author. He was just a man who wrote this very funny play, end of story. I went to the school library and looked him up in the encyclopedia, making sure no one saw who I was searching for in the "W's." To my disappointment, there were references to Wilde's imprisonment on "moral" charges but nothing more specific than that. I wanted to know if Oscar Wilde slept with other men.

In college, by the time I was sleeping with other men, I think even a fifteen year old knew that Oscar Wilde was a homosexual. He was suddenly out of the closet, along with a lot of other cultural and moral shibboleths, and the world very quickly became a very different place.

The other plays in this volume are less interesting. They are chock-full of Wilde's delicious, immortal epigrams (and that is imperative enough to read and enjoy them, and sufficient reason for their continuing revivals and occasional filmings), but they rarely transcend the characters' conventionality or the now-tedious melodramatic situations in which they find themselves. (Ibsen worked these same situations with more dramatic cunning if a good deal less humor.) If Wilde's reputation rested solely on these other works, there would be little reason for this new edition.

As for *Salomé*, it is best read as what my teachers used to call a "closet" drama; i.e., a play that is best experienced in the study and not performed. The title role was written for the great Sarah Bernhardt, who deemed it "unplayable." Dramatic history would seem to have proved her right.

"My name has two 'O's', two 'F's', and two 'W's'," Wilde wrote in 1885. He had been christened Oscar Fingal O'Flahertie Wills Wilde in Dublin in 1854. "A name which is destined to be in everyone's mouth must not be too long," he continued. "It comes too expensive in the advertisements. . . . All but two of my names have already been thrown overboard. Soon I shall discard another and be known as 'The Wilde' or 'The Oscar.' "

It is ironic that Wilde, an Irishman, is generally thought of as some sort of *über* Englishman. Like many Irish writers, Wilde was quick to get the hell out of Ireland and never look back. But if braggadocio is an Irish trait, Wilde was Irish to his fingertips. He never doubted his genius or his success, both of which were considerable. At one point in his relatively short life (he died at forty-six), he was arguably the most famous man of letters in the world and yet he had written relatively little. His greatest play, *Importance,* was thirteen years in the future when he toured America as a personality and lecturer on the Aesthete. Jaded New Yorkers and unwashed gold prospectors turned out in record numbers to see him: Oscar Wilde was famous for being Oscar Wilde. If that isn't the beginning of the cult of literary personality and the author as celebrity, I don't know what is. (Truman Capote and Lillian Hellman were latecomers to that particular game.) If there had been a Blackglama Mink "What Becomes A Celebrity Most?" photo-ad campaign in 1895, the year of *Importance*'s sensational premiere—just weeks before his even more sensational downfall at the hands of Lord Alfred Douglas's enraged father, the Marquess of Queensberry—Wilde would have been the most likely candidate for this tabloid immortalization.

Instead, he was banished to anonymity for the rest of his sad life, and then some. He was reviled, forgotten, and then reviled all over again. Today, his disgrace in the courtroom would have only increased his stature as a celebrity and his drawing power at the box office.

Oscar would have had something to say about all this, of course. Something amusing.

———

TERRENCE MCNALLY'S plays include *Love! Valour! Compassion!* and *Master Class.* In addition to four Tony Awards, McNally has received two Guggenheim Fellowships and a Rockefeller Grant, among many other honors. He lives in New York City.

# A NOTE ON THE TEXT

The text is set from the first published edition of each play. After theatre productions of the plays, Wilde had time to implement changes, often substantial ones, in time for their first publications. While *Lady Windermere's Fan* appeared in print approximately a year and a half after its stage debut, in 1893, in an edition by E. Mathews and J. Lane, *An Ideal Husband* and *The Importance of Being Earnest* were not published until 1899, by Leonard Smithers, as a result of Wilde's trial, imprisonment, and exile.

# Lady Windermere's Fan

## Fan

A PLAY ABOUT A GOOD WOMAN

To

THE DEAR MEMORY

OF

ROBERT EARL OF LYTTON

IN AFFECTION

AND

ADMIRATION

# THE PERSONS OF THE PLAY

LORD WINDERMERE
LORD DARLINGTON
LORD AUGUSTUS LORTON
MR. DUMBY
MR. CECIL GRAHAM
MR. HOPPER
PARKER, Butler

LADY WINDERMERE
THE DUCHESS OF BERWICK
LADY AGATHA CARLISLE
LADY PLYMDALE
LADY STUTFIELD
LADY JEDBURGH
MRS. COWPER-COWPER
MRS. ERLYNNE
ROSALIE, Maid

# LONDON: ST. JAMES'S THEATRE

*Lessee and Manager: Mr. George Alexander*
*February 22nd, 1892*

LORD WINDERMERE  *Mr. George Alexander*
LORD DARLINGTON  *Mr. Nutcombe Gould*
LORD AUGUSTUS LORTON  *Mr. H. H. Vincent*
MR. CECIL GRAHAM  *Mr. Ben. Webster*
MR. DUMBY  *Mr. Vane-Tempest*
MR. HOPPER  *Mr. Alfred Holles*
PARKER (*Butler*)  *Mr. V. Sansbury*
LADY WINDERMERE  *Miss Lily Hanbury*
THE DUCHESS OF BERWICK  *Miss Fanny Coleman*
LADY AGATHA CARLISLE  *Miss Laura Graves*
LADY PLYMDALE  *Miss Granville*
LADY JEDBURGH  *Miss B. Page*
LADY STUTFIELD  *Miss Madge Girdlestone*
MRS. COWPER-COWPER  *Miss A. De Winton*
MRS. ERLYNNE  *Miss Marion Terry*
ROSALIE (*Maid*)  *Miss Winifred Dolan*

# FIRST ACT

SCENE—*Morning-room of Lord Windermere's house in Carlton House Ter-race. Doors C. and R. Bureau with books and papers R. Sofa with small tea-table L. Window opening on to terrace L. Table R.*
    *(Lady Windermere is at table R., arranging roses in a blue bowl.)*
    *(Enter Parker.*

PARKER. Is your ladyship at home this afternoon?

LADY WINDERMERE. Yes—who has called?

PARKER. Lord Darlington, my lady.

LADY WINDERMERE. *(Hesitates for a moment.)* Show him up—and I'm at home to any one who calls.

PARKER. Yes, my lady.

*(Exit C.*

LADY WINDERMERE. It's best for me to see him before to-night. I'm glad he's come.

*(Enter Parker C.*

PARKER. Lord Darlington.

*(Enter Lord Darlington C.*

*(Exit Parker.*

LORD DARLINGTON. How do you do, Lady Windermere?

LADY WINDERMERE. How do you do, Lord Darlington? No, I can't shake hands with you. My hands are all wet with these roses. Aren't they lovely? They came up from Selby this morning.

LORD DARLINGTON. They are quite perfect. *(Sees a fan lying on the table.)* And what a wonderful fan! May I look at it?

LADY WINDERMERE. Do. Pretty, isn't it! It's got my name on it, and everything. I have only just seen it myself. It's my husband's birthday present to me. You know to-day is my birthday?

LORD DARLINGTON. No? Is it really?

LADY WINDERMERE. Yes, I'm of age to-day. Quite an important day in my life, isn't it? That is why I am giving this party to-night. Do sit down. *(Still arranging flowers.)*

LORD DARLINGTON. *(Sitting down.)* I wish I had known it was your birthday, Lady Windermere. I would have covered the whole street in front of your house with flowers for you to walk on. They are made for you. *(A short pause.)*

LADY WINDERMERE. Lord Darlington, you annoyed me last night at the Foreign Office. I am afraid you are going to annoy me again.

LORD DARLINGTON. I, Lady Windermere?

*(Enter Parker and Footman C., with tray and tea things.*

LADY WINDERMERE. Put it there, Parker. That will do. *(Wipes her hands with her pocket-handkerchief, goes to tea-table L., and sits down.)* Won't you come over, Lord Darlington?

*(Exit Parker C.*

LORD DARLINGTON. *(Takes chair and goes across L.C.)* I am quite miserable, Lady Windermere. You must tell me what I did. *(Sits down at table L.)*

LADY WINDERMERE. Well, you kept paying me elaborate compliments the whole evening.

LORD DARLINGTON. *(Smiling.)* Ah, now-a-days we are all of us so hard up, that the only pleasant things to pay *are* compliments. They're the only things we *can* pay.

LADY WINDERMERE. *(Shaking her head.)* No, I am talking very seriously. You mustn't laugh, I am quite serious. I don't like compliments, and I don't see why a man should think he is pleasing a woman enormously when he says to her a whole heap of things that he doesn't mean.

LORD DARLINGTON. Ah, but I did mean them. *(Takes tea which she offers him.)*

LADY WINDERMERE. *(Gravely.)* I hope not. I should be sorry to have to quarrel with you, Lord Darlington. I like you very much, you know that. But I shouldn't like you at all if I thought you were what most other men are. Believe me, you are better than most other men, and I sometimes think you pretend to be worse.

LORD DARLINGTON. We all have our little vanities, Lady Windermere.

LADY WINDERMERE. Why do you make that your special one? *(Still seated at table L.)*

LORD DARLINGTON. *(Still seated L.C.)* Oh, now-a-days so many conceited people go about Society pretending to be good, that I think it shows rather a sweet and modest disposition to pretend to be bad. Besides, there is this to be said. If you pretend to be good, the world takes you very seriously. If you pretend to be bad, it doesn't. Such is the astounding stupidity of optimism.

LADY WINDERMERE. Don't you *want* the world to take you seriously then, Lord Darlington?

LORD DARLINGTON. No, not the world. Who are the people the world takes seriously? All the dull people one can think of, from the Bishops down to the bores. I should like *you* to take me very seriously, Lady Windermere, *you* more than any one else in life.

LADY WINDERMERE. Why—why me?

LORD DARLINGTON. *(After a slight hesitation.)* Because I think we might be great friends. Let us be great friends. You may want a friend some day.

LADY WINDERMERE. Why do you say that?

LORD DARLINGTON. Oh!—we all want friends at times.

LADY WINDERMERE. I think we're very good friends already, Lord Darlington. We can always remain so as long as you don't——

LORD DARLINGTON. Don't what?

LADY WINDERMERE. Don't spoil it by saying extravagant silly things to me. You think I am a Puritan, I suppose? Well, I have something of the Puritan in me. I was brought up like that. I am glad of it. My mother died when I was a mere child. I lived always with Lady Julia, my father's elder sister you know. She was stern to me, but she taught me, what the world is forgetting, the difference that there is between what is right and what is wrong. *She* allowed of no compromise. *I* allow of none.

LORD DARLINGTON. My dear Lady Windermere!

LADY WINDERMERE. *(Leaning back on the sofa.)* You look on me as being behind the age.—Well, I am! I should be sorry to be on the same level as an age like this.

LORD DARLINGTON. You think the age very bad?

LADY WINDERMERE. Yes. Now-a-days people seem to look on life as a speculation. It is not a speculation. It is a sacrament. Its ideal is Love. Its purification is sacrifice.

LORD DARLINGTON. *(Smiling.)* Oh, anything is better than being sacrificed!

LADY WINDERMERE. *(Leaning forward.)* Don't say that.

LORD DARLINGTON. I do say it. I feel it—I know it.

*(Enter Parker C.*

PARKER. The men want to know if they are to put the carpets on the terrace for to-night, my lady?

LADY WINDERMERE. You don't think it will rain, Lord Darlington, do you?

LORD DARLINGTON. I won't hear of its raining on your birthday!

LADY WINDERMERE. Tell them to do it at once, Parker.

*(Exit Parker C.*

LORD DARLINGTON. *(Still seated.)* Do you think then—of course I am only putting an imaginary instance—do you think that in the case of a young married couple, say about two years married, if the husband suddenly becomes the intimate friend of a woman of—well, more than doubtful character, is always calling upon her, lunching with her, and probably paying her bills—do you think that the wife should not console herself?

LADY WINDERMERE. *(Frowning.)* Console herself?

LORD DARLINGTON. Yes, I think she should—I think she has the right.

LADY WINDERMERE. Because the husband is vile—should the wife be vile also?

LORD DARLINGTON. Vileness is a terrible word, Lady Windermere.

LADY WINDERMERE. It is a terrible thing, Lord Darlington.

LORD DARLINGTON. Do you know I am afraid that good people do a great deal of harm in this world. Certainly the greatest harm they do is that they make badness of such extraordinary importance. It is absurd to divide people into good and bad. People are either charming or tedious. I take the side of the charming, and you, Lady Windermere, can't help belonging to them.

LADY WINDERMERE. Now, Lord Darlington. *(Rising and crossing R., front of him.)* Don't stir, I am merely going to finish my flowers. *(Goes to table R.C.)*

LORD DARLINGTON. *(Rising and moving chair.)* And I must say I think you are very hard on modern life, Lady Windermere. Of course there is much against it, I admit. Most women, for instance, now-a-days, are rather mercenary.

LADY WINDERMERE. Don't talk about such people.

LORD DARLINGTON. Well then, setting mercenary people aside, who, of course, are dreadful, do you think seriously that women who have committed what the world calls a fault should never be forgiven?

LADY WINDERMERE. *(Standing at table.)* I think they should never be forgiven.

LORD DARLINGTON. And men? Do you think that there should be the same laws for men as there are for women?

LADY WINDERMERE. Certainly!

LORD DARLINGTON. I think life too complex a thing to be settled by these hard and fast rules.

LADY WINDERMERE. If we had "these hard and fast rules," we should find life much more simple.

LORD DARLINGTON. You allow of no exceptions?

LADY WINDERMERE. None!

LORD DARLINGTON. Ah, what a fascinating Puritan you are, Lady Windermere!

LADY WINDERMERE. The adjective was unnecessary, Lord Darlington.

LORD DARLINGTON. I couldn't help it. I can resist everything except temptation.

LADY WINDERMERE. You have the modern affectation of weakness.

LORD DARLINGTON. *(Looking at her.)* It's only an affectation, Lady Windermere.

*(Enter Parker C.*

PARKER. The Duchess of Berwick and Lady Agatha Carlisle.

*(Enter the Duchess of Berwick and Lady Agatha Carlisle C.*

*(Exit Parker C.*

DUCHESS OF BERWICK. *(Coming down C., and shaking hands.)* Dear Margaret, I am so pleased to see you. You remember Agatha, don't you? *(Crossing L.C.)* How do you do, Lord Darlington? I won't let you know my daughter, you are far too wicked.

LORD DARLINGTON. Don't say that, Duchess. As a wicked man I am a complete failure. Why, there are lots of people who say I have never really done anything wrong in the whole course of my life. Of course they only say it behind my back.

DUCHESS OF BERWICK. Isn't he dreadful? Agatha, this is Lord Darlington. Mind you don't believe a word he says. *(Lord Darlington crosses R.C.)* No, no tea, thank you, dear. *(Crosses and sits on sofa.)* We have just had tea at Lady Markby's. Such bad tea, too. It was quite undrinkable. I wasn't at all surprised. Her own son-in-law supplies it. Agatha is looking forward so much to your ball to-night, dear Margaret.

LADY WINDERMERE. *(Seated L.C.)* Oh, you mustn't think it is going to be a ball, Duchess. It is only a dance in honour of my birthday. A small and early.

LORD DARLINGTON. *(Standing L.C.)* Very small, very early, and very select, Duchess.

DUCHESS OF BERWICK. *(On sofa L.)* Of course it's going to be select. But we know *that,* dear Margaret, about *your* house. It is really one of the few houses in London where I can take Agatha, and where I feel perfectly secure about dear Berwick. I don't know what society is coming to. The most dreadful people seem to go everywhere. They certainly come to my parties—the men get quite furious if one doesn't ask them. Really, some one should make a stand against it.

LADY WINDERMERE. *I* will, Duchess. I will have no one in my house about whom there is any scandal.

LORD DARLINGTON. *(R.C.)* Oh, don't say that, Lady Windermere. I should never be admitted! *(Sitting.)*

DUCHESS OF BERWICK. Oh, men don't matter. With women it is different. We're good. Some of us are, at least. But we are positively getting elbowed into the corner. Our husbands would really forget our existence if we didn't nag at them from time to time, just to remind them that we have a perfect legal right to do so.

LORD DARLINGTON. It's a curious thing, Duchess, about the game of marriage—a game, by the way, that is going out of fashion—the wives hold all the honours, and invariably lose the odd trick.

DUCHESS OF BERWICK. The odd trick? Is that the husband, Lord Darlington?

LORD DARLINGTON. It would be rather a good name for the modern husband.

DUCHESS OF BERWICK. Dear Lord Darlington, how thoroughly depraved you are!

LADY WINDERMERE. Lord Darlington is trivial.

LORD DARLINGTON. Ah, don't say that, Lady Windermere.

LADY WINDERMERE. Why do you *talk* so trivially about life, then?

LORD DARLINGTON. Because I think that life is far too important a thing ever to talk seriously about it. *(Moves up C.)*

DUCHESS OF BERWICK. What does he mean? Do, as a concession to my poor wits, Lord Darlington, just explain to me what you really mean.

LORD DARLINGTON. *(Coming down back of table.)* I think I had better not, Duchess. Now-a-days to be intelligible is to be found out. Good-bye! *(Shakes hands with Duchess.)* And now—*(goes up stage)* Lady Windermere, good-bye. I may come to-night, mayn't I? Do let me come.

LADY WINDERMERE. *(Standing up stage with Lord Darlington.)* Yes, certainly. But you are not to say foolish, insincere things to people.

LORD DARLINGTON. *(Smiling.)* Ah! you are beginning to reform me. It is a dangerous thing to reform any one, Lady Windermere.

*(Bows, and exit C.*

DUCHESS OF BERWICK. *(Who has risen, goes C.)* What a charming, wicked creature! I like him so much. I'm quite delighted he's gone! How sweet you're looking! Where *do* you get your gowns? And now I must tell you how sorry I am for you, dear Margaret. *(Crosses to sofa and sits with Lady Windermere.)* Agatha darling!

LADY AGATHA. Yes, mamma. *(Rises.)*

DUCHESS OF BERWICK. Will you go and look over the photograph album that I see there?

LADY AGATHA. Yes, mamma. *(Goes to table up L.)*

DUCHESS OF BERWICK. Dear girl! She is so fond of photographs of Switzerland. Such a pure taste, I think. But I really am so sorry for you, Margaret.

LADY WINDERMERE. *(Smiling.)* Why, Duchess?

DUCHESS OF BERWICK. Oh, on account of that horrid woman. She dresses so well, too, which makes it much worse, sets such a dreadful example. Augustus—you know my disreputable brother—such a trial to us all—well, Augustus is completely infatuated about her. It is quite scandalous, for she is absolutely inadmissible into society. Many a woman has a past, but I am told that she has at least a dozen, and that they all fit.

LADY WINDERMERE. Whom are you talking about, Duchess?

DUCHESS OF BERWICK. About Mrs. Erlynne.

LADY WINDERMERE. Mrs. Erlynne? I never heard of her, Duchess. And what *has* she to do with me?

DUCHESS OF BERWICK. My poor child! Agatha, darling!

LADY AGATHA. Yes, mamma.

DUCHESS OF BERWICK. Will you go out on the terrace and look at the sunset?

LADY AGATHA. Yes, mamma.

*(Exit through window L.*

DUCHESS OF BERWICK. Sweet girl! So devoted to sunsets! Shows such refinement of feeling, does it not? After all, there is nothing like Nature, is there?

LADY WINDERMERE. But what is it, Duchess? Why do you talk to me about this person?

DUCHESS OF BERWICK. Don't you really know? I assure you we're all so distressed about it. Only last night at dear Lady Jansen's every one was saying how extraordinary it was that, of all men in London, Windermere should behave in such a way.

LADY WINDERMERE. My husband—what has *he* got to do with any woman of that kind?

DUCHESS OF BERWICK. Ah, what indeed, dear? That is the point. He goes to see her continually, and stops for hours at a time, and while he is there she is not at home to any one. Not that many ladies call on her, dear, but she has a great many disreputable men friends—my own brother particularly, as I told you—and that is what makes it so dreadful about Windermere. We looked upon *him* as being such a model husband, but I am afraid there is no doubt about it. My dear nieces—you know the Saville girls, don't you?—such nice domestic creatures—plain, dreadfully plain, but so good—well, they're always at the window doing fancy work, and making ugly things for the poor, which I think so useful of them in these dreadful socialistic days, and this terrible woman has taken a house in Curzon Street, right opposite them—such a respectable street, too. I don't know what we're coming to! And they tell me that Windermere goes there four and five times a week—they *see* him. They can't help it—and although they never talk scandal, they—well, of course—they remark on it to every one. And the worst of it all is that I have been told that this woman has got a great deal of money out of somebody, for it seems that she came to London six months ago without anything at all to speak of, and now she has this charming house in Mayfair, drives her ponies in the Park every afternoon and all—well, all—since she has known poor dear Windermere.

LADY WINDERMERE. Oh, I can't believe it!

DUCHESS OF BERWICK. But it's quite true, my dear. The whole of London knows it. That is why I felt it was better to come and talk to you, and advise you to take Windermere away at once to Homburg or to Aix, where he'll have something to amuse him, and where you can watch him all day long. I assure you, my dear, that on several occasions after I was first married, I had to pretend to be very ill, and was obliged to drink the most unpleasant mineral waters, merely to get Berwick out of town. He was so extremely susceptible. Though I am bound to say he never gave away any large sums of money to anybody. He is far too high-principled for that!

LADY WINDERMERE. *(Interrupting.)* Duchess, Duchess, it's *impossible*! *(Rising and crossing stage to C.)* We are only married two years. Our child is but six months old. *(Sits in chair R. of L. table.)*

DUCHESS OF BERWICK. Ah, the dear pretty baby! How is the little darling? Is it a boy or a girl? I hope a girl—Ah, no, I remember it's a boy! I'm so sorry. Boys are so wicked. My boy is excessively immoral. You wouldn't believe at what hours he comes home. And he's only left Oxford a few months—I really don't know what they teach them there.

LADY WINDERMERE. Are *all* men bad?

DUCHESS OF BERWICK. Oh, all of them, my dear, all of them, without any exception. And they never grow any better. Men become old, but they never become good.

LADY WINDERMERE. Windermere and I married for love.

DUCHESS OF BERWICK. Yes, we begin like that. It was only Berwick's brutal and incessant threats of suicide that made me accept him at all, and before the year was out, he was running after all kinds of petticoats, every colour, every shape, every material. In fact, before the honeymoon was over, I caught him winking at my maid, a most pretty, respectable girl. I dismissed her at once without a character.—No, I remember I passed her on to my sister; poor dear Sir George is so short-sighted, I thought it wouldn't matter. But it did, though—it was most unfortunate. *(Rises.)* And now, my dear child, I must go, as we are dining out. And mind you don't take this little aberration of Windermere's too much to heart. Just take him abroad, and he'll come back to you all right.

LADY WINDERMERE. Come back to me? *(C.)*

DUCHESS OF BERWICK. *(L.C.)* Yes, dear, these wicked women get our husbands away from us, but they always come back, slightly damaged, of course. And don't make scenes, men hate them!

LADY WINDERMERE. It is very kind of you, Duchess, to come and tell me all this. But I can't believe that my husband is untrue to me.

DUCHESS OF BERWICK. Pretty child! I was like that once. Now I know that all men are monsters. *(Lady Windermere rings bell.)* The only thing to do is to feed the wretches well. A good cook does wonders, and that I know you have. My dear Margaret, you are not going to cry?

LADY WINDERMERE. You needn't be afraid, Duchess, I never cry.

DUCHESS OF BERWICK. That's quite right, dear. Crying is the refuge of plain women but the ruin of pretty ones. Agatha, darling!

LADY AGATHA. *(Entering L.)* Yes, mamma. *(Stands back of table L.C.)*

DUCHESS OF BERWICK. Come and bid good-bye to Lady Winder-mere, and thank her for your charming visit. *(Coming down again.)* And by the way, I must thank you for sending a card to Mr. Hopper—he's that rich young Australian people are taking such notice of just at present. His father made a great fortune by selling some kind of food in circular tins—most palatable, I believe—I fancy it is the thing the servants always refuse to eat. But the son is quite interesting. I think he's attracted by dear Agatha's clever talk. Of course, we should be very sorry to lose her, but I think that a mother who doesn't part with a daughter every season has no real affection. We're coming to-night, dear. *(Parker opens C. doors.)* And remember my advice, take the poor fellow out of town at once, it is the only thing to do. Good-bye, once more; come, Agatha.

*(Exeunt Duchess and Lady Agatha C.*

LADY WINDERMERE. How horrible! I understand now what Lord Darlington meant by the imaginary instance of the couple not two years married. Oh! it can't be true—she spoke of enormous sums of money paid to this woman. I know where Arthur keeps his bank book—in one of the drawers of that desk. I might find out by that. I *will* find out. *(Opens drawer.)* No, it is some hideous mistake. *(Rises and goes C.)* Some silly scandal! He loves *me*! He loves *me*! But why should I not look? I am his wife, I have a right to look! *(Returns to bureau, takes out book and examines it, page by page, smiles and gives a sigh of relief.)* I knew it! there is not a word of

truth in this stupid story. *(Puts book back in drawer. As she does so, starts and takes out another book.)* A second book—private—locked! *(Tries to open it, but fails. Sees paper knife on bureau, and with it cuts cover from book. Begins to start at the first page.)* "Mrs. Erlynne—£600—Mrs. Erlynne—£700—Mrs. Erlynne—£400." Oh! it is true! it is true! How horrible! *(Throws book on floor.)*
*(Enter Lord Windermere C.*

LORD WINDERMERE. Well, dear, has the fan been sent home yet? *(Going R.C. Sees book.)* Margaret, you have cut open my bank book. You have no right to do such a thing!

LADY WINDERMERE. You think it wrong that you are found out, don't you?

LORD WINDERMERE. I think it wrong that a wife should spy on her husband.

LADY WINDERMERE. I did not spy on you. I never knew of this woman's existence till half an hour ago. Some one who pitied me was kind enough to tell me what every one in London knows already—your daily visits to Curzon Street, your mad infatuation, the monstrous sums of money you squander on this infamous woman! *(Crossing L.)*

LORD WINDERMERE. Margaret! don't talk like that of Mrs. Erlynne, you don't know how unjust it is!

LADY WINDERMERE. *(Turning to him.)* You are very jealous of Mrs. Erlynne's honour. I wish you had been as jealous of mine.

LORD WINDERMERE. Your honour is untouched, Margaret. You don't think for a moment that——*(Puts book back into desk.)*

LADY WINDERMERE. I think that you spend your money strangely. That is all. Oh, don't imagine I mind about the money. As far as I am concerned, you may squander everything we have. But what I *do* mind is that you who have loved me, you who have taught me to love you, should pass from the love that is given to the love that is bought. Oh, it's horrible! *(Sits on sofa.)* And it is I who feel degraded! *You* don't feel anything. I feel stained, utterly stained. You can't realise how hideous the last six months seem to me now—every kiss you have given me is tainted in my memory.

LORD WINDERMERE. *(Crossing to her.)* Don't say that, Margaret. I never loved any one in the whole world but you.

LADY WINDERMERE. *(Rises.)* Who is this woman, then? Why do you take a house for her?

LORD WINDERMERE. I did not take a house for her.

LADY WINDERMERE. You gave her the money to do it, which is the same thing.

LORD WINDERMERE. Margaret, as far as I have known Mrs. Erlynne——

LADY WINDERMERE. Is there a Mr. Erlynne—or is he a myth?

LORD WINDERMERE. Her husband died many years ago. She is alone in the world.

LADY WINDERMERE. No relations? *(A pause.)*

LORD WINDERMERE. None.

LADY WINDERMERE. Rather curious, isn't it? *(L.)*

LORD WINDERMERE. *(L.C.)* Margaret, I was saying to you—and I beg you to listen to me—that as far as I have known Mrs. Erlynne, she has conducted herself well. If years ago——

LADY WINDERMERE. Oh! *(Crossing R.C.)* I don't want details about her life!

LORD WINDERMERE. *(C.)* I am not going to give you any details about her life. I tell you simply this—Mrs. Erlynne was once honoured, loved, respected. She was well born, she had position—she lost everything—threw it away, if you like. That makes it all the more bitter. Misfortunes one can endure—they come from outside, they are accidents. But to suffer for one's own faults—ah!—there is the sting of life. It was twenty years ago, too. She was little more than a girl then. She had been a wife for even less time than you have.

LADY WINDERMERE. I am not interested in her—and—you should not mention this woman and me in the same breath. It is an error of taste. *(Sitting R. at desk.)*

LORD WINDERMERE. Margaret, you could save this woman. She wants to get back into society, and she wants you to help her. *(Crossing to her.)*

LADY WINDERMERE. Me!

LORD WINDERMERE. Yes, you.

LADY WINDERMERE. How impertinent of her! *(A pause.)*

LORD WINDERMERE. Margaret, I came to ask you a great favour, and I still ask it of you, though you have discovered what I had intended you should never have known, that I have given Mrs. Erlynne a large sum of money. I want you to send her an invitation for our party to-night. *(Standing L. of her.)*

LADY WINDERMERE. You are mad! *(Rises.)*

LORD WINDERMERE. I entreat you. People may chatter about her, do chatter about her, of course, but they don't know anything definite against her. She has been to several houses—not to houses where you would go, I admit, but still to houses where women who are in what is called Society now-a-days do go. That does not content her. She wants you to receive her once.

LADY WINDERMERE. As a triumph for her, I suppose?

LORD WINDERMERE. No; but because she knows that you are a good woman—and that if she comes here once she will have a chance of a happier, a surer life than she has had. She will make no further effort to know you. Won't you help a woman who is trying to get back?

LADY WINDERMERE. No! If a woman really repents, she never wishes to return to the society that has made or seen her ruin.

LORD WINDERMERE. I beg of you.

LADY WINDERMERE. *(Crossing to door R.)* I am going to dress for dinner, and don't mention the subject again this evening. Arthur *(Going to him C.)*, you fancy because I have no father or mother that I am alone in the world, and that you can treat me as you choose. You are wrong, I have friends, many friends.

LORD WINDERMERE. *(L.C.)* Margaret, you are talking foolishly, recklessly. I won't argue with you, but I insist upon your asking Mrs. Erlynne to-night.

LADY WINDERMERE. *(R.C.)* I shall do nothing of the kind. *(Crossing L.C.)*

LORD WINDERMERE. You refuse? *(C.)*

LADY WINDERMERE. Absolutely!

LORD WINDERMERE. Ah, Margaret, do this for my sake; it is her last chance.

LADY WINDERMERE. What has that to do with me?

LORD WINDERMERE. How hard good women are!

LADY WINDERMERE. How weak bad men are!

LORD WINDERMERE. Margaret, none of us men may be good enough for the women we marry—that is quite true—but you don't imagine I would ever—oh, the suggestion is monstrous!

LADY WINDERMERE. Why should *you* be different from other men? I am told that there is hardly a husband in London who does not waste his life over *some* shameful passion.

LORD WINDERMERE. I am not one of them.

LADY WINDERMERE. I am not sure of that!

LORD WINDERMERE. You are sure in your heart. But don't make chasm after chasm between us. God knows the last few minutes have thrust us wide enough apart. Sit down and write the card.

LADY WINDERMERE. Nothing in the whole world would induce me.

LORD WINDERMERE. *(Crossing to bureau.)* Then I will! *(Rings electric bell, sits and writes card.)*

LADY WINDERMERE. You are going to invite this woman? *(Crossing to him.)*

LORD WINDERMERE. Yes.

*(Pause. Enter Parker.*

Parker!

PARKER. Yes, my lord. *(Comes down L.C.)*

LORD WINDERMERE. Have this note sent to Mrs. Erlynne at No. 84A Curzon Street. *(Crossing to L.C. and giving note to Parker.)* There is no answer!

*(Exit Parker C.*

LADY WINDERMERE. Arthur, if that woman comes here, I shall insult her.

LORD WINDERMERE. Margaret, don't say that.

LADY WINDERMERE. I mean it.

LORD WINDERMERE. Child, if you did such a thing, there's not a woman in London who wouldn't pity you.

LADY WINDERMERE. There is not a *good* woman in London who would not applaud me. We have been too lax. We must make an example. I propose to begin to-night. *(Picking up fan.)* Yes, you gave me this fan to-day; it was your birthday present. If that woman crosses my threshold, I shall strike her across the face with it.

LORD WINDERMERE. Margaret, you couldn't do such a thing.

LADY WINDERMERE. You don't know me! *(Moves R.)*

*(Enter Parker.*

Parker!

PARKER. Yes, my lady.

LADY WINDERMERE. I shall dine in my own room. I don't want dinner, in fact. See that everything is ready by half-past ten. And, Parker, be sure you pronounce the names of the guests very distinctly to-night. Sometimes you speak so fast that I miss them. I am particularly anxious to hear the names quite clearly, so as to make no mistake. You understand, Parker?

PARKER. Yes, my lady.

LADY WINDERMERE. That will do!

*(Exit Parker C.*

*(Speaking to Lord Windermere.)* Arthur, if that woman comes here—I warn you——

LORD WINDERMERE. Margaret, you'll ruin us!

LADY WINDERMERE. Us! From this moment my life is separate from yours. But if you wish to avoid a public scandal, write at once to this woman, and tell her that I forbid her to come here!

LORD WINDERMERE. I will not—I cannot—she must come!

LADY WINDERMERE. Then I shall do exactly as I have said. *(Goes R.)* You leave me no choice.

*(Exit R.*

LORD WINDERMERE. *(Calling after her.)* Margaret! Margaret! *(A pause.)* My God! What shall I do? I dare not tell her who this woman really is. The shame would kill her. *(Sinks down into a chair and buries his face in his hands.)*

## ACT DROP

# SECOND ACT

*SCENE—Drawing-room in Lord Windermere's house. Door R.U. opening into ball-room, where band is playing. Door L. through which guests are entering. Door L.U. opens on to illuminated terrace. Palms, flowers, and brilliant lights. Room crowded with guests. Lady Windermere is receiving them.*

DUCHESS OF BERWICK. *(Up C.)* So strange Lord Windermere isn't here. Mr. Hopper is very late, too. You have kept those five dances for him, Agatha? *(Comes down.)*

LADY AGATHA. Yes, mamma.

DUCHESS OF BERWICK. *(Sitting on sofa.)* Just let me see your card. I'm so glad Lady Windermere has revived cards.—They're a mother's only safeguard. You dear simple little thing! *(Scratches out two names.)* No nice girl should ever waltz with such particularly younger sons! It looks so fast! The last two dances you might pass on the terrace with Mr. Hopper.

*(Enter Mr. Dumby and Lady Plymdale from the ball-room.*

LADY AGATHA. Yes, mamma.

DUCHESS OF BERWICK. *(Fanning herself.)* The air is so pleasant there.

PARKER. Mrs. Cowper-Cowper. Lady Stutfield. Sir James Royston. Mr. Guy Berkeley.

*(These people enter as announced.)*

DUMBY. Good evening, Lady Stutfield. I suppose this will be the last ball of the season?

LADY STUTFIELD. I suppose so, Mr. Dumby. It's been a delightful season, hasn't it?

DUMBY. Quite delightful! Good evening, Duchess. I suppose this will be the last ball of the season?

DUCHESS OF BERWICK. I suppose so, Mr. Dumby. It has been a very dull season, hasn't it?

DUMBY. Dreadfully dull! Dreadfully dull!

MRS. COWPER-COWPER. Good evening, Mr. Dumby. I suppose this will be the last ball of the season?

DUMBY. Oh, I think not. There'll probably be two more. *(Wanders back to Lady Plymdale.)*

PARKER. Mr. Rufford. Lady Jedburgh and Miss Graham. Mr. Hopper.

*(These people enter as announced.)*

HOPPER. How do you do, Lady Windermere? How do you do, Duchess? *(Bows to Lady Agatha.)*

DUCHESS OF BERWICK. Dear Mr. Hopper, how nice of you to come so early. We all know how you are run after in London.

HOPPER. Capital place, London! They are not nearly so exclusive in London as they are in Sydney.

DUCHESS OF BERWICK. Ah! we know your value, Mr. Hopper. We wish there were more like you. It would make life so much easier. Do you know, Mr. Hopper, dear Agatha and I are so much interested in Australia. It must be so pretty with all the dear little kangaroos flying about. Agatha has found it on the map. What a curious shape it is! Just like a large packing case. However, it is a very young country, isn't it?

HOPPER. Wasn't it made at the same time as the others, Duchess?

DUCHESS OF BERWICK. How clever you are, Mr. Hopper. You have a cleverness quite of your own. Now I mustn't keep you.

HOPPER. But I should like to dance with Lady Agatha, Duchess.

DUCHESS OF BERWICK. Well, I *hope* she has a dance left. Have you a dance left, Agatha?

LADY AGATHA. Yes, mamma.

DUCHESS OF BERWICK. The next one?

LADY AGATHA. Yes, mamma.

HOPPER. May I have the pleasure? *(Lady Agatha bows.)*

DUCHESS OF BERWICK. Mind you take great care of my little chatterbox, Mr. Hopper.

*(Lady Agatha and Mr. Hopper pass into ball-room.)*

*(Enter Lord Windermere L.*

LORD WINDERMERE. Margaret, I want to speak to you.

LADY WINDERMERE. In a moment. *(The music stops.)*

PARKER. Lord Augustus Lorton.

*(Enter Lord Augustus.*

LORD AUGUSTUS. Good evening, Lady Windermere.

DUCHESS OF BERWICK. Sir James, will you take me into the ball-room? Augustus has been dining with us to-night. I really have had quite enough of dear Augustus for the moment.

*(Sir James Royston gives the Duchess his arm and escorts her into the ball-room.)*

PARKER. Mr. and Mrs. Arthur Bowden. Lord and Lady Paisley. Lord Darlington.

*(These people enter as announced.*

LORD AUGUSTUS. *(Coming up to Lord Windermere.)* Want to speak to you particularly, dear boy. I'm worn to a shadow. Know I don't look it. None of us men do look what we really are. *Demmed* good thing, too. What I want to know is this. Who is she? Where does she come from? Why hasn't she got any demmed relations? Demmed nuisance, relations! But they make one so demmed respectable.

LORD WINDERMERE. You are talking of Mrs. Erlynne, I suppose? I only met her six months ago. Till then, I never knew of her existence.

LORD AUGUSTUS. You have seen a good deal of her since then.

LORD WINDERMERE. *(Coldly.)* Yes, I have seen a good deal of her since then. I have just seen her.

LORD AUGUSTUS. Egad! the women are very down on her. I have been dining with Arabella this evening! By Jove! you should have heard what she said about Mrs. Erlynne. She didn't leave a rag on her. . . . *(Aside.)* Berwick and I told her that didn't matter much, as the lady in question must have an extremely fine figure. You should have seen Arabella's expression! . . . But, look here, dear boy. I don't know what to do about Mrs. Erlynne. Egad! I might be married to her; she treats me with such demmed indifference. She's deuced clever, too! She explains everything. Egad! she explains you. She has got any amount of explanations for you—and all of them different.

LORD WINDERMERE. No explanations are necessary about my friendship with Mrs. Erlynne.

LORD AUGUSTUS. Hem! Well, look here, dear old fellow. Do you think she will ever get into this demmed thing called Society? Would you introduce her to your wife? No use beating about the confounded bush. Would you do that?

LORD WINDERMERE. Mrs. Erlynne is coming here to-night.

LORD AUGUSTUS. Your wife has sent her a card?

LORD WINDERMERE. Mrs. Erlynne has received a card.

LORD AUGUSTUS. Then she's all right, dear boy. But why didn't you tell me that before. It would have saved me a heap of worry and demmed misunderstandings!

*(Lady Agatha and Mr. Hopper cross and exit on terrace L.U.E.*

PARKER. Mr. Cecil Graham!

*(Enter Mr. Cecil Graham.*

CECIL GRAHAM. *(Bows to Lady Windermere, passes over and shakes hands with Lord Windermere.)* Good evening, Arthur. Why don't you ask me how I am? I like people to ask me how I am. It shows a wide-spread interest in my health. Now, to-night I am not at all well. Been dining with my people. Wonder why it is one's people are always so tedious? My father would talk morality after dinner. I told him he was old enough to know better. But my experience is that as soon as people are old enough to know better, they don't know anything at all. Hullo, Tuppy! Hear you're going to be married again; thought you were tired of that game.

LORD AUGUSTUS. You're excessively trivial, my dear boy, excessively trivial!

CECIL GRAHAM. By the way, Tuppy, which is it? Have you been twice married and once divorced, or twice divorced and once married? I say you've been twice divorced and once married. It seems so much more probable.

LORD AUGUSTUS. I have a very bad memory. I really don't remember which. *(Moves away R.)*

LADY PLYMDALE. Lord Windermere, I've something most particular to ask you.

LORD WINDERMERE. I am afraid—if you will excuse me—I must join my wife.

LADY PLYMDALE. Oh, you mustn't dream of such a thing. It's most dangerous now-a-days for a husband to pay any attention to his wife in public. It always makes people think that he beats her when they're alone. The world has grown so suspicious of anything that looks like a happy married life. But I'll tell you what it is at supper. *(Moves towards door of ball-room.)*

LORD WINDERMERE. *(C.)* Margaret! I *must* speak to you.

LADY WINDERMERE. Will you hold my fan for me, Lord Darlington? Thanks. *(Comes down to him.)*

LORD WINDERMERE. *(Crossing to her.)* Margaret, what you said before dinner was, of course, impossible?

LADY WINDERMERE. That woman is not coming here to-night!

LORD WINDERMERE. *(R.C.)* Mrs. Erlynne is coming here, and if you in any way annoy or wound her, you will bring shame and sorrow on us both. Remember that! Ah, Margaret! only trust me! A wife should trust her husband!

LADY WINDERMERE. *(C.)* London is full of women who trust their husbands. One can always recognise them. They look so thoroughly unhappy. I am not going to be one of them. *(Moves up.)* Lord Darlington, will you give me back my fan, please? Thanks. . . . A useful thing a fan, isn't it? . . . I want a friend to-night, Lord Darlington: I didn't know I would want one so soon.

LORD DARLINGTON. Lady Windermere! I knew the time would come some day; but why to-night?

LORD WINDERMERE. I *will* tell her. I must. It would be terrible if there were any scene. Margaret . . .

PARKER. Mrs. Erlynne!

*(Lord Windermere starts. Mrs. Erlynne enters, very beautifully dressed and very dignified. Lady Windermere clutches at her fan, then lets it drop on the floor. She bows coldly to Mrs. Erlynne, who bows to her sweetly in turn, and sails into the room.)*

LORD DARLINGTON. You have dropped your fan, Lady Windermere. *(Picks it up and hands it to her.)*

MRS. ERLYNNE. *(C.)* How do you do, again, Lord Windermere? How charming your sweet wife looks! Quite a picture!

LORD WINDERMERE. *(In a low voice.)* It was terribly rash of you to come!

MRS. ERLYNNE. *(Smiling.)* The wisest thing I ever did in my life. And, by the way, you must pay me a good deal of attention this evening. I am afraid of the women. You must introduce me to some of them. The men I can always manage. How do you do, Lord Augustus? You have quite neglected me lately. I have not seen you since yesterday. I am afraid you're faithless. Every one told me so.

LORD AUGUSTUS. *(R.)* Now really, Mrs. Erlynne, allow me to explain.

MRS. ERLYNNE. *(R.C.)* No, dear Lord Augustus, you can't explain anything. It is your chief charm.

LORD AUGUSTUS. Ah! if you find charms in me, Mrs. Erlynne——

*(They converse together. Lord Windermere moves uneasily about the room watching Mrs. Erlynne.)*

LORD DARLINGTON. *(To Lady Windermere.)* How pale you are!

LADY WINDERMERE. Cowards are always pale!

LORD DARLINGTON. You look faint. Come out on the terrace.

LADY WINDERMERE. Yes. *(To Parker.)* Parker, send my cloak out.

MRS. ERLYNNE. *(Crossing to her.)* Lady Windermere, how beautifully your terrace is illuminated. Reminds me of Prince Doria's at Rome.

*(Lady Windermere bows coldly, and goes off with Lord Darlington.)*

Oh, how do you do, Mr. Graham? Isn't that your aunt, Lady Jedburgh? I should so much like to know her.

CECIL GRAHAM. *(After a moment's hesitation and embarrassment.)* Oh, certainly, if you wish it. Aunt Caroline, allow me to introduce Mrs. Erlynne.

MRS. ERLYNNE. So pleased to meet you, Lady Jedburgh. *(Sits beside her on the sofa.)* Your nephew and I are great friends. I am so much interested in his political career. I think he's sure to be a wonderful success. He thinks like a Tory and talks like a Radical, and that's so important now-a-days. He's such a brilliant talker, too. But we all know from whom he inherits that. Lord Allandale was saying to me only yesterday, in the Park, that Mr. Graham talks almost as well as his aunt.

LADY JEDBURGH. *(R.)* Most kind of you to say these charming things to me! *(Mrs. Erlynne smiles, and continues conversation.)*

DUMBY. *(To Cecil Graham.)* Did you introduce Mrs. Erlynne to Lady Jedburgh?

CECIL GRAHAM. Had to, my dear fellow. Couldn't help it! That woman can make one do anything she wants. How, I don't know.

DUMBY. Hope to goodness she won't speak to me! *(Saunters towards Lady Plymdale.)*

MRS. ERLYNNE. *(C. to Lady Jedburgh.)* On Thursday? With great pleasure. *(Rises, and speaks to Lord Windermere, laughing.)* What a bore it is to have to be civil to these old dowagers! But they always insist on it!

LADY PLYMDALE. *(To Mr. Dumby.)* Who is that well-dressed woman talking to Windermere?

DUMBY. Haven't got the slightest idea! Looks like an *édition de luxe* of a wicked French novel, meant specially for the English market.

MRS. ERLYNNE. So that is poor Dumby with Lady Plymdale? I hear she is frightfully jealous of him. He doesn't seem anxious to speak to me to-night. I suppose he is afraid of her. Those straw-coloured women have dreadful tempers. Do you know, I think I'll dance with you first, Windermere. *(Lord Windermere bites his lip and frowns.)* It will make Lord Augustus so jealous! Lord Augustus! *(Lord Augustus comes down.)* Lord Windermere insists on my dancing with him first, and, as it's his own house, I can't well refuse. You know I would much sooner dance with you.

LORD AUGUSTUS. *(With a low bow.)* I wish I could think so, Mrs. Erlynne.

MRS. ERLYNNE. You know it far too well. I can fancy a person dancing through life with you and finding it charming.

LORD AUGUSTUS. *(Placing his hand on his white waistcoat.)* Oh, thank you, thank you. You are the most adorable of all ladies!

MRS. ERLYNNE. What a nice speech! So simple and so sincere! Just the sort of speech I like. Well, you shall hold my bouquet. *(Goes towards ball-room on Lord Windermere's arm.)* Ah, Mr. Dumby, how are you? I am so sorry I have been out the last three times you have called. Come and lunch on Friday.

DUMBY. *(With perfect nonchalance.)* Delighted!

*(Lady Plymdale glares with indignation at Mr. Dumby. Lord Augustus follows Mrs. Erlynne and Lord Windermere into the ball-room holding bouquet.)*

LADY PLYMDALE. *(To Mr. Dumby.)* What an absolute brute you are! I never can believe a word you say! Why did you tell me you didn't know her? What do you mean by calling on her three times running? You are not to go to lunch there; of course you understand that?

DUMBY. My dear Laura, I wouldn't dream of going!

LADY PLYMDALE. You haven't told me her name yet! Who is she?

DUMBY. *(Coughs slightly and smooths his hair.)* She's a Mrs. Erlynne.

LADY PLYMDALE. *That* woman!

DUMBY. Yes; that is what every one calls her.

LADY PLYMDALE. How very interesting! How intensely interesting! I really must have a good stare at her. *(Goes to door of ball-room and looks in.)* I have heard the most shocking things about her. They say she is ruining poor Windermere. And Lady Windermere, who goes in for being so proper, invites her! How extremely amusing! It takes a thoroughly good woman to do a thoroughly stupid thing. You are to lunch there on Friday!

DUMBY. Why?

LADY PLYMDALE. Because I want you to take my husband with you. He has been so attentive lately, that he has become a perfect nuisance. Now, this woman is just the thing for him. He'll dance attendance upon her as long as she lets him, and won't bother me. I assure you, women of that kind are most useful. They form the basis of other people's marriages.

DUMBY. What a mystery you are!

LADY PLYMDALE. *(Looking at him.)* I wish *you* were!

DUMBY. I am—to myself. I am the only person in the world I should like to know thoroughly; but I don't see any chance of it just at present.

*(They pass into the ball-room, and Lady Windermere and Lord Darlington enter from the terrace.)*

LADY WINDERMERE. Yes. Her coming here is monstrous, unbearable. I know now what you meant to-day at tea time. Why didn't you tell me right out? You should have!

LORD DARLINGTON. I couldn't! A man can't tell these things about another man! But if I had known he was going to make you ask her here to-night, I think I would have told you. That insult, at any rate, you would have been spared.

LADY WINDERMERE. I did not ask her. He insisted on her coming—against my entreaties—against my commands. Oh! the house is tainted for me! I feel that every woman here sneers at me as she dances by with my husband! What have I done to deserve this? I gave him all my life. He took it—used it—spoiled it! I am degraded in my own eyes; and I lack courage—I am a coward! *(Sits down on sofa.)*

LORD DARLINGTON. If I know you at all, I know that you can't live with a man who treats you like this! What sort of life would you have with him? You would feel that he was lying to you every moment of the day. You would feel that the look in his eyes was false, his voice false, his touch false, his passion false. He would come to you when he was weary of others; you would have to comfort him. He would come to you when he was devoted to others; you would have to charm him. You would have to be to him the mask of his real life, the cloak to hide his secret.

LADY WINDERMERE. You are right—you are terribly right. But where am I to turn? You said you would be my friend, Lord Darlington.—Tell me, what am I to do? Be my friend now.

LORD DARLINGTON. Between men and women there is no friendship possible. There is passion, enmity, worship, love, but no friendship. I love you——

LADY WINDERMERE. No, no! *(Rises.)*

LORD DARLINGTON. Yes, I love you! You are more to me than anything in the whole world. What does your husband give you?

Nothing. Whatever is in him he gives to this wretched woman, whom he has thrust into your society, into your home, to shame you before every one. I offer you my life——

LADY WINDERMERE. Lord Darlington!

LORD DARLINGTON. My life—my whole life. Take it, and do with it what you will. . . . I love you—love you as I have never loved any living thing. From the moment I met you I loved you, loved you blindly, adoringly, madly! You did not know it then—you know it now! Leave this house to-night. I won't tell you that the world matters nothing, or the world's voice, or the voice of society. They matter a great deal. They matter far too much. But there are moments when one has to choose between living one's own life, fully, entirely, completely—or dragging out some false, shallow, degrading existence that the world in its hypocrisy demands. You have that moment now. Choose! Oh, my love, choose!

LADY WINDERMERE. *(Moving slowly away from him, and looking at him with startled eyes.)* I have not the courage.

LORD DARLINGTON. *(Following her.)* Yes; you have the courage. There may be six months of pain, of disgrace even, but when you no longer bear his name, when you bear mine, all will be well. Margaret, my love, my wife that shall be some day—yes, my wife! You know it! What are you now? This woman has the place that belongs by right to you. Oh! go—go out of this house, with head erect, with a smile upon your lips, with courage in your eyes. All London will know why you did it; and who will blame you? No one. If they do, what matter? Wrong? What is wrong? It's wrong for a man to abandon his wife for a shameless woman. It is wrong for a wife to remain with a man who so dishonours her. You said once you would make no compromise with things. Make none now. Be brave! Be yourself!

LADY WINDERMERE. I am afraid of being myself. Let me think! Let me wait! My husband may return to me. *(Sits down on sofa.)*

LORD DARLINGTON. And you would take him back! You are not what I thought you were. You are just the same as every other woman. You would stand anything rather than face the censure of a world, whose praise you would despise. In a week you will

be driving with this woman in the Park. She will be your constant
guest—your dearest friend. You would endure anything rather
than break with one blow this monstrous tie. You are right. You
have no courage; none!

LADY WINDERMERE. Ah, give me time to think. I cannot answer you
now. *(Passes her hand nervously over her brow.)*

LORD DARLINGTON. It must be now or not at all.

LADY WINDERMERE. *(Rising from the sofa.)* Then, not at all! *(A pause.)*

LORD DARLINGTON. You break my heart!

LADY WINDERMERE. Mine is already broken. *(A pause.)*

LORD DARLINGTON. To-morrow I leave England. This is the last
time I shall ever look on you. You will never see me again. For
one moment our lives met—our souls touched. They must never
meet or touch again. Good-bye, Margaret.

*(Exit.*

LADY WINDERMERE. How alone I am in life! How terribly alone!
*(The music stops. Enter the Duchess of Berwick and Lord Paisley laugh-
ing and talking. Other guests come on from ball-room.)*

DUCHESS OF BERWICK. Dear Margaret, I've just been having such a
delightful chat with Mrs. Erlynne. I am so sorry for what I said to
you this afternoon about her. Of course, she must be all right if
*you* invite her. A most attractive woman, and has such sensible
views on life. Told me she entirely disapproved of people marrying more than once, so I feel quite safe about poor Augustus.
Can't imagine why people speak against her. It's those horrid
nieces of mine—the Saville girls—they're always talking scandal. Still, I should go to Homburg, dear, I really should. She is
just a little too attractive. But where is Agatha? Oh, there she
is! *(Lady Agatha and Mr. Hopper enter from terrace L.U.E.)* Mr. Hopper, I am very, very angry with you. You have taken Agatha out
on the terrace, and she is so delicate.

HOPPER. *(L.C.)* Awfully sorry, Duchess. We went out for a moment
and then got chatting together.

DUCHESS OF BERWICK. *(C.)* Ah, about dear Australia, I suppose?

HOPPER. Yes!

DUCHESS OF BERWICK. Agatha, darling! *(Beckons her over.)*

LADY AGATHA. Yes, mamma!

DUCHESS OF BERWICK. *(Aside.)* Did Mr. Hopper definitely——

LADY AGATHA. Yes, mamma.

DUCHESS OF BERWICK. And what answer did you give him, dear child?

LADY AGATHA. Yes, mamma.

DUCHESS OF BERWICK. *(Affectionately.)* My dear one! You always say the right thing. Mr. Hopper! James! Agatha has told me everything. How cleverly you have both kept your secret.

HOPPER. You don't mind my taking Agatha off to Australia, then, Duchess?

DUCHESS OF BERWICK. *(Indignantly.)* To Australia? Oh, don't mention that dreadful vulgar place.

HOPPER. But she said she'd like to come with me.

DUCHESS OF BERWICK. *(Severely.)* Did you say that, Agatha?

LADY AGATHA. Yes, mamma.

DUCHESS OF BERWICK. Agatha, you say the most silly things possible. I think on the whole that Grosvenor Square would be a more healthy place to reside in. There are lots of vulgar people live in Grosvenor Square, but at any rate there are no horrid kangaroos crawling about. But we'll talk about that to-morrow. James, you can take Agatha down. You'll come to lunch, of course, James. At half-past one, instead of two. The Duke will wish to say a few words to you, I am sure.

HOPPER. I should like to have a chat with the Duke, Duchess. He has not said a single word to me yet.

DUCHESS OF BERWICK. I think you'll find he will have a great deal to say to you to-morrow. *(Exit Lady Agatha with Mr. Hopper.)* And now good-night, Margaret. I'm afraid it's the old, old story, dear. Love—well, not love at first sight, but love at the end of the season, which is so much more satisfactory.

LADY WINDERMERE. Good-night, Duchess.

*(Exit the Duchess of Berwick on Lord Paisley's arm.)*

LADY PLYMDALE. My dear Margaret, what a handsome woman your husband has been dancing with! I should be quite jealous if I were you! Is she a great friend of yours?

LADY WINDERMERE. No!

LADY PLYMDALE. Really? Good-night, dear. *(Looks at Mr. Dumby and exits.)*

DUMBY. Awful manners young Hopper has!

CECIL GRAHAM. Ah! Hopper is one of Nature's gentlemen, the worst type of gentleman I know.

DUMBY. Sensible woman, Lady Windermere. Lots of wives would have objected to Mrs. Erlynne coming. But Lady Windermere has that uncommon thing called common sense.

CECIL GRAHAM. And Windermere knows that nothing looks so like innocence as an indiscretion.

DUMBY. Yes; dear Windermere is becoming almost modern. Never thought he would.                    *(Bows to Lady Windermere and exit.)*

LADY JEDBURGH. Good-night, Lady Windermere. What a fascinating woman Mrs. Erlynne is! She is coming to lunch on Thursday, won't you come too? I expect the Bishop and dear Lady Merton.

LADY WINDERMERE. I am afraid I am engaged, Lady Jedburgh.

LADY JEDBURGH. So sorry. Come, dear.

                    *(Exeunt Lady Jedburgh and Miss Graham.*
*(Enter Mrs. Erlynne and Lord Windermere.*

MRS. ERLYNNE. Charming ball it has been! Quite reminds me of old days. *(Sits on sofa.)* And I see that there are just as many fools in society as there used to be. So pleased to find that nothing has altered! Except Margaret. She's grown quite pretty. The last time I saw her—twenty years ago, she was a fright in flannel. Positive fright, I assure you. The dear Duchess! and that sweet Lady Agatha! Just the type of girl I like! Well, really, Windermere, if I am to be the Duchess's sister-in-law——

LORD WINDERMERE. *(Sitting L. of her)* But are you——?

*(Exit Mr. Cecil Graham with rest of guests. Lady Windermere watches, with a look of scorn and pain, Mrs. Erlynne and her husband. They are unconscious of her presence.)*

MRS. ERLYNNE. Oh, yes! He's to call to-morrow at twelve o'clock! He wanted to propose to-night. In fact he did. He kept on proposing. Poor Augustus, you know how he repeats himself. Such a bad habit! But I told him I wouldn't give him an answer till to-morrow. Of course I am going to take him. And I daresay I'll make him an admirable wife, as wives go. And there is a great deal of good in Lord Augustus. Fortunately it is all on the surface. Just where good qualities should be. Of course you must help me in this matter.

LORD WINDERMERE. I am not called on to encourage Lord Augustus, I suppose?

MRS. ERLYNNE. Oh, no! I do the encouraging. But you will make me a handsome settlement, Windermere, won't you?

LORD WINDERMERE. *(Frowning.)* Is that what you want to talk to me about to-night?

MRS. ERLYNNE. Yes.

LORD WINDERMERE. *(With a gesture of impatience.)* I will not talk of it here.

MRS. ERLYNNE. *(Laughing.)* Then we will talk of it on the terrace. Even business should have a picturesque background. Should it not, Windermere? With a proper background women can do anything.

LORD WINDERMERE. Won't to-morrow do as well?

MRS. ERLYNNE. No; you see, to-morrow I am going to accept him. And I think it would be a good thing if I was able to tell him that I had—well, what shall I say?—£2000 a year left to me by a third cousin—or a second husband—or some distant relative of that kind. It would be an additional attraction, wouldn't it? You have a delightful opportunity now of paying me a compliment, Windermere. But you are not very clever at paying compliments. I am afraid Margaret doesn't encourage you in that excellent habit. It's a great mistake on her part. When men give up saying what is charming, they give up thinking what is charming. But seriously, what do you say to £2000? £2500, I think. In modern life margin is everything. Windermere, don't you think the world an intensely amusing place? I do!

*(Exit on terrace with Lord Windermere. Music strikes up in ball-room.)*

LADY WINDERMERE. To stay in this house any longer is impossible. To-night a man who loves me offered me his whole life. I refused it. It was foolish of me. I will offer him mine now. I will give him mine. I will go to him! *(Puts on cloak and goes to the door, then turns back. Sits down at table and writes a letter, puts it into an envelope, and leaves it on table.)* Arthur has never understood me. When he reads this, he will. He may do as he chooses now with his life. I have done with mine as I think best, as I think right. It is he who has broken the bond of marriage—not I. I only break its bondage.

*(Exit.*

*(Parker enters L. and crosses towards the ball-room R. Enter Mrs. Erlynne.)*

MRS. ERLYNNE. Is Lady Windermere in the ball-room?

PARKER. Her ladyship has just gone out.

MRS. ERLYNNE. Gone out? She's not on the terrace?

PARKER. No, madam. Her ladyship has just gone out of the house.

MRS. ERLYNNE. *(Starts, and looks at the servant with a puzzled expression in her face.)* Out of the house?

PARKER. Yes, madam—her ladyship told me she had left a letter for his lordship on the table.

MRS. ERLYNNE. A letter for Lord Windermere?

PARKER. Yes, madam.

MRS. ERLYNNE. Thank you.

*(Exit Parker. The music in the ball-room stops.)*

Gone out of her house! A letter addressed to her husband! *(Goes over to bureau and looks at letter. Takes it up and lays it down again with a shudder of fear.)* No, no! It would be impossible! Life doesn't repeat its tragedies like that! Oh, why does this horrible fancy come across me? Why do I remember now the one moment of my life I most wish to forget? Does life repeat its tragedies? *(Tears letter open and reads it, then sinks down into a chair with a gesture of anguish.)* Oh, how terrible! The same words that twenty years ago I wrote to her father! and how bitterly I have been punished for it! No; my punishment, my real punishment is to-night, is now! *(Still seated R.)*

*(Enter Lord Windermere L.U.E.*

LORD WINDERMERE. Have you said good-night to my wife? *(Comes C.)*

MRS. ERLYNNE. *(Crushing letter in her hand.)* Yes.

LORD WINDERMERE. Where is she?

MRS. ERLYNNE. She is very tired. She has gone to bed. She said she had a headache.

LORD WINDERMERE. I must go to her. You'll excuse me?

MRS. ERLYNNE. *(Rising hurriedly.)* Oh, no! It's nothing serious. She's only very tired, that is all. Besides, there are people still in the supper room. She wants you to make her apologies to them. She said she didn't wish to be disturbed. *(Drops letter.)* She asked me to tell you!

LORD WINDERMERE. *(Picks up letter.)* You have dropped something.

MRS ERLYNNE. Oh yes, thank you, that is mine. *(Puts out her hand to take it.)*

LORD WINDERMERE. *(Still looking at letter.)* But it's my wife's hand-writing, isn't it?

MRS. ERLYNNE. *(Takes the letter quickly.)* Yes, it's—an address. Will you ask them to call my carriage, please?

LORD WINDERMERE. Certainly. *(Goes L. and exit.*

MRS. ERLYNNE. Thanks? What can I do? What can I do? I feel a passion awakening within me that I never felt before. What can it mean? The daughter must not be like the mother—that would be terrible. How can I save her? How can I save my child? A moment may ruin a life. Who knows that better than I? Windermere must be got out of the house; that is absolutely necessary. *(Goes L.)* But how shall I do it? It must be done somehow. Ah!

*(Enter Lord Augustus R.U.E. carrying bouquet.*

LORD AUGUSTUS. Dear lady, I am in such suspense! May I not have an answer to my request?

MRS. ERLYNNE. Lord Augustus, listen to me. You are to take Lord Windermere down to your club at once, and keep him there as long as possible. You understand?

LORD AUGUSTUS. But you said you wished me to keep early hours!

MRS. ERLYNNE. *(Nervously.)* Do what I tell you. Do what I tell you.

LORD AUGUSTUS. And my reward?

MRS. ERLYNNE. Your reward? Your reward? Oh! ask me that to-morrow. But don't let Windermere out of your sight to-night. If you do I will never forgive you. I will never speak to you again. I'll have nothing to do with you. Remember you are to keep Windermere at your club, and don't let him come back to-night.

*(Exit L.*

LORD AUGUSTUS. Well, really. I might be her husband already. Positively I might. *(Follows her in a bewildered manner.)*

ACT DROP

# THIRD ACT

*SCENE—Lord Darlington's Rooms. A large sofa is in front of fireplace R. At the back of the stage a curtain is drawn across the window. Doors L. and R. Table R. with writing materials. Table C. with syphons, glasses, and Tantalus frame. Table L. with cigar and cigarette box. Lamps lit.*

LADY WINDERMERE. *(Standing by the fireplace.)* Why doesn't he come? This waiting is horrible. He should be here. Why is he not here, to wake by passionate words some fire within me? I am cold—cold as a loveless thing. Arthur must have read my letter by this time. If he cared for me, he would have come after me, would have taken me back by force. But he doesn't care. He's entrammelled by this woman—fascinated by her—dominated by her. If a woman wants to hold a man, she has merely to appeal to what is worst in him. We make gods of men and they leave us. Others make brutes of them and they fawn and are faithful. How hideous life is! . . . Oh! it was mad of me to come here, horribly mad. And yet, which is the worst, I wonder, to be at the mercy of a man who loves one, or the wife of a man who in one's own house dishonours one? What woman knows? What woman in the whole world? But will he love me always, this man to whom I am giving my life? What do I bring him? Lips that have lost the note of joy, eyes that are blinded by tears, chill hands and icy heart. I bring him nothing. I must go back—no; I can't go back, my letter has put me in their power—Arthur would not take me back! That fatal letter! No! Lord Darlington leaves England to-morrow. I will go with him—I have no choice. *(Sits down for a few moments. Then starts up and puts on her cloak.)* No, no! I will go back, let Arthur do with me what he pleases. I can't wait here. It has been

madness my coming. I must go at once. As for Lord Darlington—
Oh! here he is! What shall I do? What can I say to him? Will he
let me go away at all? I have heard that men are brutal, horrible . . .
Oh! *(Hides her face in her hands.)*
*(Enter Mrs. Erlynne L.*

MRS. ERLYNNE. Lady Windermere! *(Lady Windermere starts and looks
up. Then recoils in contempt.)* Thank Heaven I am in time. You must
go back to your husband's house immediately.

LADY WINDERMERE. Must?

MRS. ERLYNNE. *(Authoritatively.)* Yes, you must! There is not a second
to be lost. Lord Darlington may return at any moment.

LADY WINDERMERE. Don't come near me!

MRS. ERLYNNE. Oh! You are on the brink of ruin, you are on the
brink of a hideous precipice. You must leave this place at once,
my carriage is waiting at the corner of the street. You must come
with me and drive straight home.
*(Lady Windermere throws off her cloak and flings it on the sofa.)*
What are you doing?

LADY WINDERMERE. Mrs. Erlynne—if you had not come here, I
would have gone back. But now that I see you, I feel that nothing
in the whole world would induce me to live under the same roof
as Lord Windermere. You fill me with horror. There is something about you that stirs the wildest—rage within me. And I
know why you are here. My husband sent you to lure me back
that I might serve as a blind to whatever relations exist between
you and him.

MRS. ERLYNNE. Oh! You don't think that—you can't.

LADY WINDERMERE. Go back to my husband, Mrs. Erlynne. He belongs to you and not to me. I suppose he is afraid of a scandal.
Men are such cowards. They outrage every law of the world, and
are afraid of the world's tongue. But he had better prepare himself. He shall have a scandal. He shall have the worst scandal
there has been in London for years. He shall see his name in
every vile paper, mine on every hideous placard.

MRS. ERLYNNE. No—no——

LADY WINDERMERE. Yes! he shall. Had he come himself, I admit I would have gone back to the life of degradation you and he had prepared for me—I was going back—but to stay himself at home, and to send you as his messenger—oh! it was infamous—infamous.

MRS. ERLYNNE. *(C.)* Lady Windermere, you wrong me horribly—you wrong your husband horribly. He doesn't know you are here—he thinks you are safe in your own house. He thinks you are asleep in your own room. He never read the mad letter you wrote to him!

LADY WINDERMERE. *(R.)* Never read it!

MRS. ERLYNNE. No—he knows nothing about it.

LADY WINDERMERE. How simple you think me! *(Going to her.)* You are lying to me!

MRS. ERLYNNE. *(Restraining herself.)* I am not. I am telling you the truth.

LADY WINDERMERE. If my husband didn't read my letter, how is it that you are here? Who told you I had left the house you were shameless enough to enter? Who told you where I had gone to? My husband told you, and sent you to decoy me back. *(Crosses L.)*

MRS. ERLYNNE. *(R.C.)* Your husband has never seen the letter. I—saw it, I opened it. I—read it.

LADY WINDERMERE. *(Turning to her.)* You opened a letter of mine to my husband? You wouldn't dare!

MRS. ERLYNNE. Dare! Oh! to save you from the abyss into which you are falling, there is nothing in the world I would not dare, nothing in the whole world. Here is the letter. Your husband has never read it. He never shall read it. *(Going to fireplace.)* It should never have been written. *(Tears it and throws it into the fire.)*

LADY WINDERMERE. *(With infinite contempt in her voice and look.)* How do I know that that was my letter after all? You seem to think the commonest device can take me in!

MRS. ERLYNNE. Oh! why do you disbelieve everything I tell you? What object do you think I have in coming here, except to save you from utter ruin, to save you from the consequence of a hideous mistake? That letter that is burnt now *was* your letter. I swear it to you!

LADY WINDERMERE. *(Slowly.)* You took good care to burn it before I had examined it. I cannot trust you. You, whose whole life is a lie, how could you speak the truth about anything? *(Sits down.)*

MRS. ERLYNNE. *(Hurriedly.)* Think as you like about me—say what you choose against me, but go back, go back to the husband you love.

LADY WINDERMERE. *(Sullenly.)* I do *not* love him!

MRS. ERLYNNE. You do, and you know that he loves you.

LADY WINDERMERE. He does not understand what love is. He understands it as little as you—but I see what you want. It would be a great advantage for you to get me back. Dear Heaven! what a life I would have then! Living at the mercy of a woman who has neither mercy nor pity in her, a woman whom it is an infamy to meet, a degradation to know, a vile woman, a woman who comes between husband and wife!

MRS. ERLYNNE. *(With a gesture of despair.)* Lady Windermere, Lady Windermere, don't say such terrible things. You don't know how terrible they are, how terrible and how unjust. Listen, you must listen! Only go back to your husband, and I promise you never to communicate with him again on any pretext—never to see him—never to have anything to do with his life or yours. The money that he gave me, he gave me not through love, but through hatred, not in worship, but in contempt. The hold I have over him——

LADY WINDERMERE. *(Rising.)* Ah! you admit you have a hold!

MRS. ERLYNNE. Yes, and I will tell you what it is. It is his love for you, Lady Windermere.

LADY WINDERMERE. You expect me to believe that?

MRS. ERLYNNE. You must believe it! It is true. It is his love for you that has made him submit to—oh! call it what you like, tyranny, threats, anything you choose. But it is his love for you. His desire to spare you—shame, yes, shame and disgrace.

LADY WINDERMERE. What do you mean? You are insolent! What have I to do with you?

MRS. ERLYNNE. *(Humbly.)* Nothing. I know it—but I tell you that your husband loves you—that you may never meet with such love again in your whole life—that such love you will never meet—and that if you throw it away, the day may come when you will starve for love and it will not be given to you, beg for love and it will be denied you—Oh! Arthur loves you!

LADY WINDERMERE. Arthur? And you tell me there is nothing between you?

MRS. ERLYNNE. Lady Windermere, before Heaven your husband is guiltless of all offence towards you! And I—I tell you that had it ever occurred to me that such a monstrous suspicion would have entered your mind, I would have died rather than have crossed your life or his—oh! died, gladly died! *(Moves away to sofa R.)*

LADY WINDERMERE. You talk as if you had a heart. Women like you have no hearts. Heart is not in you. You are bought and sold. *(Sits L.C.)*

MRS. ERLYNNE. *(Starts, with a gesture of pain. Then restrains herself, and comes over to where Lady Windermere is sitting. As she speaks, she stretches out her hands towards her, but does not dare to touch her.)* Believe what you choose about me. I am not worth a moment's sorrow. But don't spoil your beautiful young life on my account! You don't know what may be in store for you, unless you leave this house at once. You don't know what it is to fall into the pit, to be despised, mocked, abandoned, sneered at—to be an outcast! to find the door shut against one, to have to creep in by hideous by-ways, afraid every moment lest the mask should be stripped from one's face, and all the while to hear the laughter, the horrible laughter of the world, a thing more tragic than all the tears the world has ever shed. You don't know what it is. One pays for one's sin, and then one pays again, and all one's life one pays. You must never know that—As for me, if suffering be an expiation, then at this moment I have expiated all my faults, whatever they have been, for to-night you have made a heart in one who had it not, made it and broken it.—But let that pass. I may have wrecked my own life, but I will not let you wreck yours. You—why, you are a mere girl, you would be lost. You haven't got the kind of brains that enables a woman to get back. You have neither the wit nor the courage. You couldn't stand dishonour. No! Go back, Lady Windermere, to the husband who loves you, whom you love. You have a child, Lady Windermere. Go back to that child who even now, in pain or in joy, may be calling to you. *(Lady Windermere rises.)* God gave you that child. He will require from you that you make his life fine, that you watch over him. What answer will you make to God if his life is ruined through you? Back to your house, Lady Windermere—your husband loves you! He has never swerved for a moment from the love he bears you. But even if he had a thousand loves, you must stay with your child. If he was harsh to you, you must stay with your child. If he ill-treated you, you must stay with your child. If he abandoned you, your place is with your child.

*(Lady Windermere bursts into tears and buries her face in her hands.)*

*(Rushing to her.)* Lady Windermere!

LADY WINDERMERE. *(Holding out her hands to her, helplessly, as a child might do.)* Take me home. Take me home.

MRS. ERLYNNE. *(Is about to embrace her. Then restrains herself. There is a look of wonderful joy in her face.)* Come! Where is your cloak? *(Getting it from sofa.)* Here. Put it on. Come at once!

*(They go to the door.)*

LADY WINDERMERE. Stop! Don't you hear voices?

MRS. ERLYNNE. No, no! There is no one!

LADY WINDERMERE. Yes, there is! Listen! Oh! that is my husband's voice! He is coming in! Save me! Oh, it's some plot! You have sent for him.

*(Voices outside.)*

MRS. ERLYNNE. Silence! I'm here to save you, if I can. But I fear it is too late! There! *(Points to the curtain across the window.)* The first chance you have, slip out, if you ever get a chance!

LADY WINDERMERE. But you?

MRS. ERLYNNE. Oh! never mind me. I'll face them.

*(Lady Windermere hides herself behind the curtain.)*

LORD AUGUSTUS. *(Outside.)* Nonsense, dear Windermere, you must not leave me!

MRS. ERLYNNE. Lord Augustus! Then it is I who am lost! *(Hesitates for a moment, then looks round and sees door R., and exit through it.)*
*(Enter Lord Darlington, Mr. Dumby, Lord Windermere, Lord Augustus Lorton, and Mr. Cecil Graham.*

DUMBY. What a nuisance their turning us out of the club at this hour! It's only two o'clock. *(Sinks into a chair.)* The lively part of the evening is only just beginning. *(Yawns and closes his eyes.)*

LORD WINDERMERE. It is very good of you, Lord Darlington, allowing Augustus to force our company on you, but I'm afraid I can't stay long.

LORD DARLINGTON. Really! I am so sorry! You'll take a cigar, won't you?

LORD WINDERMERE. Thanks! *(Sits down.)*

LORD AUGUSTUS. *(To Lord Windermere.)* My dear boy, you must not dream of going. I have a great deal to talk to you about, of demmed importance, too. *(Sits down with him at L. table.)*

CECIL GRAHAM. Oh! We all know what that is! Tuppy can't talk about anything but Mrs. Erlynne!

LORD WINDERMERE. Well, that is no business of yours, is it, Cecil?

CECIL GRAHAM. None! That is why it interests me. My own business always bores me to death. I prefer other people's.

LORD DARLINGTON. Have something to drink, you fellows. Cecil, you'll have a whisky and soda?

CECIL GRAHAM. Thanks. *(Goes to table with Lord Darlington.)* Mrs. Erlynne looked very handsome to-night, didn't she?

LORD DARLINGTON. I am not one of her admirers.

CECIL GRAHAM. I usen't to be, but I am now. Why! she actually made me introduce her to poor dear Aunt Caroline. I believe she is going to lunch there.

LORD DARLINGTON. *(In surprise.)* No?

CECIL GRAHAM. She is, really.

LORD DARLINGTON. Excuse me, you fellows. I'm going away to-morrow. And I have to write a few letters. *(Goes to writing table and sits down.)*

DUMBY. Clever woman, Mrs. Erlynne.

CECIL GRAHAM. Hallo, Dumby! I thought you were asleep.

DUMBY. I am, I usually am!

LORD AUGUSTUS. A very clever woman. Knows perfectly well what a demmed fool I am—knows it as well as I do myself.

*(Cecil Graham comes towards him laughing.)*

Ah! you may laugh, my boy, but it is a great thing to come across a woman who thoroughly understands one.

DUMBY. It is an awfully dangerous thing. They always end by marrying one.

CECIL GRAHAM. But I thought, Tuppy, you were never going to see her again. Yes! you told me so yesterday evening at the club. You said you'd heard——*(Whispering to him.)*

LORD AUGUSTUS. Oh, she's explained that.

CECIL GRAHAM. And the Wiesbaden affair?

LORD AUGUSTUS. She's explained that too.

DUMBY. And her income, Tuppy? Has she explained that?

LORD AUGUSTUS. *(In a very serious voice.)* She's going to explain that to-morrow.

*(Cecil Graham goes back to C. table.)*

DUMBY. Awfully commercial, women now-a-days. Our grandmothers threw their caps over the mills, of course, but, by Jove, their granddaughters only throw their caps over mills that can raise the wind for them.

LORD AUGUSTUS. You want to make her out a wicked woman. She is not!

CECIL GRAHAM. Oh! Wicked women bother one. Good women bore one. That is the only difference between them.

LORD AUGUSTUS. *(Puffing a cigar.)* Mrs. Erlynne has a future before her.

DUMBY. Mrs. Erlynne has a past before her.

LORD AUGUSTUS. I prefer women with a past. They're always so demmed amusing to talk to.

CECIL GRAHAM. Well, you'll have lots of topics of conversation with *her*, Tuppy. *(Rising and going to him.)*

LORD AUGUSTUS. You're getting annoying, dear boy; you're getting demmed annoying.

CECIL GRAHAM. *(Puts his hands on his shoulders.)* Now, Tuppy, you've lost your figure and you've lost your character. Don't lose your temper; you have only got one.

LORD AUGUSTUS. My dear boy, if I wasn't the most good-natured man in London——

CECIL GRAHAM. We'd treat you with more respect, wouldn't we, Tuppy? *(Strolls away.)*

DUMBY. The youth of the present day are quite monstrous. They have absolutely no respect for dyed hair. *(Lord Augustus looks round angrily.)*

CECIL GRAHAM. Mrs. Erlynne has a very great respect for dear Tuppy.

DUMBY. Then Mrs. Erlynne sets an admirable example to the rest of her sex. It is perfectly brutal the way most women now-a-days behave to men who are not their husbands.

LORD WINDERMERE. Dumby, you are ridiculous, and Cecil, you let your tongue run away with you. You must leave Mrs. Erlynne alone. You don't really know anything about her, and you're always talking scandal against her.

CECIL GRAHAM. *(Coming towards him L.C.)* My dear Arthur, I never talk scandal. *I* only talk gossip.

LORD WINDERMERE. What is the difference between scandal and gossip?

CECIL GRAHAM. Oh! gossip is charming! History is merely gossip. But scandal is gossip made tedious by morality. Now, I never moralise. A man who moralises is usually a hypocrite, and a woman who moralises is invariably plain. There is nothing in the whole world so unbecoming to a woman as a Nonconformist conscience. And most women know it, I'm glad to say.

LORD AUGUSTUS. Just my sentiments, dear boy, just my sentiments.

CECIL GRAHAM. Sorry to hear it, Tuppy; whenever people agree with me, I always feel I must be wrong.

LORD AUGUSTUS. My dear boy, when I was your age——

CECIL GRAHAM. But you never were, Tuppy, and you never will be. *(Goes up C.)* I say, Darlington, let us have some cards. You'll play, Arthur, won't you.

LORD WINDERMERE. No, thanks, Cecil.

instinct about life. I have got it. Tuppy hasn't. Experience is the name Tuppy gives to his mistakes. That is all. *(Lord Augustus looks round indignantly.)*

DUMBY. Experience is the name every one gives to their mistakes.

CECIL GRAHAM. *(Standing with his back to the fireplace.)* One shouldn't commit any. *(Sees Lady Windermere's fan on sofa.)*

DUMBY. Life would be very dull without them.

CECIL GRAHAM. Of course you are quite faithful to this woman you are in love with, Darlington, to this good woman?

LORD DARLINGTON. Cecil, if one really loves a woman, all other women in the world become absolutely meaningless to one. Love changes one—*I* am changed.

CECIL GRAHAM. Dear me! How very interesting! Tuppy, I want to talk to you. *(Lord Augustus takes no notice.)*

DUMBY. It's no use talking to Tuppy. You might just as well talk to a brick wall.

CECIL GRAHAM. But I like talking to a brick wall—it's the only thing in the world that never contradicts me! Tuppy!

LORD AUGUSTUS. Well, what is it? What is it? *(Rising and going over to Cecil Graham.)*

CECIL GRAHAM. Come over here. I want you particularly. *(Aside.)* Darlington has been moralising and talking about the purity of love, and that sort of thing, and he has got some woman in his rooms all the time.

LORD AUGUSTUS. No, really! really!

CECIL GRAHAM. *(In a low voice.)* Yes, here is her fan. *(Points to the fan.)*

LORD AUGUSTUS. *(Chuckling.)* By Jove! By Jove!

LORD WINDERMERE. *(Up by door.)* I am really off now, Lord Darlington. I am sorry you are leaving England so soon. Pray call on us when you come back! My wife and I will be charmed to see you!

LORD DARLINGTON. *(Up stage with Lord Windermere.)* I am afraid I shall be away for many years. Good-night!

CECIL GRAHAM. Arthur!

LORD WINDERMERE. What?

CECIL GRAHAM. I want to speak to you for a moment. No, do come!

LORD WINDERMERE. *(Putting on his coat.)* I can't—I'm off!

CECIL GRAHAM. It is something very particular. It will interest you enormously.

LORD WINDERMERE. *(Smiling.)* It is some of your nonsense, Cecil.

CECIL GRAHAM. It isn't! It isn't really.

LORD AUGUSTUS. *(Going to him.)* My dear fellow, you mustn't go yet. I have a lot to talk to you about. And Cecil has something to show you.

LORD WINDERMERE. *(Walking over.)* Well, what is it?

CECIL GRAHAM. Darlington has got a woman here in his rooms. Here is her fan. Amusing, isn't it? *(A pause.)*

LORD WINDERMERE. Good God! *(Seizes the fan—Dumby rises.)*

CECIL GRAHAM. What is the matter?

LORD WINDERMERE. Lord Darlington!

LORD DARLINGTON. *(Turning round.)* Yes!

LORD WINDERMERE. What is my wife's fan doing here in your rooms? Hands off, Cecil. Don't touch me.

LORD DARLINGTON. Your wife's fan?

LORD WINDERMERE. Yes, here it is!

LORD DARLINGTON. *(Walking towards him.)* I don't know!

LORD WINDERMERE. You must know. I demand an explanation. Don't hold me, you fool. *(To Cecil Graham.)*

LORD DARLINGTON. *(Aside.)* She is here after all!

LORD WINDERMERE. Speak, sir! Why is my wife's fan here? Answer me! By God! I'll search your rooms, and if my wife's here, I'll—— *(Moves.)*

LORD DARLINGTON. You shall not search my rooms. You have no right to do so. I forbid you!

LORD WINDERMERE. You scoundrel! I'll not leave your room till I have searched every corner of it! What moves behind that curtain? *(Rushes towards the curtain C.)*

MRS. ERLYNNE. *(Enters behind R.)* Lord Windermere!

LORD WINDERMERE. Mrs. Erlynne!

*(Every one starts and turns round. Lady Windermere slips out from behind the curtain and glides from the room L.)*

MRS. ERLYNNE. I am afraid I took your wife's fan in mistake for my own, when I was leaving your house to-night. I am so sorry. *(Takes fan from him. Lord Windermere looks at her in contempt. Lord Darlington in mingled astonishment and anger. Lord Augustus turns away. The other men smile at each other.)*

ACT DROP

# Fourth Act

SCENE—*Same as in Act I.*

LADY WINDERMERE. *(Lying on sofa.)* How can I tell him? I can't tell him. It would kill me. I wonder what happened after I escaped from that horrible room. Perhaps she told them the true reason of her being there, and the real meaning of that—fatal fan of mine. Oh, if he knows—how can I look him in the face again? He would never forgive me. *(Touches bell.)* How securely one thinks one lives—out of reach of temptation, sin, folly. And then suddenly—Oh! Life is terrible. It rules us, we do not rule it.
*(Enter Rosalie R.*

ROSALIE. Did your ladyship ring for me?

LADY WINDERMERE. Yes. Have you found out at what time Lord Windermere came in last night?

ROSALIE. His lordship did not come in till five o'clock.

LADY WINDERMERE. Five o'clock? He knocked at my door this morning, didn't he?

ROSALIE. Yes, my lady—at half-past nine. I told him your ladyship was not awake yet.

LADY WINDERMERE. Did he say anything?

ROSALIE. Something about your ladyship's fan. I didn't quite catch what his lordship said. Has the fan been lost, my lady? I can't find it, and Parker says it was not left in any of the rooms. He has looked in all of them and on the terrace as well.

LADY WINDERMERE. It doesn't matter. Tell Parker not to trouble. That will do.

*(Exit Rosalie.*

LADY WINDERMERE. *(Rising.)* She is sure to tell him. I can fancy a person doing a wonderful act of self-sacrifice, doing it spontaneously, recklessly, nobly—and afterwards finding out that it costs too much. Why should she hesitate between her ruin and mine? . . . How strange! I would have publicly disgraced her in my own house. She accepts public disgrace in the house of another to save me. . . . There is a bitter irony in things, a bitter irony in the way we talk of good and bad women. . . . Oh, what a lesson! and what a pity that in life we only get our lessons when they are of no use to us! For even if she doesn't tell, I must. Oh! the shame of it, the shame of it. To tell it is to live through it all again. Actions are the first tragedy in life, words are the second. Words are perhaps the worst. Words are merciless. . . . Oh! *(Starts as Lord Windermere enters.)*

LORD WINDERMERE. *(Kisses her.)* Margaret—how pale you look!

LADY WINDERMERE. I slept very badly.

LORD WINDERMERE. *(Sitting on sofa with her.)* I am so sorry. I came in dreadfully late, and didn't like to wake you. You are crying, dear.

LADY WINDERMERE. Yes, I am crying, for I have something to tell you, Arthur.

LORD WINDERMERE. My dear child, you are not well. You've been doing too much. Let us go away to the country. You'll be all right at Selby. The season is almost over. There is no use staying on. Poor darling! We'll go away to-day, if you like. *(Rises.)* We can easily catch the 3.40. I'll send a wire to Fannen.

*(Crosses and sits down at table to write a telegram.)*

LADY WINDERMERE. Yes; let us go away to-day. No; I can't go to-day, Arthur. There is some one I must see before I leave town—some one who has been kind to me.

LORD WINDERMERE. *(Rising and leaning over sofa.)* Kind to you?

LADY WINDERMERE. Far more than that. *(Rises and goes to him.)* I will tell you, Arthur, but only love me, love me as you used to love me.

LORD WINDERMERE. Used to? You are not thinking of that wretched woman who came here last night? *(Coming round and sitting R. of her.)* You don't still imagine—no, you couldn't.

LADY WINDERMERE. I don't. I know now I was wrong and foolish.

LORD WINDERMERE. It was very good of you to receive her last night—but you are never to see her again.

LADY WINDERMERE. Why do you say that? *(A pause.)*

LORD WINDERMERE. *(Holding her hand.)* Margaret, I thought Mrs. Erlynne was a woman more sinned against than sinning, as the phrase goes. I thought she wanted to be good, to get back into a place that she had lost by a moment's folly, to lead again a decent life. I believed what she told me—I was mistaken in her. She is bad—as bad as a woman can be.

LADY WINDERMERE. Arthur, Arthur, don't talk so bitterly about any woman. I don't think now that people can be divided into the good and the bad, as though they were two separate races or creations. What are called good women may have terrible things in them, mad moods of recklessness, assertion, jealousy, sin. Bad women, as they are termed, may have in them sorrow, repentance, pity, sacrifice. And I don't think Mrs. Erlynne a bad woman—I know she's not.

LORD WINDERMERE. My dear child, the woman's impossible. No matter what harm she tries to do us, you must never see her again. She is inadmissible anywhere.

LADY WINDERMERE. But I want to see her. I want her to come here.

LORD WINDERMERE. Never!

LADY WINDERMERE. She came here once as *your* guest. She must come now as *mine.* That is but fair.

LORD WINDERMERE. She should never have come here.

LADY WINDERMERE. *(Rising.)* It is too late, Arthur, to say that now. *(Moves away.)*

LORD WINDERMERE. *(Rising.)* Margaret, if you knew where Mrs. Erlynne went last night, after she left this house, you would not sit in the same room with her. It was absolutely shameless, the whole thing.

LADY WINDERMERE. Arthur, I can't bear it any longer. I must tell you. Last night——

*(Enter Parker with a tray on which lie Lady Windermere's fan and a card.*

PARKER. Mrs. Erlynne has called to return your ladyship's fan which she took away by mistake last night. Mrs. Erlynne has written a message on the card.

LADY WINDERMERE. Oh, ask Mrs. Erlynne to be kind enough to come up. *(Reads card.)* Say I shall be very glad to see her.

*(Exit Parker.*

She wants to see me, Arthur.

LORD WINDERMERE. *(Takes card and looks at it.)* Margaret, I *beg* you not to. Let me see her first, at any rate. She's a very dangerous woman. She is the most dangerous woman I know. You don't realise what you're doing.

LADY WINDERMERE. It is right that I should see her.

LORD WINDERMERE. My child, you may be on the brink of a great sorrow. Don't go to meet it. It is absolutely necessary that I should see her before you do.

LADY WINDERMERE. Why should it be necessary?

*(Enter Parker.*

PARKER. Mrs. Erlynne.

*(Enter Mrs. Erlynne.*

MRS. ERLYNNE. *(Exit Parker.*

How do you do, Lady Windermere? *(To Lord Windermere.)* How do you do? Do you know, Lady Windermere, I am so sorry about your fan. I can't imagine how I made such a silly mistake. Most stupid of me. And as I was driving in your direction, I thought I would take the opportunity of returning your property in person with many apologies for my carelessness, and of bidding you good-bye.

LADY WINDERMERE. Good-bye? *(Moves towards sofa with Mrs. Erlynne and sits down beside her.)* Are you going away, then, Mrs. Erlynne?

MRS. ERLYNNE. Yes; I am going to live abroad again. The English climate doesn't suit me. My—heart is affected here, and that I don't like. I prefer living in the south. London is too full of fogs and—and serious people, Lord Windermere. Whether the fogs produce the serious people or whether the serious people produce the fogs, I don't know, but the whole thing rather gets on my nerves, and so I'm leaving this afternoon by the Club Train.

LADY WINDERMERE. This afternoon? But I wanted so much to come and see you.

MRS. ERLYNNE. How kind of you! But I am afraid I have to go.

LADY WINDERMERE. Shall I never see you again, Mrs. Erlynne?

MRS. ERLYNNE. I am afraid not. Our lives lie too far apart. But this is a little thing I would like you to do for me. I want a photograph of you, Lady Windermere—would you give me one? You don't know how gratified I should be.

LADY WINDERMERE. Oh, with pleasure. There is one on that table. I'll show it to you. *(Goes across to the table.)*

LORD WINDERMERE. *(Coming up to Mrs. Erlynne and speaking in a low voice.)* It is monstrous your intruding yourself here after your conduct last night.

MRS. ERLYNNE. *(With an amused smile.)* My dear Windermere, manners before morals!

LADY WINDERMERE. *(Returning.)* I'm afraid it is very flattering—I am not so pretty as that. *(Showing photograph.)*

MRS. ERLYNNE. You are much prettier. But haven't you got one of yourself with your little boy?

LADY WINDERMERE. I have. Would you prefer one of those?

MRS. ERLYNNE. Yes.

LADY WINDERMERE. I'll go and get it for you, if you'll excuse me for a moment. I have one upstairs.

MRS. ERLYNNE. So sorry, Lady Windermere, to give you so much trouble.

LADY WINDERMERE. *(Moves to door R.)* No trouble at all, Mrs. Erlynne.

MRS. ERLYNNE. Thanks so much.

*(Exit Lady Windermere R.*

You seem rather out of temper this morning, Windermere. Why should you be? Margaret and I get on charmingly together.

LORD WINDERMERE. I can't bear to see you with her. Besides, you have not told me the truth, Mrs. Erlynne.

MRS. ERLYNNE. I have not told *her* the truth, you mean.

LORD WINDERMERE. *(Standing C.)* I sometimes wish you had. I should have been spared then the misery, the anxiety, the annoyance of the last six months. But rather than my wife should know—that the mother whom she was taught to consider as dead, the mother whom she has mourned as dead, is living—a divorced woman, going about under an assumed name, a bad woman preying upon life, as I know you now to be—rather than that, I was ready to supply you with money to pay bill after bill, extravagance after extravagance, to risk what occurred yesterday, the first quarrel I have ever had with my wife. You don't understand what that means to me. How could you? But I tell you that the only bitter words that ever came from those sweet lips of hers were on your account, and I hate to see you next her. You sully the innocence that is in her. *(Moves L.C.)* And then I used to think that with all your faults you were frank and honest. You are not.

MRS. ERLYNNE. Why do you say that?

LORD WINDERMERE. You made me get you an invitation to my wife's ball.

MRS. ERLYNNE. For my daughter's ball—yes.

LORD WINDERMERE. You came, and within an hour of your leaving the house you are found in a man's rooms—you are disgraced before every one. *(Goes up stage C.)*

MRS. ERLYNNE. Yes.

LORD WINDERMERE. *(Turning round on her.)* Therefore I have a right to look upon you as what you are—a worthless, vicious woman. I have the right to tell you never to enter this house, never to attempt to come near my wife——

MRS. ERLYNNE. *(Coldly.)* My daughter, you mean.

LORD WINDERMERE. You have no right to claim her as your daughter. You left her, abandoned her when she was but a child in the cradle, abandoned her for your lover, who abandoned you in turn.

MRS. ERLYNNE. *(Rising.)* Do you count that to his credit, Lord Windermere—or to mine?

LORD WINDERMERE. To his, now that I know you.

MRS. ERLYNNE. Take care—you had better be careful.

LORD WINDERMERE. Oh, I am not going to mince words for you. I know you thoroughly.

MRS. ERLYNNE. *(Looking steadily at him.)* I question that.

LORD WINDERMERE. I *do* know you. For twenty years of your life you lived without your child, without a thought of your child. One day you read in the papers that she had married a rich man. You saw your hideous chance. You knew that to spare her the ignominy of learning that a woman like you was her mother, I would endure anything. You began your blackmailing.

MRS. ERLYNNE. *(Shrugging her shoulders.)* Don't use ugly words, Windermere. They are vulgar. I saw my chance, it is true, and took it.

LORD WINDERMERE. Yes, you took it—and spoiled it all last night by being found out.

MRS. ERLYNNE. *(With a strange smile.)* You are quite right, I spoiled it all last night.

LORD WINDERMERE. And as for your blunder in taking my wife's fan from here and then leaving it about in Darlington's rooms, it is unpardonable. I can't bear the sight of it now. I shall never let my wife use it again. The thing is soiled for me. You should have kept it and not brought it back.

MRS. ERLYNNE. I think I *shall* keep it. *(Goes up.)* It's extremely pretty. *(Takes up fan.)* I shall ask Margaret to give it to me.

LORD WINDERMERE. I hope my wife will give it to you.

MRS. ERLYNNE. Oh, I'm sure she will have no objection.

LORD WINDERMERE. I wish that at the same time she would give you a miniature she kisses every night before she prays—It's the miniature of a young innocent-looking girl with beautiful dark hair.

MRS. ERLYNNE. Ah, yes, I remember. How long ago that seems! *(Goes to sofa and sits down.)* It was done before I was married. Dark hair and an innocent expression were the fashion then, Windermere! *(A pause.)*

LORD WINDERMERE. What do you mean by coming here this morning? What is your object? *(Crossing L.C. and sitting.)*

MRS. ERLYNNE. *(With a note of irony in her voice.)* To bid good-bye to my dear daughter, of course. *(Lord Windermere bites his under lip in anger. MRS. ERLYNNE looks at him, and her voice and manner become serious. In her accents as she talks there is a note of deep tragedy. For a moment she reveals herself.)* Oh, don't imagine I am going to have a pathetic scene with her, weep on her neck and tell her who I am, and all that kind of thing. I have no ambition to play the part of a mother. Only once in my life have I known a mother's feelings. That was last night. They were terrible—they made me suffer— they made me suffer too much. For twenty years, as you say, I have lived childless,—I want to live childless still. *(Hiding her feelings with a trivial laugh.)* Besides, my dear Windermere, how on earth could I pose as a mother with a grown-up daughter? Margaret is twenty-one, and I have never admitted that I am more than twenty-nine, or thirty at the most. Twenty-nine when there are pink shades, thirty when there are not. So you see what difficulties it would involve. No, as far as I am concerned, let your wife cherish the memory of this dead, stainless mother. Why should I interfere with her illusions? I find it hard enough to keep my own. I lost one illusion last night. I thought I had no heart. I find I have, and a heart doesn't suit me, Windermere. Somehow it doesn't go with modern dress. It makes one look old. *(Takes up hand-mirror from table and looks into it.)* And it spoils one's career at critical moments.

LORD WINDERMERE. You fill me with horror—with absolute horror.

MRS. ERLYNNE. *(Rising.)* I suppose, Windermere, you would like me to retire into a convent or become a hospital nurse, or something of that kind, as people do in silly modern novels. That is stupid of you, Arthur; in real life we don't do such things—not as long as we have any good looks left, at any rate. No—what consoles one now-a-days is not repentance, but pleasure. Repentance is quite out of date. And besides, if a woman really repents, she has to go to a bad dressmaker, otherwise no one believes in her. And nothing in the world would induce me to do that. No; I am going to pass entirely out of your two lives. My coming into them has been a mistake—I discovered that last night.

LORD WINDERMERE. A fatal mistake.

MRS. ERLYNNE. *(Smiling.)* Almost fatal.

LORD WINDERMERE. I am sorry now I did not tell my wife the whole thing at once.

MRS. ERLYNNE. I regret my bad actions. You regret your good ones—that is the difference between us.

LORD WINDERMERE. I don't trust you. I *will* tell my wife. It's better for her to know, and from me. It will cause her infinite pain—it will humiliate her terribly, but it's right that she should know.

MRS. ERLYNNE. You propose to tell her?

LORD WINDERMERE. I am going to tell her.

MRS. ERLYNNE. *(Going up to him.)* If you do, I will make my name so infamous that it will mar every moment of her life. It will ruin her, and make her wretched. If you dare to tell her, there is no depth of degradation I will not sink to, no pit of shame I will not enter. You shall not tell her—I forbid you.

LORD WINDERMERE. Why?

MRS. ERLYNNE. *(After a pause.)* If I said to you that I cared for her, perhaps loved her even—you would sneer at me, wouldn't you?

LORD WINDERMERE. I should feel it was not true. A mother's love means devotion, unselfishness, sacrifice. What could you know of such things?

MRS. ERLYNNE. You are right. What could I know of such things? Don't let us talk any more about it—as for telling my daughter who I am, that I do not allow. It is my secret, it is not yours. If I make up my mind to tell her, and I think I will, I shall tell her before I leave the house—if not, I shall never tell her.

LORD WINDERMERE. *(Angrily.)* Then let me beg of you to leave our house at once. I will make your excuses to Margaret.

*(Enter Lady Windermere R. She goes over to Mrs. Erlynne with the photograph in her hand. Lord Windermere moves to back of sofa, and anxiously watches Mrs. Erlynne as the scene progresses.)*

LADY WINDERMERE. I am so sorry, Mrs. Erlynne, to have kept you waiting. I couldn't find the photograph anywhere. At last I discovered it in my husband's dressing-room—he had stolen it.

MRS. ERLYNNE. *(Takes the photograph from her and looks at it.)* I am not surprised—it is charming. *(Goes over to sofa with Lady Windermere, and sits down beside her. Looks again at the photograph.)* And so that is your little boy! What is he called?

LADY WINDERMERE. Gerard, after my dear father.

MRS. ERLYNNE. *(Laying the photograph down.)* Really?

LADY WINDERMERE. Yes. If it had been a girl, I would have called it after my mother. My mother had the same name as myself, Margaret.

MRS. ERLYNNE. My name is Margaret too.

LADY WINDERMERE. Indeed!

MRS. ERLYNNE. Yes. *(Pause.)* You are devoted to your mother's memory, Lady Windermere, your husband tells me.

LADY WINDERMERE. We all have ideals in life. At least we all should have. Mine is my mother.

MRS. ERLYNNE. Ideals are dangerous things. Realities are better. They wound, but they're better.

LADY WINDERMERE. *(Shaking her head.)* If I lost my ideals, I should lose everything.

MRS. ERLYNNE. Everything?

LADY WINDERMERE. Yes. *(Pause.)*

MRS. ERLYNNE. Did your father often speak to you of your mother?

LADY WINDERMERE. No, it gave him too much pain. He told me how my mother had died a few months after I was born. His eyes filled with tears as he spoke. Then he begged me never to mention her name to him again. It made him suffer even to hear it. My father—my father really died of a broken heart. His was the most ruined life I know.

MRS. ERLYNNE. *(Rising.)* I am afraid I must go now, Lady Windermere.

LADY WINDERMERE. *(Rising.)* Oh no, don't.

MRS. ERLYNNE. I think I had better. My carriage must have come back by this time. I sent it to Lady Jedburgh's with a note.

LADY WINDERMERE. Arthur, would you mind seeing if Mrs. Erlynne's carriage has come back?

MRS. ERLYNNE. Pray don't trouble, Lord Windermere.

LADY WINDERMERE. Yes, Arthur, do go, please.

*(Lord Windermere hesitates for a moment and looks at Mrs. Erlynne. She remains quite impassive. He leaves the room.)*

*(To Mrs. Erlynne.)* Oh! What am I to say to you? You saved me last night? *(Goes towards her.)*

MRS. ERLYNNE. Hush—don't speak of it.

LADY WINDERMERE. I must speak of it. I can't let you think that I am going to accept this sacrifice. I am not. It is too great. I am going to tell my husband everything. It is my duty.

MRS. ERLYNNE. It is not your duty—at least you have duties to others besides him. You say you owe me something?

LADY WINDERMERE. I owe you everything.

MRS. ERLYNNE. Then pay your debt by silence. That is the only way in which it can be paid. Don't spoil the one good thing I have done in my life by telling it to any one. Promise me that what passed last night will remain a secret between us. You must not bring misery into your husband's life. Why spoil his love? You must not spoil it. Love is easily killed. Oh! how easily love is killed! Pledge me your word, Lady Windermere, that you will *never* tell him. I insist upon it.

LADY WINDERMERE. *(With bowed head.)* It is your will, not mine.

MRS. ERLYNNE. Yes, it is my will. And never forget your child—I like to think of you as a mother. I like you to think of yourself as one.

LADY WINDERMERE. *(Looking up.)* I always will now. Only once in my life I have forgotten my own mother—that was last night. Oh, if I had remembered her I should not have been so foolish, so wicked.

MRS. ERLYNNE. *(With a slight shudder.)* Hush, last night is quite over.
*(Enter Lord Windermere.*

LORD WINDERMERE. Your carriage has not come back yet, Mrs. Erlynne.

MRS. ERLYNNE. It makes no matter. I'll take a hansom. There is nothing in the world so respectable as a good Shrewsbury and Talbot. And now, dear Lady Windermere, I am afraid it is really good-bye. *(Moves up C.)* Oh, I remember. You'll think me absurd, but do you know I've taken a great fancy to this fan that I was silly enough to run away with last night from your ball. Now, I wonder would you give it to me? Lord Windermere says you may. I know it is his present.

LADY WINDERMERE. Oh, certainly, if it will give you any pleasure. But it has my name on it. It has 'Margaret' on it.

MRS. ERLYNNE. But we have the same Christian name.

LADY WINDERMERE. Oh, I forgot. Of course, do have it. What a wonderful chance our names being the same!

MRS. ERLYNNE. Quite wonderful. Thanks—it will always remind me of you. *(Shakes hands with her.)*
*(Enter Parker.*

PARKER. Lord Augustus Lorton. Mrs. Erlynne's carriage has come.
*(Enter Lord Augustus.*

LORD AUGUSTUS. Good morning, dear boy. Good morning, Lady Windermere. *(Sees Mrs. Erlynne.)* Mrs. Erlynne!

MRS. ERLYNNE. How do you do, Lord Augustus? Are you quite well this morning?

LORD AUGUSTUS. *(Coldly.)* Quite well, thank you, Mrs. Erlynne.

MRS. ERLYNNE. You don't look at all well, Lord Augustus. You stop up too late—it is so bad for you. You really should take more care of yourself. Good-bye, Lord Windermere. *(Goes towards door with a bow to Lord Augustus. Suddenly smiles and looks back at him.)* Lord Augustus! Won't you see me to my carriage? You might carry the fan.

LORD WINDERMERE. Allow me!

MRS. ERLYNNE. No; I want Lord Augustus. I have a special message for the dear Duchess. Won't you carry the fan, Lord Augustus?

LORD AUGUSTUS. If you really desire it, Mrs. Erlynne.

MRS. ERLYNNE. *(Laughing.)* Of course I do. You'll carry it so gracefully. You would carry off anything gracefully, dear Lord Augustus.
*(When she reaches the door she looks back for a moment at Lady Windermere. Their eyes meet. Then she turns, and exit C. followed by Lord Augustus.)*

LADY WINDERMERE. You will never speak against Mrs. Erlynne again, Arthur, will you?

LORD WINDERMERE. *(Gravely.)* She is better than one thought her.

LADY WINDERMERE. She is better than I am.

LORD WINDERMERE. *(Smiling as he strokes her hair.)* Child, you and she belong to different worlds. Into your world evil has never entered.

LADY WINDERMERE. Don't say that, Arthur. There is the same world for all of us, and good and evil, sin and innocence, go through it hand in hand. To shut one's eyes to half of life that one may live securely is as though one blinded oneself that one might walk with more safety in a land of pit and precipice.

LORD WINDERMERE. *(Moves down with her.)* Darling, why do you say that?

LADY WINDERMERE. *(Sits on sofa.)* Because I, who had shut my eyes to life, came to the brink. And one who had separated us——

LORD WINDERMERE. We were never separated.

LADY WINDERMERE. We never must be again. Oh Arthur, don't love me less, and I will trust you more. I will trust you absolutely. Let us go to Selby. In the Rose Garden at Selby the roses are white and red.

*(Enter Lord Augustus C.*

LORD AUGUSTUS. Arthur, she has explained everything!

*(Lady Windermere looks horribly frightened at this. Lord Windermere starts.* LORD AUGUSTUS *takes Windermere by the arm and brings him to front of stage. He talks rapidly and in a low voice. Lady Windermere stands watching them in terror.)*

My dear fellow, she has explained every demmed thing. We all wronged her immensely. It was entirely for my sake she went to Darlington's rooms. Called first at the Club—fact is, wanted to put me out of suspense—and being told I had gone on—followed—naturally frightened when she heard a lot of us coming in—retired to another room—I assure you, most gratifying to me, the whole thing. We all behaved brutally to her. She is just the woman for me. Suits me down to the ground. All the conditions she makes are that we live entirely out of England. A very good thing, too. Demmed clubs, demmed climate, demmed cooks, demmed everything. Sick of it all!

LADY WINDERMERE. *(Frightened.)* Has Mrs. Erlynne——?

LORD AUGUSTUS. *(Advancing towards her with a low bow.)* Yes, Lady

Windermere—Mrs. Erlynne has done me the honour of accepting my hand.

LORD WINDERMERE. Well, you are certainly marrying a very clever woman!

LADY WINDERMERE. *(Taking her husband's hand.)* Ah, you're marrying a very good woman!

CURTAIN

# AN IDEAL HUSBAND

# THE PERSONS OF THE PLAY

THE EARL OF CAVERSHAM, K.G.
VISCOUNT GORING, his Son
SIR ROBERT CHILTERN, Bart., Under-Secretary for Foreign
    Affairs
VICOMTE DE NANJAC, Attaché at the French Embassy in
    London
MR. MONTFORD
MASON, Butler to Sir Robert Chiltern
PHIPPS, Lord Gorin's Servant
JAMES    ⎫
          ⎬ FOOTMEN
HAROLD ⎭

LADY CHILTERN
LADY MARKBY
THE COUNTESS OF BASILDON
MRS. MARCHMONT
MISS MABEL CHILTERN, Sir Robert Chiltern's Sister
MRS. CHEVELEY

# THE SCENES OF THE PLAY

*Time .... The Present*
*Place .... London*

*The Action of the Play is completed within twenty-four hours.*

# THEATRE ROYAL, HAYMARKET

*Sole Lessee: Mr. Herbert Beerbohm Tree*
*Managers: Mr. Lewis Waller and Mr. H. H. Morell*
*January 3rd, 1895*

THE EARL OF CAVERSHAM   *Mr. Alfred Bishop*
VISCOUNT GORING   *Mr. Charles H. Hawtrey*
SIR ROBERT CHILTERN   *Mr. Lewis Waller*
VICOMTE DE NANJAC   *Mr. Cosmo Stuart*
MR. MONTFORD   *Mr. Harry Stanford*
MASON   *Mr. H. Deane*
PHIPPS   *Mr. C. H. Brookfield*
JAMES (FOOTMAN)   *Mr. Charles Meyrick*
HAROLD (FOOTMAN)   *Mr. Goodhart*

LADY CHILTERN   *Miss Julia Neilson*
LADY MARKBY   *Miss Fanny Brough*
COUNTESS OF BASILDON   *Miss Vane Featherston*

MRS. MARCHMONT   *Miss Helen Forsyth*
MISS MABEL CHILTERN   *Miss Maude Millett*
MRS. CHEVELEY   *Miss Florence West*

# FIRST ACT

SCENE—*The octagon room at Sir Robert Chiltern's house in Grosvenor Square.*

*(The room is brilliantly lighted and full of guests. At the top of the staircase stands Lady Chiltern, a woman of grave Greek beauty, about twenty-seven years of age. She receives the guests as they come up. Over the well of the staircase hangs a great chandelier with wax lights, which illumine a large eighteenth-century French tapestry—representing the Triumph of Love, from a design by Boucher—that is stretched on the staircase wall. On the right is the entrance to the music-room. The sound of a string quartette is faintly heard. The entrance on the left leads to other reception-rooms. Mrs. Marchmont and Lady Basildon, two very pretty women, are seated together on a Louis Seize sofa. They are types of exquisite fragility. Their affectation of manner has a delicate charm. Watteau would have loved to paint them.)*

MRS. MARCHMONT. Going on to the Hartlocks' to-night, Margaret?

LADY BASILDON. I suppose so. Are you?

MRS. MARCHMONT. Yes. Horribly tedious parties they give, don't they?

LADY BASILDON. Horribly tedious! Never know why I go. Never know why I go anywhere.

MRS. MARCHMONT. I come here to be educated.

LADY BASILDON. Ah! I hate being educated!

MRS. MARCHMONT. So do I. It puts one almost on a level with the commercial classes, doesn't it? But dear Gertrude Chiltern is always telling me that I should have some serious purpose in life. So I come here to try to find one.

LADY BASILDON. *(Looking round through her lorgnette.)* I don't see anybody here to-night whom one could possibly call a serious purpose. The man who took me in to dinner talked to me about his wife the whole time.

MRS. MARCHMONT. How very trivial of him!

LADY BASILDON. Terribly trivial! What did your man talk about?

MRS. MARCHMONT. About myself.

LADY BASILDON. *(Languidly.)* And were you interested?

MRS. MARCHMONT. *(Shaking her head.)* Not in the smallest degree.

LADY BASILDON. What martyrs we are, dear Margaret!

MRS. MARCHMONT. *(Rising.)* And how well it becomes us, Olivia!

*(They rise and go towards the music-room. The Vicomte de Nanjac, a young attaché known for his neckties and his Anglomania, approaches with a low bow, and enters into conversation.)*

MASON. *(Announcing guests from the top of the staircase.)* Mr. and Lady Jane Barford. Lord Caversham.

*(Enter Lord Caversham, an old gentleman of seventy, wearing the riband and star of the Garter. A fine Whig type. Rather like a portrait by Lawrence.)*

LORD CAVERSHAM. Good evening, Lady Chiltern! Has my good-for-nothing young son been here?

LADY CHILTERN. *(Smiling.)* I don't think Lord Goring has arrived yet.

MABEL CHILTERN. *(Coming up to Lord Caversham.)* Why do you call Lord Goring good-for-nothing?

*(Mabel Chiltern is a perfect example of the English type of prettiness, the apple-blossom type. She has all the fragrance and freedom of a flower. There is ripple after ripple of sunlight in her hair, and the little mouth, with its parted lips, is expectant, like the mouth of a child. She has the fascinating tyranny of youth, and the astonishing courage of innocence. To sane people she is not reminiscent of any work of art. But she is really like a Tanagra statuette, and would be rather annoyed if she were told so.)*

LORD CAVERSHAM. Because he leads such an idle life.

MABEL CHILTERN. How can you say such a thing? Why, he rides in the Row at ten o'clock in the morning, goes to the Opera three times a week, changes his clothes at least five times a day, and dines out every night of the season. You don't call that leading an idle life, do you?

LORD CAVERSHAM. *(Looking at her with a kindly twinkle in his eyes.)* You are a very charming young lady!

MABEL CHILTERN. How sweet of you to say that, Lord Caversham! Do come to us more often. You know we are always at home on Wednesdays, and you look so well with your star!

LORD CAVERSHAM. Never go anywhere now. Sick of London Society. Shouldn't mind being introduced to my own tailor; he always votes on the right side. But object strongly to being sent down to dinner with my wife's milliner. Never could stand Lady Caversham's bonnets.

MABEL CHILTERN. Oh, I love London Society! I think it has immensely improved. It is entirely composed now of beautiful idiots and brilliant lunatics. Just what Society should be.

LORD CAVERSHAM. Hum! Which is Goring? Beautiful idiot, or the other thing?

MABEL CHILTERN. *(Gravely.)* I have been obliged for the present to put Lord Goring into a class quite by himself. But he is developing charmingly!

LORD CAVERSHAM. Into what?

MABEL CHILTERN. *(With a little curtsey.)* I hope to let you know very soon, Lord Caversham!

MASON. *(Announcing guests.)* Lady Markby. Mrs. Cheveley.

*(Enter Lady Markby and Mrs. Cheveley. Lady Markby is a pleasant, kindly, popular woman, with gray hair à la marquise and good lace. Mrs. Cheveley, who accompanies her, is tall and rather slight. Lips very thin and highly-coloured, a line of scarlet on a pallid face. Venetian red hair, aquiline nose, and long throat. Rouge accentuates the natural paleness of her complexion. Gray-green eyes that move restlessly. She is in heliotrope, with diamonds. She looks rather like an orchid, and makes great demands on one's curiosity. In all her movements she is extremely graceful. A work of art, on the whole, but showing the influence of too many schools.)*

LADY MARKBY. Good evening, dear Gertrude! So kind of you to let me bring my friend, Mrs. Cheveley. Two such charming women should know each other!

LADY CHILTERN. *(Advances towards Mrs. Cheveley with a sweet smile. Then suddenly stops, and bows rather distantly.)* I think Mrs. Cheveley and I have met before. I did not know she had married a second time.

LADY MARKBY. *(Genially.)* Ah, nowadays people marry as often as they can, don't they? It is most fashionable. *(To Duchess of Maryborough.)* Dear Duchess, and how is the Duke? Brain still weak, I suppose? Well, that is only to be expected, is it not? His good father was just the same. There is nothing like race, is there?

MRS. CHEVELEY. *(Playing with her fan.)* But have we really met before, Lady Chiltern? I can't remember where. I have been out of England for so long.

LADY CHILTERN. We were at school together, Mrs. Cheveley.

MRS. CHEVELEY. *(Superciliously.)* Indeed? I have forgotten all about my schooldays. I have a vague impression that they were detestable.

LADY CHILTERN. *(Coldly.)* I am not surprised!

MRS. CHEVELEY. *(In her sweetest manner.)* Do you know, I am quite looking forward to meeting your clever husband, Lady Chiltern. Since he had been at the Foreign Office, he has been so much talked of in Vienna. They actually succeed in spelling his name right in the newspapers. That in itself is fame, on the continent.

LADY CHILTERN. I hardly think there will be much in common between you and my husband, Mrs. Cheveley! *(Moves away.)*

VICOMTE DE NANJAC. Ah! Chère Madame, quelle surprise! I have not seen you since Berlin!

MRS. CHEVELEY. Not since Berlin, Vicomte. Five years ago!

VICOMTE DE NANJAC. And you are younger and more beautiful than ever. How do you manage it?

MRS. CHEVELEY. By making it a rule only to talk to perfectly charming people like yourself.

VICOMTE DE NANJAC. Ah! you flatter me. You butter me, as they say here.

MRS. CHEVELEY. Do they say that here? How dreadful of them!

VICOMTE DE NANJAC. Yes, they have a wonderful language. It should be more widely known.

*(Sir Robert Chiltern enters. A man of forty, but looking somewhat younger. Clean-shaven, with finely-cut features, dark-haired and dark-eyed. A personality of mark. Not popular—few personalities are. But intensely admired by the few, and deeply respected by the many. The note of his manner is that of perfect distinction, with a slight touch of pride. One feels that he is conscious of the success he has made in life. A nervous temperament, with a tired look. The firmly-chiselled mouth and chin contrast strikingly with the romantic expression in the deep-set eyes. The variance is suggestive of an almost complete separation of passion and intellect, as though thought and emotion were each isolated in its own sphere through some violence of will-power. There is nervousness in the nostrils, and in the pale, thin, pointed hands. It would be inaccurate to call him picturesque. Picturesqueness cannot survive the House of Commons. But Vandyck would have liked to have painted his head.)*

SIR ROBERT CHILTERN. Good evening, Lady Markby! I hope you have brought Sir John with you?

LADY MARKBY. Oh! I have brought a much more charming person than Sir John. Sir John's temper since he has taken seriously to politics has become quite unbearable. Really, now that the House of Commons is trying to become useful, it does a great deal of harm.

SIR ROBERT CHILTERN. I hope not, Lady Markby. At any rate we do our best to waste the public time, don't we? But who is this charming person you have been kind enough to bring to us?

LADY MARKBY. Her name is Mrs. Cheveley! One of the Dorsetshire Cheveleys, I suppose. But I really don't know. Families are so mixed nowadays. Indeed, as a rule, everybody turns out to be somebody else.

SIR ROBERT CHILTERN. Mrs. Cheveley? I seem to know the name.

LADY MARKBY. She has just arrived from Vienna.

SIR ROBERT CHILTERN. Ah! yes. I think I know whom you mean.

LADY MARKBY. Oh! she goes everywhere there, and has such pleasant scandals about all her friends. I really must go to Vienna next winter. I hope there is a good chef at the Embassy.

SIR ROBERT CHILTERN. If there is not, the Ambassador will certainly have to be recalled. Pray point out Mrs. Cheveley to me. I should like to see her.

LADY MARKBY. Let me introduce you. *(To Mrs. Cheveley.)* My dear, Sir Robert Chiltern is dying to know you!

SIR ROBERT CHILTERN. *(Bowing.)* Everyone is dying to know the brilliant Mrs. Cheveley. Our attachés at Vienna write to us about nothing else.

MRS. CHEVELEY. Thank you, Sir Robert. An acquaintance that begins with a compliment is sure to develop into a real friendship. It starts in the right manner. And I find that I know Lady Chiltern already.

SIR ROBERT CHILTERN. Really?

MRS. CHEVELEY. Yes. She has just reminded me that we were at school together. I remember it perfectly now. She always got the good conduct prize. I have a distinct recollection of Lady Chiltern always getting the good conduct prize!

SIR ROBERT CHILTERN. *(Smiling.)* And what prizes did you get, Mrs. Cheveley?

MRS. CHEVELEY. My prizes came a little later on in life. I don't think any of them were for good conduct. I forget!

SIR ROBERT CHILTERN. I am sure they were for something charming!

MRS. CHEVELEY. I don't know that women are always rewarded for being charming. I think they are usually punished for it! Certainly, more women grow old nowadays through the faithfulness of their admirers than through anything else! At least that is the only way I can account for the terribly haggard look of most of your pretty women in London!

SIR ROBERT CHILTERN. What an appalling philosophy that sounds! To attempt to classify you, Mrs. Cheveley, would be an impertinence. But may I ask, at heart, are you an optimist or a pessimist? Those seem to be the only two fashionable religions left to us nowadays.

MRS. CHEVELEY. Oh, I'm neither. Optimism begins in a broad grin, and Pessimism ends with blue spectacles. Besides, they are both of them merely poses.

SIR ROBERT CHILTERN. You prefer to be natural?

MRS. CHEVELEY. Sometimes. But it is such a very difficult pose to keep up.

SIR ROBERT CHILTERN. What would those modern psychological novelists, of whom we hear so much, say to such a theory as that?

MRS. CHEVELEY. Ah! the strength of women comes from the fact that psychology cannot explain us. Men can be analyzed, women ... merely adored.

SIR ROBERT CHILTERN. You think science cannot grapple with the problem of women?

MRS. CHEVELEY. Science can never grapple with the irrational. That is why it has no future before it, in this world.

SIR ROBERT CHILTERN. And women represent the irrational.

MRS. CHEVELEY. Well-dressed women do.

SIR ROBERT CHILTERN. *(With a polite bow.)* I fear I could hardly agree with you there. But do sit down. And now tell me, what makes you leave your brilliant Vienna for our gloomy London—or perhaps the question is indiscreet?

MRS. CHEVELEY. Questions are never indiscreet. Answers sometimes are.

SIR ROBERT CHILTERN. Well, at any rate, may I know if it is politics or pleasure?

MRS. CHEVELEY. Politics are my only pleasure. You see nowadays it is not fashionable to flirt till one is forty, or to be romantic till one is forty-five, so we poor women who are under thirty, or say we are, have nothing open to us but politics or philanthropy. And philanthropy seems to me to have become simply the refuge of people who wish to annoy their fellow-creatures. I prefer politics. I think they are more ... becoming!

SIR ROBERT CHILTERN. A political life is a noble career!

MRS. CHEVELEY. Sometimes. And sometimes it is a clever game, Sir Robert. And sometimes it is a great nuisance.

SIR ROBERT CHILTERN. Which do you find it?

MRS. CHEVELEY. I? A combination of all three. *(Drops her fan.)*

SIR ROBERT CHILTERN. *(Picks up fan.)* Allow me!

MRS. CHEVELEY. Thanks.

SIR ROBERT CHILTERN. But you have not told me yet what makes you honour London so suddenly. Our season is almost over.

MRS. CHEVELEY. Oh! I don't care about the London season! It is too matrimonial. People are either hunting for husbands, or hiding from them. I wanted to meet you. It is quite true. You know what a woman's curiosity is. Almost as great as a man's! I wanted immensely to meet you, and ... to ask you to do something for me.

SIR ROBERT CHILTERN. I hope it is not a little thing, Mrs. Cheveley. I find that little things are so very difficult to do.

MRS. CHEVELEY. *(After a moment's reflection.)* No, I don't think it is quite a little thing.

SIR ROBERT CHILTERN. I am so glad. Do tell me what it is.

MRS. CHEVELEY. Later on. *(Rises.)* And now may I walk through your beautiful house? I hear your pictures are charming. Poor Baron Arnheim—you remember the Baron?—used to tell me you had some wonderful Corots.

SIR ROBERT CHILTERN. *(With an almost imperceptible start.)* Did you know Baron Arnheim well?

MRS. CHEVELEY. *(Smiling.)* Intimately. Did you?

SIR ROBERT CHILTERN. At one time.

MRS. CHEVELEY. Wonderful man, wasn't he?

SIR ROBERT CHILTERN. *(After a pause.)* He was very remarkable, in many ways.

MRS. CHEVELEY. I often think it such a pity he never wrote his memoirs. They would have been most interesting.

SIR ROBERT CHILTERN. Yes: he knew men and cities well, like the old Greek.

MRS. CHEVELEY. Without the dreadful disadvantage of having a Penelope waiting at home for him.

MASON. Lord Goring.

*(Enter Lord Goring. Thirty-four, but always says he is younger. A well-bred, expressionless face. He is clever, but would not like to be thought so. A flawless dandy, he would be annoyed if he were considered romantic. He plays with life, and is on perfectly good terms with the world. He is fond of being misunderstood. It gives him a post of vantage.)*

SIR ROBERT CHILTERN. Good evening, my dear Arthur! Mrs. Cheveley, allow me to introduce to you Lord Goring, the idlest man in London.

MRS. CHEVELEY. I have met Lord Goring before.

LORD GORING. *(Bowing.)* I did not think you would remember me, Mrs. Cheveley.

MRS. CHEVELEY. My memory is under admirable control. And are you still a bachelor?

LORD GORING. I . . . believe so.

MRS. CHEVELEY. How very romantic!

LORD GORING. Oh! I am not at all romantic. I am not old enough. I leave romance to my seniors.

SIR ROBERT CHILTERN. Lord Goring is the result of Boodle's Club, Mrs. Cheveley.

MRS. CHEVELEY. He reflects every credit on the institution.

LORD GORING. May I ask are you staying in London long?

MRS. CHEVELEY. That depends partly on the weather, partly on the cooking, and partly on Sir Robert.

SIR ROBERT CHILTERN. You are not going to plunge us into a European war, I hope?

MRS. CHEVELEY. There is no danger, at present!

*(She nods to Lord Goring, with a look of amusement in her eyes, and goes out with Sir Robert Chiltern. Lord Goring saunters over to Mabel Chiltern.)*

MABEL CHILTERN. You are very late!

LORD GORING. Have you missed me?

MABEL CHILTERN. Awfully!

LORD GORING. Then I am sorry I did not stay away longer. I like being missed.

MABEL CHILTERN. How very selfish of you!

LORD GORING. I am very selfish.

MABEL CHILTERN. You are always telling me of your bad qualities, Lord Goring.

LORD GORING. I have only told you half of them as yet, Miss Mabel!

MABEL CHILTERN. Are the others very bad?

LORD GORING. Quite dreadful! When I think of them at night I go to sleep at once.

MABEL CHILTERN. Well, I delight in your bad qualities. I wouldn't have you part with one of them.

LORD GORING. How very nice of you! But then you are always nice. By the way, I want to ask you a question, Miss Mabel. Who brought Mrs. Cheveley here? That woman in heliotrope, who has just gone out of the room with your brother?

MABEL CHILTERN. Oh, I think Lady Markby brought her. Why do you ask?

LORD GORING. I hadn't seen her for years, that is all.

MABEL CHILTERN. What an absurd reason!

LORD GORING. All reasons are absurd.

MABEL CHILTERN. What sort of woman is she?

LORD GORING. Oh! a genius in the daytime and a beauty at night!

MABEL CHILTERN. I dislike her already.

LORD GORING. That shows your admirable good taste.

VICOMTE DE NANJAC. *(Approaching.)* Ah, the English young lady is the dragon of good taste, is she not? Quite the dragon of good taste.

LORD GORING. So the newspapers are always telling us.

VICOMTE DE NANJAC. I read all your English newspapers. I find them so amusing.

LORD GORING. Then, my dear Nanjac, you must certainly read between the lines.

VICOMTE DE NANJAC. I should like to, but my professor objects. *(To Mabel Chiltern.)* May I have the pleasure of escorting you to the music-room, Mademoiselle?

MABEL CHILTERN. *(Looking very disappointed.)* Delighted, Vicomte, quite delighted! *(Turning to Lord Goring.)* Aren't you coming to the music-room?

LORD GORING. Not if there is any music going on, Miss Mabel.

MABEL CHILTERN. *(Severely.)* The music is in German. You would not understand it.

*(Goes out with the Vicomte de Nanjac. Lord Caversham comes up to his son.)*

LORD CAVERSHAM. Well, sir! what are you doing here? Wasting your life as usual! You should be in bed, sir. You keep too late hours! I heard of you the other night at Lady Rufford's dancing till four o'clock in the morning!

LORD GORING. Only a quarter to four, father.

LORD CAVERSHAM. Can't make out how you stand London Society. The thing has gone to the dogs, a lot of damned nobodies talking about nothing.

LORD GORING. I love talking about nothing, father. It is the only thing I know anything about.

LORD CAVERSHAM. You seem to me to be living entirely for pleasure.

LORD GORING. What else is there to live for, father? Nothing ages like happiness.

LORD CAVERSHAM. You are heartless, sir, very heartless!

LORD GORING. I hope not, father. Good evening, Lady Basildon!

LADY BASILDON. *(Arching two pretty eyebrows.)* Are you here? I had no idea you ever came to political parties!

LORD GORING. I adore political parties. They are the only place left to us where people don't talk politics.

LADY BASILDON. I delight in talking politics. I talk them all day long. But I can't bear listening to them. I don't know how the unfortunate men in the House stand these long debates.

LORD GORING. By never listening.

LADY BASILDON. Really?

LORD GORING. *(In his most serious manner.)* Of course. You see, it is a very dangerous thing to listen. If one listens one may be convinced; and a man who allows himself to be convinced by an argument is a thoroughly unreasonable person.

LADY BASILDON. Ah! that accounts for so much in men that I have never understood, and so much in women that their husbands never appreciate in them!

MRS. MARCHMONT. *(With a sigh.)* Our husbands never appreciate anything in us. We have to go to others for that!

LADY BASILDON. *(Emphatically.)* Yes, always to others, have we not?

LORD GORING. *(Smiling.)* And those are the views of the two ladies who are known to have the most admirable husbands in London.

MRS. MARCHMONT. That is exactly what we can't stand. My Reginald is quite hopelessly faultless. He is really unendurably so, at times! There is not the smallest element of excitement in knowing him.

LORD GORING. How terrible! Really, the thing should be more widely known!

LADY BASILDON. Basildon is quite as bad; he is as domestic as if he was a bachelor.

MRS. MARCHMONT. *(Pressing Lady Basildon's hand.)* My poor Olivia! We have married perfect husbands, and we are well punished for it.

LORD GORING. I should have thought it was the husbands who were punished.

MRS. MARCHMONT. *(Drawing herself up.)* Oh, dear no! They are as happy as possible! And as for trusting us, it is tragic how much they trust us.

LADY BASILDON. Perfectly tragic!

LORD GORING. Or comic, Lady Basildon?

LADY BASILDON. Certainly not comic, Lord Goring. How unkind of you to suggest such a thing!

MRS. MARCHMONT. I am afraid Lord Goring is in the camp of the enemy, as usual. I saw him talking to that Mrs. Cheveley when he came in.

LORD GORING. Handsome woman, Mrs. Cheveley!

LADY BASILDON. *(Stiffly.)* Please don't praise other women in our presence. You might wait for us to do that!

LORD GORING. I did wait.

MRS. MARCHMONT. Well, we are not going to praise her. I hear she went to the Opera on Monday night, and told Tommy Rufford at supper that, as far as she could see, London Society was entirely made up of dowdies and dandies.

LORD GORING. She is quite right, too. The men are all dowdies and the women are all dandies, aren't they?

MRS. MARCHMONT. *(After a pause.)* Oh! do you really think that is what Mrs. Cheveley meant?

LORD GORING. Of course. And a very sensible remark for Mrs. Cheveley to make, too.

*(Enter Mabel Chiltern. She joins the group.)*

MABEL CHILTERN. Why are you talking about Mrs. Cheveley? Everybody is talking about Mrs. Cheveley! Lord Goring says—what did you say, Lord Goring, about Mrs. Cheveley? Oh! I remember, that she was a genius in the daytime and a beauty at night.

LADY BASILDON. What a horrid combination! So very unnatural!

MRS. MARCHMONT. *(In her most dreamy manner.)* I like looking at geniuses, and listening to beautiful people.

LORD GORING. Ah! that is morbid of you, Mrs. Marchmont!

MRS. MARCHMONT. *(Brightening to a look of real pleasure.)* I am so glad to hear you say that. Marchmont and I have been married for seven years, and he has never once told me that I was morbid. Men are so painfully unobservant!

LADY BASILDON. *(Turning to her.)* I have always said, dear Margaret, that you were the most morbid person in London.

MRS. MARCHMONT. Ah! but you are always sympathetic, Olivia!

MABEL CHILTERN. Is it morbid to have a desire for food? I have a great desire for food. Lord Goring, will you give me some supper?

LORD GORING. With pleasure, Miss Mabel. *(Moves away with her.)*

MABEL CHILTERN. How horrid you have been! You have never talked to me the whole evening!

LORD GORING. How could I? You went away with the child-diplomatist.

MABEL CHILTERN. You might have followed us. Pursuit would have been only polite. I don't think I like you at all this evening!

LORD GORING. I like you immensely.

MABEL CHILTERN. Well, I wish you'd show it in a more marked way!

*(They go downstairs.)*

MRS. MARCHMONT. Olivia, I have a curious feeling of absolute faintness. I think I should like some supper very much. I know I should like some supper.

LADY BASILDON. I am positively dying for supper, Margaret!

MRS. MARCHMONT. Men are so horribly selfish, they never think of these things.

LADY BASILDON. Men are grossly material, grossly material!

*(The Vicomte de Nanjac enters from the music-room with some other guests. After having carefully examined all the people present, he approaches Lady Basildon.)*

VICOMTE DE NANJAC. May I have the honour of taking you down to supper, Comtesse?

LADY BASILDON. *(Coldly.)* I never take supper, thank you, Vicomte.

*(The Vicomte is about to retire. Lady Basildon, seeing this, rises at once and takes his arm.)* But I will come down with you with pleasure.

VICOMTE DE NANJAC. I am so fond of eating! I am very English in all my tastes.

LADY BASILDON. You look quite English, Vicomte, quite English.

*(They pass out. Mr. Montford, a perfectly groomed young dandy, approaches Mrs. Marchmont.)*

MR. MONTFORD. Like some supper, Mrs. Marchmont?

MRS. MARCHMONT. *(Languidly.)* Thank you, Mr. Montford, I never touch supper. *(Rises hastily and takes his arm.)* But I will sit beside you, and watch you.

MR. MONTFORD. I don't know that I like being watched when I am eating!

MRS. MARCHMONT. Then I will watch some one else.

MR. MONTFORD. I don't know that I should like that either.

MRS. MARCHMONT. *(Severely.)* Pray, Mr. Montford, do not make these painful scenes of jealousy in public!

*(They go downstairs with the other guests, passing Sir Robert Chiltern and Mrs. Cheveley, who now enter.)*

SIR ROBERT CHILTERN. And are you going to any of our country houses before you leave England, Mrs. Cheveley?

MRS. CHEVELEY. Oh, no! I can't stand your English house-parties. In England people actually try to be brilliant at breakfast. That is so dreadful of them! Only dull people are brilliant at breakfast. And then the family skeleton is always reading family prayers. My stay in England really depends on you, Sir Robert. *(Sits down on the sofa.)*

SIR ROBERT CHILTERN. *(Taking a seat beside her.)* Seriously?

MRS. CHEVELEY. Quite seriously. I want to talk to you about a great political and financial scheme, about this Argentine Canal Company, in fact.

SIR ROBERT CHILTERN. What a tedious, practical subject for you to talk about, Mrs. Cheveley!

MRS. CHEVELEY. Oh, I like tedious, practical subjects. What I don't like are tedious, practical people. There is a wide difference. Besides, you are interested, I know, in International Canal schemes. You were Lord Radley's secretary, weren't you, when the Government bought the Suez Canal shares?

SIR ROBERT CHILTERN. Yes. But the Suez Canal was a very great and splendid undertaking. It gave us our direct route to India. It had imperial value. It was necessary that we should have control. This Argentine scheme is a commonplace Stock Exchange swindle.

MRS. CHEVELEY. A speculation, Sir Robert! A brilliant, daring speculation.

SIR ROBERT CHILTERN. Believe me, Mrs. Cheveley, it is a swindle. Let us call things by their proper names. It makes matters simpler. We have all the information about it at the Foreign Office. In fact, I sent out a special Commission to inquire into the matter privately, and they report that the works are hardly begun, and as for the money already subscribed, no one seems to know what has become of it. The whole thing is a second Panama, and with not a quarter of the chance of success that miserable affair ever had. I hope you have not invested in it. I am sure you are far too clever to have done that.

MRS. CHEVELEY. I have invested very largely in it.

SIR ROBERT CHILTERN. Who could have advised you to do such a foolish thing?

MRS. CHEVELEY. Your old friend—and mine.

SIR ROBERT CHILTERN. Who?

MRS. CHEVELEY. Baron Arnheim.

SIR ROBERT CHILTERN. *(Frowning.)* Ah! yes. I remember hearing, at the time of his death, that he had been mixed up in the whole affair.

MRS. CHEVELEY. It was his last romance. His last but one, to do him justice.

SIR ROBERT CHILTERN. *(Rising.)* But you have not seen my Corots yet. They are in the music-room. Corots seem to go with music, don't they? May I show them to you?

MRS. CHEVELEY. *(Shaking her head.)* I am not in a mood to-night for silver twilights, or rose-pink dawns. I want to talk business. *(Motions to him with her fan to sit down again beside her.)*

SIR ROBERT CHILTERN. I fear I have no advice to give you, Mrs. Cheveley, except to interest yourself in something less dangerous. The success of the Canal depends, of course, on the attitude of England, and I am going to lay the report of the Commissioners before the House to-morrow night.

MRS. CHEVELEY. That you must not do. In your own interests, Sir Robert, to say nothing of mine, you must not do that.

SIR ROBERT CHILTERN. *(Looking at her in wonder.)* In my own interests? My dear Mrs. Cheveley, what do you mean? *(Sits down beside her.)*

MRS. CHEVELEY. Sir Robert, I will be quite frank with you. I want you to withdraw the report that you had intended to lay before the House, on the ground that you have reasons to believe that the Commissioners have been prejudiced or misinformed, or something. Then I want you to say a few words to the effect that the Government is going to reconsider the question, and that you have reason to believe that the Canal, if completed, will be of great international value. You know the sort of things ministers say in cases of this kind. A few ordinary platitudes will do. In modern life nothing produces such an effect as a good platitude. It makes the whole world kin. Will you do that for me?

SIR ROBERT CHILTERN. Mrs. Cheveley, you cannot be serious in making me such a proposition!

MRS. CHEVELEY. I am quite serious.

SIR ROBERT CHILTERN. *(Coldly.)* Pray allow me to believe that you are not!

MRS. CHEVELEY. *(Speaking with great deliberation and emphasis.)* Ah! but I am. And, if you do what I ask you, I . . . will pay you very handsomely!

SIR ROBERT CHILTERN. Pay me!

MRS. CHEVELEY. Yes.

SIR ROBERT CHILTERN. I am afraid I don't quite understand what you mean.

MRS. CHEVELEY. *(Leaning back on the sofa and looking at him.)* How very disappointing! And I have come all the way from Vienna in order that you should thoroughly understand me.

SIR ROBERT CHILTERN. I fear I don't.

MRS. CHEVELEY. *(In her most nonchalant manner.)* My dear Sir Robert, you are a man of the world, and you have your price, I suppose. Everybody has nowadays. The drawback is that most people are so dreadfully expensive. I know I am. I hope you will be more reasonable in your terms.

SIR ROBERT CHILTERN. *(Rises indignantly.)* If you will allow me, I will call your carriage for you. You have lived so long abroad, Mrs. Cheveley, that you seem to be unable to realize that you are talking to an English gentleman.

MRS. CHEVELEY. *(Detains him by touching his arm with her fan, and keeping it there while she is talking.)* I realize that I am talking to a man who laid the foundation of his fortune by selling to a Stock Exchange speculator a Cabinet secret.

SIR ROBERT CHILTERN. *(Biting his lip.)* What do you mean?

MRS. CHEVELEY. *(Rising and facing him.)* I mean that I know the real origin of your wealth and your career, and I have got your letter, too.

SIR ROBERT CHILTERN. What letter?

MRS. CHEVELEY. *(Contemptuously.)* The letter you wrote to Baron Arnheim, when you were Lord Radley's secretary, telling the Baron to buy Suez Canal shares—a letter written three days before the Government announced its own purchase.

SIR ROBERT CHILTERN. *(Hoarsely.)* It is not true.

MRS. CHEVELEY. You thought that letter had been destroyed. How foolish of you! It is in my possession.

SIR ROBERT CHILTERN. The affair to which you allude was no more than a speculation. The House of Commons had not yet passed the bill; it might have been rejected.

MRS. CHEVELEY. It was a swindle, Sir Robert. Let us call things by their proper names. It makes everything simpler. And now I am going to sell you that letter, and the price I ask for it is your public support of the Argentine scheme. You made your own fortune out of one canal. You must help me and my friends to make our fortunes out of another!

SIR ROBERT CHILTERN. It is infamous, what you propose—infamous!

MRS. CHEVELEY. Oh, no! This is the game of life as we all have to play it, Sir Robert, sooner or later!

SIR ROBERT CHILTERN. I cannot do what you ask me.

MRS. CHEVELEY. You mean you cannot help doing it. You know you are standing on the edge of a precipice. And it is not for you to make terms. It is for you to accept them. Supposing you refuse——

SIR ROBERT CHILTERN. What then?

MRS. CHEVELEY. My dear Sir Robert, what then? You are ruined, that is all! Remember to what a point your Puritanism in England has brought you. In old days nobody pretended to be a bit better than his neighbours. In fact, to be a bit better than one's neighbour was considered excessively vulgar and middle-class. Nowadays, with our modern mania for morality, everyone has to pose as a paragon of purity, incorruptibility, and all the other seven deadly virtues—and what is the result? You all go over like ninepins—one after the other. Not a year passes in England without somebody disappearing. Scandals used to lend charm, or at least interest, to a man—now they crush him. And yours is a very nasty scandal. You couldn't survive it. If it were known that as a young man, secretary to a great and important minister, you sold a Cabinet secret for a large sum of money, and that that was the origin of your wealth and career, you would be hounded out of public life, you would disappear completely.

And after all, Sir Robert, why should you sacrifice your entire future rather than deal diplomatically with your enemy? For the moment I am your enemy. I admit it! And I am much stronger than you are. The big battalions are on my side. You have a splendid position, but it is your splendid position that makes you so vulnerable. You can't defend it! And I am in attack. Of course I have not talked morality to you. You must admit in fairness that I have spared you that. Years ago you did a clever, unscrupulous thing; it turned out a great success. You owe to it your fortune and position. And now you have got to pay for it. Sooner or later we all have to pay for what we do. You have to pay now. Before I leave you to-night, you have got to promise me to suppress your report, and to speak in the House in favour of this scheme.

SIR ROBERT CHILTERN. What you ask is impossible.

MRS. CHEVELEY. You must make it possible. You are going to make it possible. Sir Robert, you know what your English newspapers are like. Suppose that when I leave this house I drive down to some newspaper office, and give them this scandal and the proofs of it! Think of their loathsome joy, of the delight they would have in dragging you down, of the mud and mire they would plunge you in. Think of the hypocrite with his greasy smile penning his leading article, and arranging the foulness of the public placard.

SIR ROBERT CHILTERN. Stop! You want me to withdraw the report and to make a short speech stating that I believe there are possibilities in the scheme?

MRS. CHEVELEY. *(Sitting down on the sofa.)* Those are my terms.

SIR ROBERT CHILTERN. *(In a low voice.)* I will give you any sum of money you want.

MRS. CHEVELEY. Even you are not rich enough, Sir Robert, to buy back your past. No man is.

SIR ROBERT CHILTERN. I will not do what you ask me. I will not.

MRS. CHEVELEY. You have to. If you don't . . . *(Rises from the sofa.)*

SIR ROBERT CHILTERN. *(Bewildered and unnerved.)* Wait a moment! What did you propose? You said that you would give me back my letter, didn't you?

Mrs. CHEVELEY. Yes. That is agreed. I will be in the Ladies' Gallery to-morrow night at half-past eleven. If by that time—and you will have had heaps of opportunity—you have made an announcement to the House in the terms I wish, I shall hand you back your letter with the prettiest thanks, and the best, or at any rate the most suitable, compliment I can think of. I intend to play quite fairly with you. One should always play fairly ... when one has the winning cards. The Baron taught me that ... amongst other things.

Sir ROBERT CHILTERN. You must let me have time to consider your proposal.

Mrs. CHEVELEY. No; you must settle now!

Sir ROBERT CHILTERN. Give me a week—three days!

Mrs. CHEVELEY. Impossible! I have got to telegraph to Vienna to-night.

Sir ROBERT CHILTERN. My God! what brought you into my life?

Mrs. CHEVELEY. Circumstances.          *(Moves towards the door.)*

Sir ROBERT CHILTERN. Don't go. I consent. The report shall be withdrawn. I will arrange for a question to be put to me on the subject.

Mrs. CHEVELEY. Thank you. I knew we should come to an amicable agreement. I understood your nature from the first. I analyzed you, though you did not adore me. And now you can get my carriage for me, Sir Robert. I see the people coming up from supper, and Englishmen always get romantic after a meal, and that bores me dreadfully.

*(Exit Sir Robert Chiltern.)*

*(Enter Guests, Lady Chiltern, Lady Markby, Lord Caversham, Lady Basildon, Mrs. Marchmont, Vicomte de Nanjac, Mr. Montford.)*

LADY MARKBY. Well, dear Mrs. Cheveley, I hope you have enjoyed yourself. Sir Robert is very entertaining, is he not?

Mrs. CHEVELEY. Most entertaining! I have enjoyed my talk with him immensely.

LADY MARKBY. He has had a very interesting and brilliant career. And he has married a most admirable wife. Lady Chiltern is a woman of the very highest principles, I am glad to say. I am a little too old now, myself, to trouble about setting a good example, but I always admire people who do. And Lady Chiltern has a very ennobling effect on life, though her dinner-parties are rather dull sometimes. But one can't have everything, can one? And now I must go, dear. Shall I call for you to-morrow?

MRS. CHEVELEY. Thanks.

LADY MARKBY. We might drive in the Park at five. Everything looks so fresh in the Park now!

MRS. CHEVELEY. Except the people!

LADY MARKBY. Perhaps the people are a little jaded. I have often observed that the Season as it goes on produces a kind of softening of the brain. However, I think anything is better than high intellectual pressure. That is the most unbecoming thing there is. It makes the noses of the young girls so particularly large. And there is nothing so difficult to marry as a large nose, men don't like them. Good-night, dear! *(To Lady Chiltern.)* Good-night, Gertrude! *(Goes out on Lord Caversham's arm.)*

MRS. CHEVELEY. What a charming house you have, Lady Chiltern! I have spent a delightful evening. It has been so interesting getting to know your husband.

LADY CHILTERN. Why did you wish to meet my husband, Mrs. Cheveley?

MRS. CHEVELEY. Oh, I will tell you. I wanted to interest him in this Argentine Canal scheme, of which I dare say you have heard. And I found him most susceptible,—susceptible to reason, I mean. A rare thing in a man. I converted him in ten minutes. He is going to make a speech in the House to-morrow night in favour of the idea. We must go to the Ladies' Gallery and hear him! It will be a great occasion!

LADY CHILTERN. There must be some mistake. That scheme could never have my husband's support.

MRS. CHEVELEY. Oh, I assure you it's all settled. I don't regret my tedious journey from Vienna now. It has been a great success. But, of course, for the next twenty-four hours the whole thing is a dead secret.

LADY CHILTERN. *(Gently.)* A secret? Between whom?

MRS. CHEVELEY. *(With a flash of amusement in her eyes.)* Between your husband and myself.

SIR ROBERT CHILTERN. *(Entering.)* Your carriage is here, Mrs. Cheveley!

MRS. CHEVELEY. Thanks! Good evening, Lady Chiltern! Goodnight, Lord Goring! I am at Claridge's. Don't you think you might leave a card?

LORD GORING. If you wish it, Mrs. Cheveley!

MRS. CHEVELEY. Oh, don't be so solemn about it, or I shall be obliged to leave a card on you. In England I suppose that would be hardly considered *en règle*. Abroad, we are more civilized. Will you see me down, Sir Robert? Now that we have both the same interests at heart we shall be great friends, I hope!

*(Sails out on Sir Robert Chiltern's arm. Lady Chiltern goes to the top of the staircase and looks down at them as they descend. Her expression is troubled. After a little time she is joined by some of the guests, and passes with them into another reception-room.)*

MABEL CHILTERN. What a horrid woman!

LORD GORING. You should go to bed, Miss Mabel.

MABEL CHILTERN. Lord Goring!

LORD GORING. My father told me to go to bed an hour ago. I don't see why I shouldn't give you the same advice. I always pass on good advice. It is the only thing to do with it. It is never of any use to oneself.

MABEL CHILTERN. Lord Goring, you are always ordering me out of the room. I think it most courageous of you. Especially as I am not going to bed for hours. *(Goes over to the sofa.)* You can come and sit down if you like, and talk about anything in the world, except the Royal Academy, Mrs. Cheveley, or novels in Scotch dialect. They are not improving subjects. *(Catches sight of something that is lying on the sofa half-hidden by the cushion.)* What is this? Some one has dropped a diamond brooch! Quite beautiful, isn't it? *(Shows it to him.)* I wish it was mine, but Gertrude won't let me wear anything but pearls, and I am thoroughly sick of pearls. They make one look so plain, so good and so intellectual. I wonder whom the brooch belongs to.

LORD GORING. I wonder who dropped it.

MABEL CHILTERN. It is a beautiful brooch.

LORD GORING. It is a handsome bracelet.

MABEL CHILTERN. It isn't a bracelet. It's a brooch.

LORD GORING. It can be used as a bracelet. *(Takes it from her, and, pulling out a green letter-case, puts the ornament carefully in it, and replaces the whole thing in his breast-pocket with the most perfect sangfroid.)*

MABEL CHILTERN. What are you doing?

LORD GORING. Miss Mabel, I am going to make a rather strange request to you.

MABEL CHILTERN. *(Eagerly.)* Oh, pray do! I have been waiting for it all the evening.

LORD GORING. *(Is a little taken aback, but recovers himself.)* Don't mention to anybody that I have taken charge of this brooch. Should anyone write and claim it, let me know at once.

MABEL CHILTERN. That is a strange request.

LORD GORING. Well, you see I gave this brooch to somebody once, years ago.

MABEL CHILTERN. You did?

LORD GORING. Yes.

*(Lady Chiltern enters alone. The other guests have gone.)*

MABEL CHILTERN. Then I shall certainly bid you good-night. Good-night, Gertrude!                                                      *(Exit.)*

LADY CHILTERN. Good-night, dear! *(To Lord Goring.)* You saw whom Lady Markby brought here to-night.

LORD GORING. Yes. It was an unpleasant surprise. What did she come here for?

LADY CHILTERN. Apparently to try and lure Robert to uphold some fraudulent scheme in which she is interested. The Argentine Canal, in fact.

LORD GORING. She has mistaken her man, hasn't she?

LADY CHILTERN. She is incapable of understanding an upright nature like my husband's!

LORD GORING. Yes. I should fancy she came to grief if she tried to get Robert into her toils. It is extraordinary what astounding mistakes clever women make.

LADY CHILTERN. I don't call women of that kind clever. I call them stupid!

LORD GORING. Same thing often. Good-night, Lady Chiltern!

LADY CHILTERN. Good-night!

*(Enter Sir Robert Chiltern.)*

SIR ROBERT CHILTERN. My dear Arthur, you are not going? Do stop a little!

LORD GORING. Afraid I can't, thanks. I have promised to look in at the Hartlocks. I believe they have got a mauve Hungarian band that plays mauve Hungarian music. See you soon. Good-bye!

*(Exit.)*

SIR ROBERT CHILTERN. How beautiful you look to-night, Gertrude!

LADY CHILTERN. Robert, it is not true, is it? You are not going to lend your support to this Argentine speculation? You couldn't!

SIR ROBERT CHILTERN. *(Starting.)* Who told you I intended to do so?

LADY CHILTERN. That woman who has just gone out, Mrs. Cheveley, as she calls herself now. She seemed to taunt me with it. Robert, I know this woman. You don't. We were at school together. She was untruthful, dishonest, an evil influence on everyone whose trust or friendship she could win. I hated, I despised her. She stole things, she was a thief. She was sent away for being a thief. Why do you let her influence you?

SIR ROBERT CHILTERN. Gertrude, what you tell me may be true, but it happened many years ago. It is best forgotten! Mrs. Cheveley may have changed since then. No one should be entirely judged by their past.

LADY CHILTERN. *(Sadly.)* One's past is what one is. It is the only way by which people should be judged.

SIR ROBERT CHILTERN. That is a hard saying, Gertrude!

LADY CHILTERN. It is a true saying, Robert. And what did she mean by boasting that she had got you to lend your support, your name to a thing I have heard you describe as the most dishonest and fraudulent scheme there has ever been in political life?

SIR ROBERT CHILTERN. *(Biting his lip.)* I was mistaken in the view I took. We all may make mistakes.

LADY CHILTERN. But you told me yesterday that you had received the report from the Commission, and that it entirely condemned the whole thing.

SIR ROBERT CHILTERN. *(Walking up and down.)* I have reasons now to believe that the Commission was prejudiced, or, at any rate, misinformed. Besides, Gertrude, public and private life are different things. They have different laws, and move on different lines.

LADY CHILTERN. They should both represent man at his highest. I see no difference between them.

SIR ROBERT CHILTERN. *(Stopping.)* In the present case, on a matter of practical politics, I have changed my mind. That is all.

LADY CHILTERN. All!

SIR ROBERT CHILTERN. *(Sternly.)* Yes!

LADY CHILTERN. Robert! Oh! it is horrible that I should have to ask you such a question—Robert, are you telling me the whole truth?

SIR ROBERT CHILTERN. Why do you ask me such a question?

LADY CHILTERN. *(After a pause.)* Why do you not answer it?

SIR ROBERT CHILTERN. *(Sitting down.)* Gertrude, truth is a very complex thing, and politics is a very complex business. There are wheels within wheels. One may be under certain obligations to people that one must pay. Sooner or later in political life one has to compromise. Everyone does.

LADY CHILTERN. Compromise? Robert, why do you talk so differently to-night from the way I have always heard you talk? Why are you changed?

SIR ROBERT CHILTERN. I am not changed. But circumstances alter things.

LADY CHILTERN. Circumstances should never alter principles!

SIR ROBERT CHILTERN. But if I told you——

LADY CHILTERN. What?

SIR ROBERT CHILTERN. That it was necessary, vitally necessary.

LADY CHILTERN. It can never be necessary to do what is not honourable. Or if it be necessary, then what is it that I have loved! But it is not, Robert; tell me it is not. Why should it be? What gain would you get? Money? We have no need of that! And money that comes from a tainted source is a degradation. Power? But power is nothing in itself. It is power to do good that is fine—that, and that only. What is it, then? Robert, tell me why you are going to do this dishonourable thing?

SIR ROBERT CHILTERN. Gertrude, you have no right to use that word. I told you it was a question of rational compromise. It is no more than that.

LADY CHILTERN. Robert, that is all very well for other men, for men who treat life simply as a sordid speculation; but not for you, Robert, not for you. You are different. All your life you have stood apart from others. You have never let the world soil you. To the world, as to myself, you have been an ideal always. Oh! be that ideal still. That great inheritance throw not away—that tower of ivory do not destroy. Robert, men can love what is beneath them—things unworthy, stained, dishonoured. We women worship when we love; and when we lose our worship, we lose everything. Oh! don't kill my love for you, don't kill that!

SIR ROBERT CHILTERN. Gertrude!

LADY CHILTERN. I know that there are men with horrible secrets in their lives—men who have done some shameful thing, and who in some critical moment have to pay for it, by doing some other act of shame—oh! don't tell me you are such as they are! Robert, is there in your life any secret dishonour or disgrace? Tell me, tell me at once, that——

SIR ROBERT CHILTERN. That what?

LADY CHILTERN. *(Speaking very slowly.)* That our lives may drift apart.

SIR ROBERT CHILTERN. Drift apart?

LADY CHILTERN. That they may be entirely separate. It would be better for us both.

SIR ROBERT CHILTERN. Gertrude, there is nothing in my past life that you might not know.

LADY CHILTERN. I was sure of it, Robert. I was sure of it. But why did you say those dreadful things, things so unlike your real self? Don't let us ever talk about the subject again. You will write, won't you, to Mrs. Cheveley, and tell her that you cannot support this scandalous scheme of hers? If you have given her any promise you must take it back, that is all!

SIR ROBERT CHILTERN. Must I write and tell her that?

LADY CHILTERN. Surely, Robert! What else is there to do?

SIR ROBERT CHILTERN. I might see her personally. It would be better.

LADY CHILTERN. You must never see her again, Robert. She is not a woman you should ever speak to. She is not worthy to talk to a man like you. No; you must write to her at once, now, this moment, and let your letter show her that your decision is quite irrevocable!

SIR ROBERT CHILTERN. Write this moment!

LADY CHILTERN. Yes.

SIR ROBERT CHILTERN. But it is too late. It is close on twelve.

LADY CHILTERN. That makes no matter. She must know at once that she has been mistaken in you—and that you are not a man to do anything base or underhand or dishonourable. Write here, Robert. Write that you decline to support this scheme of hers, as you hold it to be a dishonest scheme. Yes—write the word dishonest. She knows what that word means. *(Sir Robert Chiltern sits down and writes a letter. His wife takes it up and reads it.)* Yes; that will do. *(Rings bell.)* And now the envelope. *(He writes the envelope slowly. Enter Mason.)* Have this letter sent at once to Claridge's Hotel. There is no answer. *(Exit Mason.* LADY CHILTERN *kneels down beside her husband and puts her arms round him.)* Robert, love gives one a sort of instinct to things. I feel to-night that I have saved you from something that might have been a danger to you, from something that might have made men honour you less than they do. I don't think you realize sufficiently, Robert, that you have brought into the political life of our time a nobler atmosphere, a finer attitude towards life, a freer air of purer aims and higher ideals—I know it, and for that I love you, Robert.

SIR ROBERT CHILTERN. Oh, love me always, Gertrude, love me always!

LADY CHILTERN. I will love you always, because you will always be worthy of love. We needs must love the highest when we see it!

*(Kisses him and rises and goes out.)*

*(Sir Robert Chiltern walks up and down for a moment; then sits down and*

*buries his face in his hands. The Servant enters and begins putting out the lights. Sir Robert Chiltern looks up.)*

SIR ROBERT CHILTERN. Put out the lights, Mason, put out the lights! *(The Servant puts out the lights. The room becomes almost dark. The only light there is comes from the great chandelier that hangs over the staircase and illumines the tapestry of the Triumph of Love.)*

ACT-DROP

# Second Act

*SCENE: Morning-room at Sir Robert Chiltern's house. Lord Goring, dressed in the height of fashion, in lounging in an armchair. Sir Robert Chiltern is standing in front of the fireplace. He is evidently in a state of great mental excitement and distress. As the scene progresses he paces nervously up and down the room.*

LORD GORING. My dear Robert, it's a very awkward business, very awkward indeed. You should have told your wife the whole thing. Secrets from other people's wives are a necessary luxury in modern life. So, at least, I am always told at the club by people who are bald enough to know better. But no man should have a secret from his own wife. She invariably finds it out. Women have a wonderful instinct about things. They can discover everything except the obvious.

SIR ROBERT CHILTERN. Arthur, I couldn't tell my wife. When could I have told her? Not last night. It would have made a life-long separation between us, and I would have lost the love of the one woman in the world I worship, of the only woman who has ever stirred love within me. Last night it would have been quite impossible. She would have turned from me in horror . . . in horror and in contempt.

LORD GORING. Is Lady Chiltern as perfect as all that?

SIR ROBERT CHILTERN. Yes; my wife is as perfect as all that.

LORD GORING. *(Taking off his left-hand glove.)* What a pity! I beg your pardon, my dear fellow, I didn't quite mean that. But if what you tell me is true, I should like to have a serious talk about life with Lady Chiltern.

SIR ROBERT CHILTERN. It would be quite useless.

LORD GORING. May I try?

SIR ROBERT CHILTERN. Yes; but nothing could make her alter her views.

LORD GORING. Well, at the worst it would simply be a psychological experiment.

SIR ROBERT CHILTERN. All such experiments are terribly dangerous.

LORD GORING. Everything is dangerous, my dear fellow. If it wasn't so, life wouldn't be worth living. . . . Well, I am bound to say that I think you should have told her years ago.

SIR ROBERT CHILTERN. When? When we were engaged? Do you think she would have married me if she had known that the origin of my fortune is such as it is, the basis of my career such as it is, and that I had done a thing that I suppose most men would call shameful and dishonourable?

LORD GORING. *(Slowly.)* Yes; most men would call it ugly names. There is no doubt of that.

SIR ROBERT CHILTERN. *(Bitterly.)* Men who every day do something of the same kind themselves. Men who, each one of them, have worse secrets in their own lives.

LORD GORING. That is the reason they are so pleased to find out other people's secrets. It distracts public attention from their own.

SIR ROBERT CHILTERN. And, after all, whom did I wrong by what I did? No one.

LORD GORING. *(Looking at him steadily.)* Except yourself, Robert.

SIR ROBERT CHILTERN. *(After a pause.)* Of course I had private information about a certain transaction contemplated by the Government of the day, and I acted on it. Private information is practically the source of every large modern fortune.

LORD GORING. *(Tapping his boot with his cane.)* And public scandal invariably the result.

SIR ROBERT CHILTERN. *(Pacing up and down the room.)* Arthur, do you think that what I did nearly eighteen years ago should be brought up against me now? Do you think it fair that a man's whole career should be ruined for a fault done in one's boyhood almost? I was twenty-two at the time, and I had the double misfortune of being well-born and poor, two unforgivable things nowadays. Is it fair that the folly, the sin of one's youth, if men choose to call it a sin, should wreck a life like mine, should place me in the pillory, should shatter all that I have worked for, all that I have built up? Is it fair, Arthur?

LORD GORING. Life is never fair, Robert. And perhaps it is a good thing for most of us that it is not.

SIR ROBERT CHILTERN. Every man of ambition has to fight his century with its own weapons. What this century worships is wealth. The God of this century is wealth. To succeed one must have wealth. At all costs one must have wealth.

LORD GORING. You underrate yourself, Robert. Believe me, without wealth you could have succeeded just as well.

SIR ROBERT CHILTERN. When I was old, perhaps. When I had lost my passion for power, or could not use it. When I was tired, worn out, disappointed. I wanted my success when I was young. Youth is the time for success. I couldn't wait.

LORD GORING. Well, you certainly have had your success while you are still young. No one in our day has had such a brilliant success. Under-Secretary for Foreign Affairs at the age of forty— that's good enough for anyone, I should think.

SIR ROBERT CHILTERN. And if it is all taken away from me now? If I lose everything over a horrible scandal? If I am hounded from public life?

LORD GORING. Robert, how could you have sold yourself for money?

SIR ROBERT CHILTERN. *(Excitedly.)* I did not sell myself for money. I bought success at a great price. That is all.

LORD GORING. *(Gravely.)* Yes; you certainly paid a great price for it. But what first made you think of doing such a thing?

SIR ROBERT CHILTERN. Baron Arnheim.

LORD GORING. Damned scoundrel!

SIR ROBERT CHILTERN. No; he was a man of a most subtle and refined intellect. A man of culture, charm, and distinction. One of the most intellectual men I ever met.

LORD GORING. Ah! I prefer a gentlemanly fool any day. There is more to be said for stupidity than people imagine. Personally I have a great admiration for stupidity. It is a sort of fellow-feeling, I suppose. But how did he do it? Tell me the whole thing.

SIR ROBERT CHILTERN. *(Throws himself into an armchair by the writing-table.)* One night after dinner at Lord Radley's the Baron began talking about success in modern life as something that one could reduce to an absolutely definite science. With that wonderfully fascinating quiet voice of his he expounded to us the most terrible of all philosophies, the philosophy of power, preached to us the most marvellous of all gospels, the gospel of gold. I think he saw the effect he had produced on me, for some days afterwards he wrote and asked me to come and see him. He was living then in Park Lane, in the house Lord Woolcomb has now. I remember so well how, with a strange smile on his pale curved lips, he led me through his wonderful picture gallery, showed me his tapestries, his enamels, his jewels, his carved ivories, made me wonder at the strange loveliness of the luxury in which he lived; and then told me that luxury was nothing but a background, a painted scene in a play, and that power, power over other men, power over the world was the one thing worth having, the one supreme pleasure worth knowing, the one joy one never tired of, and that in our century only the rich possessed it.

LORD GORING. *(With great deliberation.)* A thoroughly shallow creed.

SIR ROBERT CHILTERN. *(Rising.)* I didn't think so then. I don't think so now. Wealth has given me enormous power. It gave me at the very outset of my life freedom, and freedom is everything. You have never been poor, and never known what ambition is. You cannot understand what a wonderful chance the Baron gave me. Such a chance as few men get.

LORD GORING. Fortunately for them, if one is to judge by results. But tell me definitely, how did the Baron finally persuade you to—well, to do what you did?

SIR ROBERT CHILTERN. When I was going away he said to me that if I ever could give him any private information of real value he would make me a very rich man. I was dazed at the prospect he held out to me, and my ambition and my desire for power were at that time boundless. Six weeks later certain private documents passed through my hands.

LORD GORING. *(Keeping his eyes steadily fixed on the carpet.)* State documents?

SIR ROBERT CHILTERN. Yes. *(Lord Goring sighs, then passes his hand across his forehead and looks up.)*

LORD GORING. I had no idea that you, of all men in the world, could have been so weak, Robert, as to yield to such a temptation as Baron Arnheim held out to you.

SIR ROBERT CHILTERN. Weak? Oh, I am sick of hearing that phrase. Sick of using it about others. Weak? Do you really think, Arthur, that it is weakness that yields to temptation? I tell you that there are terrible temptations that it requires strength, strength and courage, to yield to. To stake all one's life on a single moment, to risk everything on one throw, whether the stake be power or pleasure, I care not—there is no weakness in that. There is a horrible, a terrible courage. I had that courage. I sat down the same afternoon and wrote Baron Arnheim the letter this woman now holds. He made three-quarters of a million over the transaction.

LORD GORING. And you?

SIR ROBERT CHILTERN. I received from the Baron £110,000.

LORD GORING. You were worth more, Robert.

SIR ROBERT CHILTERN. No; that money gave me exactly what I wanted, power over others. I went into the House immediately. The Baron advised me in finance from time to time. Before five years I had almost trebled my fortune. Since then everything that I have touched has turned out a success. In all things connected with money I have had a luck so extraordinary that sometimes it has made me almost afraid. I remember having read somewhere, in some strange book, that when the gods wish to punish us they answer our prayers.

LORD GORING. But tell me, Robert, did you never suffer any regret for what you had done?

SIR ROBERT CHILTERN. No. I felt that I had fought the century with its own weapons, and won.

LORD GORING. *(Sadly.)* You thought you had won?

SIR ROBERT CHILTERN. I thought so. *(After a long pause.)* Arthur, do you despise me for what I have told you?

LORD GORING. *(With deep feeling in his voice.)* I am very sorry for you, Robert, very sorry indeed.

SIR ROBERT CHILTERN. I don't say that I suffered any remorse. I didn't. Not remorse in the ordinary, rather silly sense of the word. But I have paid conscience money many times. I had a wild hope that I might disarm destiny. The sum Baron Arnheim gave me I have distributed twice over in public charities since then.

LORD GORING. *(Looking up.)* In public charities? Dear me! what a lot of harm you must have done, Robert!

SIR ROBERT CHILTERN. Oh, don't say that, Arthur; don't talk like that.

LORD GORING. Never mind what I say, Robert. I am always saying what I shouldn't say. In fact, I usually say what I really think. A great misfortune nowadays. It makes one so liable to be misunderstood. As regards this dreadful business, I will help you in whatever way I can. Of course you know that.

SIR ROBERT CHILTERN. Thank you, Arthur, thank you. But what is to be done? What can be done?

LORD GORING. *(Leaning back with his hands in his pockets.)* Well, the English can't stand a man who is always saying he is in the right, but they are very fond of a man who admits that he has been in the wrong. It is one of the best things in them. However, in your case, Robert, a confession would not do. The money, if you will allow me to say so, is . . . awkward. Besides, if you did make a clean breast of the whole affair, you would never be able to talk morality again. And in England a man who can't talk morality twice a week to a large, popular, immoral audience is quite over as a serious politician. There would be nothing left for him as a profession except Botany or the Church. A confession would be of no use. It would ruin you.

SIR ROBERT CHILTERN. It would ruin me. Arthur, the only thing for me to do now is to fight the thing out.

LORD GORING. *(Rising from his chair.)* I was waiting for you to say that, Robert. It is the only thing to do now. And you must begin by telling your wife the whole story.

SIR ROBERT CHILTERN. That I will not do.

LORD GORING. Robert, believe me, you are wrong.

SIR ROBERT CHILTERN. I couldn't do it. It would kill her love for me. And now about this woman, this Mrs. Cheveley. How can I defend myself against her? You knew her before, Arthur, apparently.

LORD GORING. Yes.

SIR ROBERT CHILTERN. Did you know her well?

LORD GORING. *(Arranging his necktie.)* So little that I got engaged to be married to her once, when I was staying at the Tenbys'. The affair lasted for three days . . . nearly.

SIR ROBERT CHILTERN. Why was it broken off?

LORD GORING. *(Airily.)* Oh, I forget. At least, it makes no matter. By the way, have you tried her with money? She used to be confoundedly fond of money.

SIR ROBERT CHILTERN. I offered her any sum she wanted. She refused.

LORD GORING. Then the marvellous gospel of gold breaks down sometimes. The rich can't do everything, after all.

SIR ROBERT CHILTERN. Not everything. I suppose you are right. Arthur, I feel that public disgrace is in store for me. I feel certain of it. I never knew what terror was before. I know it now. It is as if a hand of ice were laid upon one's heart. It is as if one's heart were beating itself to death in some empty hollow.

LORD GORING. *(Striking the table.)* Robert, you must fight her. You must fight her.

SIR ROBERT CHILTERN. But how?

LORD GORING. I can't tell you how, at present. I have not the smallest idea. But everyone has some weak point. There is some flaw in each one of us. *(Strolls over to the fireplace and looks at himself in the glass.)* My father tells me that even I have faults. Perhaps I have. I don't know.

SIR ROBERT CHILTERN. In defending myself against Mrs. Cheveley, I have a right to use any weapon I can find, have I not?

LORD GORING. *(Still looking in the glass.)* In your place I don't think I should have the smallest scruple in doing so. She is thoroughly well able to take care of herself.

SIR ROBERT CHILTERN. *(Sits down at the table and takes a pen in his hand.)* Well, I shall send a cipher telegram to the Embassy at Vienna, to inquire if there is anything known against her. There may be some secret scandal she might be afraid of.

LORD GORING. *(Settling his buttonhole.)* Oh, I should fancy Mrs. Cheveley is one of those very modern women of our time who find a new scandal as becoming as a new bonnet, and air them both in the Park every afternoon at five-thirty. I am sure she adores scandals, and that the sorrow of her life at present is that she can't manage to have enough of them.

SIR ROBERT CHILTERN. *(Writing.)* Why do you say that?

LORD GORING. *(Turning round.)* Well, she wore far too much rouge last night, and not quite enough clothes. That is always a sign of despair in a woman.

SIR ROBERT CHILTERN. *(Striking a bell.)* But it is worth while my wiring to Vienna, is it not?

LORD GORING. It is always worth while asking a question, though it is not always worth while answering one.

*(Enter Mason.)*

SIR ROBERT CHILTERN. Is Mr. Trafford in his room?

MASON. Yes, Sir Robert.

SIR ROBERT CHILTERN. *(Puts what he has written into an envelope, which he then carefully closes.)* Tell him to have this sent off in cipher at once. There must not be a moment's delay.

MASON. Yes, Sir Robert.

SIR ROBERT CHILTERN. Oh! just give that back to me again.

*(Writes something on the envelope. Mason then goes out with the letter.)*

SIR ROBERT CHILTERN. She must have had some curious hold over Baron Arnheim. I wonder what it was.

LORD GORING. *(Smiling.)* I wonder.

SIR ROBERT CHILTERN. I will fight her to the death, as long as my wife knows nothing.

LORD GORING. *(Strongly.)* Oh, fight in any case—in any case.

SIR ROBERT CHILTERN. *(With a gesture of despair.)* If my wife found out, there would be little left to fight for. Well, as soon as I hear from Vienna, I shall let you know the result. It is a chance, just a chance, but I believe in it. And as I fought the age with its own weapons, I will fight her with her weapons. It is only fair, and she looks like a woman with a past, doesn't she?

LORD GORING. Most pretty women do. But there is a fashion in pasts just as there is a fashion in frocks. Perhaps Mrs. Cheveley's past is merely a slightly *décolleté* one, and they are excessively popular nowadays. Besides, my dear Robert, I should not build too high hopes on frightening Mrs. Cheveley. I should not fancy Mrs. Cheveley is a woman who would be easily frightened. She has survived all her creditors, and she shows wonderful presence of mind.

SIR ROBERT CHILTERN. Oh! I live on hopes now. I clutch at every chance. I feel like a man on a ship that is sinking. The water is round my feet, and the very air is bitter with storm. Hush! I hear my wife's voice.

*(Enter Lady Chiltern in walking dress.)*

LADY CHILTERN. Good afternoon, Lord Goring!

LORD GORING. Good afternoon, Lady Chiltern! Have you been in the Park?

LADY CHILTERN. No: I have just come from the Woman's Liberal Association, where, by the way, Robert, your name was received with loud applause, and now I have come in to have my tea. *(To Lord Goring.)* You will wait and have some tea, won't you?

LORD GORING. I'll wait for a short time, thanks.

LADY CHILTERN. I will be back in a moment. I am only going to take my hat off.

LORD GORING. *(In his most earnest manner.)* Oh! Please don't. It is so pretty. One of the prettiest hats I ever saw. I hope the Woman's Liberal Association received it with loud applause.

LADY CHILTERN. *(With a smile.)* We have much more important work to do than to look at each other's bonnets, Lord Goring.

LORD GORING. Really? What sort of work?

LADY CHILTERN. Oh! dull, useful, delightful things, Factory Acts,

Female Inspectors, the Eight Hours' Bill, the Parliamentary Franchise ... Everything, in fact, that you would find thoroughly uninteresting.

LORD GORING. And never bonnets?

LADY CHILTERN. *(With mock indignation.)* Never bonnets, never!

*(Lady Chiltern goes out through the door leading to her boudoir.)*

SIR ROBERT CHILTERN. *(Takes Lord Goring's hand.)* You have been a good friend to me, Arthur, a thoroughly good friend.

LORD GORING. I don't know that I have been able to do much for you, Robert, as yet. In fact, I have not been able to do anything for you, as far as I can see. I am thoroughly disappointed with myself.

SIR ROBERT CHILTERN. You have enabled me to tell you the truth. That is something. The truth has always stifled me.

LORD GORING. Ah! the truth is a thing I get rid of as soon as possible! Bad habit, by the way. Makes one very unpopular at the club ... with the older members. They call it being conceited. Perhaps it is.

SIR ROBERT CHILTERN. I would to God that I had been able to tell the truth ... to live the truth. Ah! that is the great thing in life, to live the truth. *(Sighs, and goes towards the door.)* I'll see you soon again, Arthur, shan't I?

LORD GORING. Certainly. Whenever you like. I'm going to look in at the Bachelors' Ball to-night, unless I find something better to do. But I'll come round to-morrow morning. If you should want me to-night by any chance, send round a note to Curzon Street.

SIR ROBERT CHILTERN. Thank you.

*(As he reaches the door, Lady Chiltern enters from her boudoir.)*

LADY CHILTERN. You are not going, Robert?

SIR ROBERT CHILTERN. I have some letters to write, dear.

LADY CHILTERN. *(Going to him.)* You work too hard, Robert. You seem never to think of yourself, and you are looking so tired.

SIR ROBERT CHILTERN. It is nothing, dear, nothing.

*(He kisses her and goes out.)*

LADY CHILTERN. *(To Lord Goring.)* Do sit down. I am so glad you have called. I want to talk to you about . . . well, not about bonnets, or the Woman's Liberal Association. You take far too much interest in the first subject, and not nearly enough in the second.

LORD GORING. You want to talk to me about Mrs. Cheveley?

LADY CHILTERN. Yes. You have guessed it. After you left last night I found out that what she had said was really true. Of course I made Robert write her a letter at once, withdrawing his promise.

LORD GORING. So he gave me to understand.

LADY CHILTERN. To have kept it would have been the first stain on a career that has been stainless always. Robert must be above reproach. He is not like other men. He cannot afford to do what other men do. *(She looks at Lord Goring, who remains silent.)* Don't you agree with me? You are Robert's greatest friend. You are our greatest friend, Lord Goring. No one, except myself, knows Robert better than you do. He has no secrets from me, and I don't think he has any from you.

LORD GORING. He certainly has no secrets from me. At least I don't think so.

LADY CHILTERN. Then I am not right in my estimate of him? I know I am right. But speak to me frankly.

LORD GORING. *(Looking straight at her.)* Quite frankly?

LADY CHILTERN. Surely. You have nothing to conceal, have you?

LORD GORING. Nothing. But, my dear Lady Chiltern, I think, if you will allow me to say so, that in practical life——

LADY CHILTERN. *(Smiling.)* Of which you know so little, Lord Goring——

LORD GORING. Of which I know nothing by experience, though I know something by observation. I think that in practical life there is something about success, actual success, that is a little unscrupulous, something about ambition that is unscrupulous always. Once a man has set his heart and soul on getting to a certain point, if he has to climb the crag, he climbs the crag; if he has to walk in the mire——

LADY CHILTERN. Well?

LORD GORING. He walks in the mire. Of course I am only talking generally about life.

LADY CHILTERN. *(Gravely.)* I hope so. Why do you look at me so strangely, Lord Goring?

LORD GORING. Lady Chiltern, I have sometimes thought that . . . perhaps you are a little hard in some of your views on life. I think that . . . often you don't make sufficient allowances. In every nature there are elements of weakness, or worse than weakness. Supposing, for instance, that—that any public man, my father, or Lord Merton, or Robert, say, had, years ago, written some foolish letter to someone . . .

LADY CHILTERN. What do you mean by a foolish letter?

LORD GORING. A letter gravely compromising one's position. I am only putting an imaginary case.

LADY CHILTERN. Robert is as incapable of doing a foolish thing as he is of doing a wrong thing.

LORD GORING. *(After a long pause.)* Nobody is incapable of doing a foolish thing. Nobody is incapable of doing a wrong thing.

LADY CHILTERN. Are you a Pessimist? What will the other dandies say? They will all have to go into mourning.

LORD GORING. *(Rising.)* No, Lady Chiltern, I am not a Pessimist. Indeed I am not sure that I quite know what Pessimism really means. All I do know is that life cannot be understood without much charity, cannot be lived without much charity. It is love, and not German philosophy, that is the true explanation of this world, whatever may be the explanation of the next. And if you are ever in trouble, Lady Chiltern, trust me absolutely, and I will help you in every way I can. If you ever want me, come to me for my assistance, and you shall have it. Come at once to me.

LADY CHILTERN. *(Looking at him in surprise.)* Lord Goring, you are talking quite seriously. I don't think I ever heard you talk seriously before.

LORD GORING. *(Laughing.)* You must excuse me, Lady Chiltern. It won't occur again, if I can help it.

LADY CHILTERN. But I like you to be serious.

*(Enter Mabel Chiltern, in the most ravishing frock.)*

MABEL CHILTERN. Dear Gertrude, don't say such a dreadful thing to Lord Goring. Seriousness would be very unbecoming to him. Good afternoon, Lord Goring! Pray be as trivial as you can.

LORD GORING. I should like to, Miss Mabel, but I am afraid I am . . . a little out of practice this morning; and besides, I have to be going now.

MABEL CHILTERN. Just when I have come in! What dreadful manners you have! I am sure you were very badly brought up.

LORD GORING. I was.

MABEL CHILTERN. I wish I had brought you up!

LORD GORING. I am so sorry you didn't.

MABEL CHILTERN. It is too late now, I suppose?

LORD GORING. *(Smiling.)* I am not so sure.

MABEL CHILTERN. Will you ride to-morrow morning?

LORD GORING. Yes, at ten.

MABEL CHILTERN. Don't forget.

LORD GORING. Of course I shan't. By the way, Lady Chiltern, there is no list of your guests in "The Morning Post" of to-day. It has apparently been crowded out by the County Council, or the Lambeth Conference, or something equally boring. Could you let me have a list? I have a particular reason for asking you.

LADY CHILTERN. I am sure Mr. Trafford will be able to give you one.

LORD GORING. Thanks, so much.

MABEL CHILTERN. Tommy is the most useful person in London.

LORD GORING. *(Turning to her.)* And who is the most ornamental?

MABEL CHILTERN. *(Triumphantly.)* I am.

LORD GORING. How clever of you to guess it! *(Takes up his hat and cane.)* Good-bye, Lady Chiltern! You will remember what I said to you, won't you?

LADY CHILTERN. Yes; but I don't know why you said it to me.

LORD GORING. I hardly know myself. Good-bye, Miss Mabel!

MABEL CHILTERN. *(With a little move of disappointment.)* I wish you were not going. I have had four wonderful adventures this morning; four and a half, in fact. You might stop and listen to some of them.

LORD GORING. How very selfish of you to have four and a half! There won't be any left for me.

MABEL CHILTERN. I don't want you to have any. They would not be good for you.

LORD GORING. That is the first unkind thing you have ever said to me. How charmingly you said it! Ten to-morrow.

MABEL CHILTERN. Sharp.

LORD GORING. Quite sharp. But don't bring Mr. Trafford.

MABEL CHILTERN. *(With a little toss of the head.)* Of course I shan't bring Tommy Trafford. Tommy Trafford is in great disgrace.

LORD GORING. I am delighted to hear it.    *(Bows and goes out.)*

MABEL CHILTERN. Gertrude, I wish you would speak to Tommy Trafford.

LADY CHILTERN. What has poor Mr. Trafford done this time? Robert says he is the best secretary he has ever had.

MABEL CHILTERN. Well, Tommy has proposed to me again. Tommy really does nothing but propose to me. He proposed to me last night in the music-room, when I was quite unprotected, as there was an elaborate trio going on. I didn't dare to make the smallest repartee, I need hardly tell you. If I had, it would have stopped the music at once. Musical people are so absurdly unreasonable. They always want one to be perfectly dumb at the very moment when one is longing to be absolutely deaf. Then he proposed to me in broad daylight this morning, in front of that dreadful statue of Achilles. Really, the things that go on in front of that work of art are quite appalling. The police should interfere. At luncheon I saw by the glare in his eye that he was going to propose again, and I just managed to check him in time by assuring him that I was a bimetallist. Fortunately I don't know what bimetallism means. And I don't believe anybody else does either. But the observation crushed Tommy for ten minutes. He looked quite shocked. And then Tommy is so annoying in the way he proposes. If he proposed at the top of his voice, I should not mind so much. That might produce some effect on the public. But he does it in a horrid confidential way. When Tommy wants to be romantic he talks to one just like a doctor. I am very fond of Tommy, but his methods of proposing are quite out of date. I wish, Gertrude, you would speak to him, and tell him that once a week is quite often enough to propose to anyone, and that it should always be done in a manner that attracts some attention.

LADY CHILTERN. Dear Mabel, don't talk like that. Besides, Robert thinks very highly of Mr. Trafford. He believes he has a brilliant future before him.

MABEL CHILTERN. Oh! I wouldn't marry a man with a future before him for anything under the sun.

LADY CHILTERN. Mabel!

MABEL CHILTERN. I know, dear. You married a man with a future, didn't you? But then Robert was a genius, and you have a noble, self-sacrificing character. You can stand geniuses. I have no character at all, and Robert is the only genius I could ever bear. As a rule, I think they are quite impossible. Geniuses talk so much, don't they? Such a bad habit! And they are always thinking about themselves, when I want them to be thinking about me. I must go round now and rehearse at Lady Basildon's. You remember, we are having tableaux, don't you? The Triumph of something, I don't know what! I hope it will be triumph of me. Only triumph I am really interested in at present. *(Kisses Lady Chiltern and goes out; then comes running back.)* Oh, Gertrude, do you know who is coming to see you? That dreadful Mrs. Cheveley, in a most lovely gown. Did you ask her?

LADY CHILTERN. *(Rising.)* Mrs. Cheveley! Coming to see me? Impossible!

MABEL CHILTERN. I assure you she is coming upstairs, as large as life and not nearly so natural.

LADY CHILTERN. You need not wait, Mabel. Remember, Lady Basildon is expecting you.

MABEL CHILTERN. Oh! I must shake hands with Lady Markby. She is delightful. I love being scolded by her.
*(Enter Mason.)*

MASON. Lady Markby. Mrs. Cheveley.
*(Enter Lady Markby and Mrs. Cheveley.)*

LADY CHILTERN. *(Advancing to meet them.)* Dear Lady Markby, how nice of you to come and see me! *(Shakes hands with her, and bows somewhat distantly to Mrs. Cheveley.)* Won't you sit down, Mrs. Cheveley?

MRS. CHEVELEY. Thanks. Isn't that Miss Chiltern? I should like so much to know her.

LADY CHILTERN. Mabel, Mrs. Cheveley wishes to know you. *(Mabel Chiltern gives a little nod.)*

MRS. CHEVELEY. *(Sitting down.)* I thought your frock so charming last night, Miss Chiltern. So simple and . . . suitable.

MABEL CHILTERN. Really? I must tell my dressmaker. It will be such a surprise to her. Good-bye, Lady Markby!

LADY MARKBY. Going already?

MABEL CHILTERN. I am so sorry but I am obliged to. I am just off to rehearsal. I have got to stand on my head in some tableaux.

LADY MARKBY. On your head, child? Oh! I hope not. I believe it is most unhealthy. *(Takes a seat on the sofa next Lady Chiltern.)*

MABEL CHILTERN. But it is for an excellent charity: in aid of the Undeserving, the only people I am really interested in. I am the secretary, and Tommy Trafford is treasurer.

MRS. CHEVELEY. And what is Lord Goring?

MABEL CHILTERN. Oh! Lord Goring is president.

MRS. CHEVELEY. The post should suit him admirably, unless he has deteriorated since I knew him first.

LADY MARKBY. *(Reflecting).* You are remarkably modern, Mabel. A little too modern, perhaps. Nothing is so dangerous as being too modern. One is apt to grow old-fashioned quite suddenly. I have known many instances of it.

MABEL CHILTERN. What a dreadful prospect!

LADY MARKBY. Ah! My dear, you need not be nervous. You will always be as pretty as possible. That is the best fashion there is, and the only fashion that England succeeds in setting.

MABEL CHILTERN. *(With a curtsey.)* Thank you so much, Lady Markby, for England . . . and myself. *(Goes out.)*

LADY MARKBY. *(Turning to Lady Chiltern.)* Dear Gertrude, we just called to know if Mrs. Cheveley's diamond brooch has been found.

LADY CHILTERN. Here?

MRS. CHEVELEY. Yes. I missed it when I got back to Claridge's, and I thought I might possibly have dropped it here.

LADY CHILTERN. I have heard nothing about it. But I will send for the butler and ask. *(Touches the bell.)*

MRS. CHEVELEY. Oh, pray don't trouble, Lady Chiltern. I daresay I lost it at the Opera, before we came on here.

LADY MARKBY. Ah yes, I suppose it must have been at the Opera. The fact is, we all scramble and jostle so much nowadays that I wonder we have anything at all left on us at the end of an evening. I know myself that, when I am coming back from the Drawing Room, I always feel as if I hadn't a shred on me, except a small shred of decent reputation, just enough to prevent the lower classes making painful observations through the windows of the carriage. The fact is that our Society is terribly overpopulated. Really, some one should arrange a proper scheme of assisted emigration. It would do a great deal of good.

MRS. CHEVELEY. I quite agree with you, Lady Markby. It is nearly six years since I have been in London for the season, and I must say Society has become dreadfully mixed. One sees the oddest people everywhere.

LADY MARKBY. That is quite true, dear. But one needn't know them. I'm sure I don't know half the people who come to my house. Indeed, from all I hear, I shouldn't like to.

*(Enter Mason.)*

LADY CHILTERN. What sort of a brooch was it that you lost, Mrs. Cheveley?

MRS. CHEVELEY. A diamond snake-brooch with a ruby, a rather large ruby.

LADY MARKBY. I thought you said there was a sapphire on the head, dear?

MRS. CHEVELEY. *(Smiling.)* No, Lady Markby—a ruby.

LADY MARKBY. *(Nodding her head.)* And very becoming, I am quite sure.

LADY CHILTERN. Has a ruby and diamond brooch been found in any of the rooms this morning, Mason?

MASON. No, my lady.

MRS. CHEVELEY. It really is of no consequence, Lady Chiltern. I am so sorry to have put you to any inconvenience.

LADY CHILTERN. *(Coldly.)* Oh, it has been no inconvenience. That will do, Mason. You can bring tea.

*(Exit Mason.)*

LADY MARKBY. Well, I must say it is most annoying to lose anything. I remember once at Bath, years ago, losing in the Pump Room an exceedingly handsome cameo bracelet that Sir John had given me. I don't think he has ever given me anything since, I am sorry to say. He has sadly degenerated. Really, this horrid House of Commons quite ruins our husbands for us. I think the Lower House by far the greatest blow to a happy married life that there has been since that terrible thing called the Higher Education of Women was invented.

LADY CHILTERN. Ah! it is heresy to say that in this house, Lady Markby. Robert is a great champion of the Higher Education of Women, and so, I am afraid, am I.

MRS. CHEVELEY. The higher education of men is what I should like to see. Men need it so sadly.

LADY MARKBY. They do, dear. But I am afraid such a scheme would be quite unpractical. I don't think man has much capacity for development. He has got as far as he can, and that is not far, is it? With regard to women, well, dear Gertrude, you belong to the younger generation, and I am sure it is all right if you approve of it. In my time, of course, we were taught not to understand anything. That was the old system, and wonderfully interesting it was. I assure you that the amount of things I and my poor dear sister were taught not to understand was quite extraordinary. But modern women understand everything, I am told.

MRS. CHEVELEY. Except their husbands. That is the one thing the modern woman never understands.

LADY MARKBY. And a very good thing too, dear, I daresay. It might break up many a happy home if they did. Not yours, I need hardly say, Gertrude. You have married a pattern husband. I wish I could say as much for myself. But since Sir John has taken to attending the debates regularly, which he never used to do in the good old days, his language has become quite impossible. He always seems to think that he is addressing the House, and consequently whenever he discusses the state of the agricultural labourer, or the Welsh Church, or something quite improper of that kind, I am obliged to send all the servants out of the room. It is not pleasant to see one's own butler, who has been with one for twenty-three years, actually blushing at the sideboard, and the footmen making contortions in corners like persons in circuses. I assure you my life will be quite ruined unless they send John at once to the Upper House. He won't take any interest in politics then, will he? The House of Lords is so sensible. An assembly of gentlemen. But in his present state, Sir John is really a great trial. Why, this morning before breakfast was half over, he stood up on the hearthrug, put his hands in his pockets, and appealed to the country at the top of his voice. I left the table as soon as I had my second cup of tea, I need hardly say. But his violent language could be heard all over the house! I trust, Gertrude, that Sir Robert is not like that?

LADY CHILTERN. But I am very much interested in politics, Lady Markby. I love to hear Robert talk about them.

LADY MARKBY. Well, I hope he is not as devoted to Blue Books as Sir John is. I don't think they can be quite improving reading for anyone.

MRS. CHEVELEY. *(Languidly)* I have never read a Blue Book. I prefer books . . . in yellow covers.

LADY MARKBY. *(Genially unconscious.)* Yellow is a gayer colour, is it not? I used to wear yellow a good deal in my early days, and would do so now if Sir John was not so painfully personal in his observations, and a man on the question of dress is always ridiculous, is he not?

MRS. CHEVELEY. Oh, no! I think men are the only authorities on dress.

LADY MARKBY. Really? One wouldn't say so from the sort of hats they wear, would one?

*(The butler enters, followed by the footman. Tea is set on a small table close to Lady Chiltern.)*

LADY CHILTERN. May I give you some tea, Mrs. Cheveley?

MRS. CHEVELEY. Thanks. *(The butler hands Mrs. Cheveley a cup of tea on a salver.)*

LADY CHILTERN. Some tea, Lady Markby?

LADY MARKBY. No thanks, dear.

*(The servants go out.* The fact is, I have promised to go round for ten minutes to see poor Lady Brancaster, who is in very great trouble. Her daughter, quite a well-brought-up girl, too, has actually become engaged to be married to a curate in Shropshire. It is very sad, very sad indeed. I can't understand this modern mania for curates. In my time we girls saw them, of course, running about the place like rabbits. But we never took any notice of them, I need hardly say. But I am told that nowadays country society is quite honeycombed with them. I think it most irreligious. And then the eldest son has quarrelled with his father, and it is said that when they meet at the club Lord Brancaster always hides himself behind the money article in "The Times." However, I believe that is quite a common occurrence nowadays and that they have to take in extra copies of "The Times" at all the clubs in St. James's Street; there are so many sons who won't have anything to do with their fathers, and so many fathers who won't speak to their sons. I think myself, it is very much to be regretted.

MRS. CHEVELEY. So do I. Fathers have so much to learn from their sons nowadays.

LADY MARKBY. Really, dear? What?

MRS. CHEVELEY. The art of living. The only really Fine Art we have produced in modern times.

LADY MARKBY. *(Shaking her head.)* Ah! I am afraid Lord Brancaster knew a good deal about that. More than his poor wife ever did. *(Turning to Lady Chiltern.)* You know Lady Brancaster, don't you, dear?

LADY CHILTERN. Just slightly. She was staying at Langton last autumn, when we were there.

LADY MARKBY. Well, like all stout women, she looks the very picture of happiness, as no doubt you noticed. But there are many tragedies in her family, besides this affair of the curate. Her own sister, Mrs. Jekyll, had a most unhappy life; through no fault of her own, I am sorry to say. She ultimately was so broken-hearted that she went into a convent, or on to the operatic stage, I forget which. No, I think it was decorative art-needlework she took up. I know she had lost all sense of pleasure in life. *(Rising.)* And now, Gertrude, if you will allow me, I shall leave Mrs. Cheveley in your charge and call back for her in a quarter of an hour. Or perhaps, dear Mrs. Cheveley, you wouldn't mind waiting in the carriage while I am with Lady Brancaster. As I intend it to be a visit of condolence, I shan't stay long.

MRS. CHEVELEY. *(Rising.)* I don't mind waiting in the carriage at all, provided there is somebody to look at one.

LADY MARKBY. Well, I hear the curate is always prowling about the house.

MRS. CHEVELEY. I am afraid I am not fond of girl friends.

LADY CHILTERN. *(Rising.)* Oh, I hope Mrs. Cheveley will stay here a little. I should like to have a few minutes' conversation with her.

MRS. CHEVELEY. How very kind of you, Lady Chiltern! Believe me, nothing would give me greater pleasure.

LADY MARKBY. Ah! no doubt you both have many pleasant reminiscences of your schooldays to talk over together. Good-bye, dear Gertrude! Shall I see you at Lady Bonar's to-night? She has discovered a wonderful new genius. He does . . . nothing at all, I believe. That is a great comfort, is it not?

LADY CHILTERN. Robert and I are dining at home by ourselves to-night, and I don't think I shall go anywhere afterwards. Robert, of course, will have to be in the House. But there is nothing interesting on.

LADY MARKBY. Dining at home by yourselves? Is that quite prudent? Ah, I forgot, your husband is an exception. Mine is the general rule, and nothing ages a woman so rapidly as having married the general rule.

*(Exit Lady Markby)*

MRS. CHEVELEY. Wonderful woman, Lady Markby, isn't she? Talks more and says less than anybody I ever met. She is made to be a public speaker. Much more so than her husband, though he is a typical Englishman, always dull and usually violent.

LADY CHILTERN. *(Makes no answer, but remains standing. There is a pause. Then the eyes of the two women meet.* LADY CHILTERN *looks stern and pale. Mrs. Cheveley seems rather amused.)* Mrs. Cheveley, I think it is right to tell you quite frankly that, had I known who you really were, I should not have invited you to my house last night.

MRS. CHEVELEY. *(With an impertinent smile.)* Really?

LADY CHILTERN. I could not have done so.

MRS. CHEVELEY. I see that after all these years you have not changed a bit, Gertrude.

LADY CHILTERN. I never change.

MRS. CHEVELEY. *(Elevating her eyebrows.)* Then life has taught you nothing?

LADY CHILTERN. It has taught me that a person who has once been guilty of a dishonest and dishonourable action may be guilty of it a second time, and should be shunned.

MRS. CHEVELEY. Would you apply that rule to everyone?

LADY CHILTERN. Yes, to everyone, without exception.

MRS. CHEVELEY. Then I am sorry for you, Gertrude, very sorry for you.

LADY CHILTERN. You see now, I am sure, that for many reasons any further acquaintance between us during your stay in London is quite impossible?

MRS. CHEVELEY. *(Leaning back in her chair.)* Do you know, Gertrude, I don't mind your talking morality a bit. Morality is simply the attitude we adopt towards people whom we personally dislike. You dislike me. I am quite aware of that. And I have always detested you. And yet I have come here to do you a service.

LADY CHILTERN. *(Contemptuously.)* Like the service you wished to render my husband last night, I suppose. Thank heaven, I saved him from that.

MRS. CHEVELEY. *(Starting to her feet.)* It was you who made him write that insolent letter to me? It was you who made him break his promise?

LADY CHILTERN. Yes.

MRS. CHEVELEY. Then you must make him keep it. I give you till to-morrow morning—no more. If by that time your husband does not solemnly bind himself to help me in this great scheme in which I am interested——

LADY CHILTERN. This fraudulent speculation——

MRS. CHEVELEY. Call it what you choose. I hold your husband in the hollow of my hand, and if you are wise you will make him do what I tell him.

LADY CHILTERN. *(Rising and going towards her.)* You are impertinent. What has my husband to do with you? With a woman like you?

MRS. CHEVELEY. *(With a bitter laugh.)* In this world like meets with like. It is because your husband is himself fraudulent and dishonest that we pair so well together. Between you and him there are chasms. He and I are closer than friends. We are enemies linked together. The same sin binds us.

LADY CHILTERN. How dare you class my husband with yourself? How dare you threaten him or me? Leave my house. You are unfit to enter it.

*(Sir Robert Chiltern enters from behind. He hears his wife's last words, and sees to whom they are addressed. He grows deadly pale.)*

MRS. CHEVELEY. Your house! A house bought with the price of dishonour. A house, everything in which has been paid for by fraud. *(Turns round and sees Sir Robert Chiltern.)* Ask him what the origin of his fortune is! Get him to tell you how he sold to a stockbroker a Cabinet secret. Learn from him to what you owe your position.

LADY CHILTERN. It is not true! Robert! It is not true!

MRS. CHEVELEY. *(Pointing at him with outstretched finger.)* Look at him! Can he deny it? Does he dare to?

SIR ROBERT CHILTERN. Go! Go at once. You have done your worst now.

MRS. CHEVELEY. My worst? I have not yet finished with you, with either of you. I give you both till to-morrow at noon. If by then you don't do what I bid you to do, the whole world shall know the origin of Sir Robert Chiltern.

*(Sir Robert Chiltern strikes the bell. Enter Mason.)*

SIR ROBERT CHILTERN. Show Mrs. Cheveley out.

*(Mrs. Cheveley starts; then bows with somewhat exaggerated politeness to Lady Chiltern, who makes no sign of response. As she passes by Sir Robert Chiltern, who is standing close to the door, she pauses for a moment and looks him straight in the face. She then goes out, followed by the servant, who closes the door after him. The husband and wife are left alone. Lady Chiltern stands like some one in a dreadful dream. Then she turns round and looks at her husband. She looks at him with strange eyes, as though she was seeing him for the first time.)*

LADY CHILTERN. You sold a Cabinet secret for money! You began your life with fraud! You built up your career on dishonour! Oh, tell me it is not true! Lie to me! Lie to me! Tell me it is not true!

SIR ROBERT CHILTERN. What this woman said is quite true. But Gertrude, listen to me. You don't realize how I was tempted. Let me tell you the whole thing. *(Goes towards her.)*

LADY CHILTERN. Don't come near me. Don't touch me. I feel as if you had soiled me forever. Oh! what a mask you have been wearing all these years! A horrible painted mask! You sold yourself for money. Oh! a common thief were better. You put yourself up to sale to the highest bidder! You were bought in the market. You lied to the whole world. And yet you will not lie to me.

SIR ROBERT CHILTERN. *(Rushing towards her.)* Gertrude! Gertrude!

LADY CHILTERN. *(Thrusting him back with outstretched hands.)* No, don't speak! Say nothing! Your voice wakes terrible memories— memories of things that made me love you—memories of words that made me love you—memories that now are horrible to me. And how I worshipped you! You were to me something apart from common life, a thing pure, noble, honest, without stain. The world seemed to me finer because you were in it, and goodness more real because you lived. And now—oh, when I think that I made of a man like you my ideal! the ideal of my life!

SIR ROBERT CHILTERN. There was your mistake. There was your error. The error all women commit. Why can't you women love us, faults and all? Why do you place us on monstrous pedestals? We have all feet of clay, women as well as men; but when we men love women, we love them knowing their weaknesses, their follies, their imperfections, love them all the more, it may be, for that reason. It is not the perfect, but the imperfect, who have need of love. It is when we are wounded by our own hands, or by the hands of others, that love should come to cure us—else what use is love at all? All sins, except a sin against itself, Love should forgive. All lives, save loveless lives, true Love should pardon. A man's love is like that. It is wider, larger, more human than a woman's. Women think that they are making ideals of men. What they are making of us are false idols merely. You made your false idol of me, and I had not the courage to come down, show you my wounds, tell you my weaknesses. I was afraid that I might lose your love, as I have lost it now. And so, last night you ruined my life for me—yes, ruined it! What this woman asked of me was nothing compared to what she offered to me. She offered security, peace, stability. The sin of my youth, that I had thought was buried, rose up in front of me, hideous, horrible, with its hands at my throat. I could have killed it for ever, sent it back into its tomb, destroyed its record, burned the one witness against me. You prevented me. No one but you, you know it. And now what is there before me but public disgrace, ruin, terrible shame, the mockery of the world, a lonely dishonoured life, a lonely dishonoured death, it may be, some day? Let women make no more ideals of men! let them not put them on altars and bow before them, or they may ruin other lives as completely as you—you whom I have so wildly loved—have ruined mine!

*(He passes from the room. Lady Chiltern rushes towards him, but the door is closed when she reaches it. Pale with anguish, bewildered, helpless, she sways like a plant in the water. Her hands, outstretched, seem to tremble in the air like blossoms in the wind. Then she flings herself down beside a sofa and buries her face. Her sobs are like the sobs of a child.)*

ACT-DROP

# THIRD ACT

SCENE—*The Library in Lord Goring's house. An Adams room. On the right is the door leading into the hall. On the left, the door of the smoking-room. A pair of folding doors at the back open into the drawing-room. The fire is lit. Phipps, the butler, is arranging some newspapers on the writing-table. The distinction of Phipps is his impassivity. He has been termed by enthusiasts the Ideal Butler. The Sphinx is not so incommunicable. He is a mask with a manner. Of his intellectual or emotional life history knows nothing. He represents the dominance of form.*

*(Enter Lord Goring in evening dress with a buttonhole. He is wearing a silk hat and Inverness cape. White-gloved, he carries a Louis Seize cane. His are all the delicate fopperies of Fashion. One sees that he stands in immediate relation to modern life, makes it indeed, and so masters it. He is the first well-dressed philosopher in the history of thought.)*

LORD GORING. Got my second buttonhole for me, Phipps?

PHIPPS. Yes, my lord. *(Takes his hat, cane and cape, and presents new buttonhole on salver.)*

LORD GORING. Rather distinguished thing, Phipps. I am the only person of the smallest importance in London at present who wears a buttonhole.

PHIPPS. Yes, my lord. I have observed that.

LORD GORING. *(Taking out old buttonhole.)* You see, Phipps, Fashion is what one wears oneself. What is unfashionable is what other people wear.

PHIPPS. Yes, my lord.

LORD GORING. Just as vulgarity is simply the conduct of other people.

PHIPPS. Yes, my lord.

LORD GORING. *(Putting in new buttonhole.)* And falsehoods the truths of other people.

PHIPPS. Yes, my lord.

LORD GORING. Other people are quite dreadful. The only possible society is oneself.

PHIPPS. Yes, my lord.

LORD GORING. To love oneself is the beginning of a life-long romance, Phipps.

PHIPPS. Yes, my lord.

LORD GORING. *(Looking at himself in the glass.)* Don't think I quite like this buttonhole, Phipps. Makes me look a little too old. Makes me almost in the prime of life, eh, Phipps?

PHIPPS. I don't observe any alteration in your lordship's appearance.

LORD GORING. You don't, Phipps?

PHIPPS. No, my lord.

LORD GORING. I am not quite sure. For the future a more trivial buttonhole, Phipps, on Thursday evenings.

PHIPPS. I will speak to the florist, my lord. She has had a loss in her family lately, which perhaps accounts for the lack of triviality your lordship complains of in the buttonhole.

LORD GORING. Extraordinary thing about the lower classes in England—they are always losing their relations.

PHIPPS. Yes, my lord! They are extremely fortunate in that respect.

LORD GORING. *(Turns round and looks at him. Phipps remains impassive.)* Hum! Any letters, Phipps?

PHIPPS. Three, my lord. *(Hands letters on a salver.)*

LORD GORING. *(Takes letters.)* Want my cab round in twenty minutes.

PHIPPS. Yes, my lord. *(Goes towards door.)*

LORD GORING. *(Holds up letter in pink envelope.)* Ahem! Phipps, when did this letter arrive?

PHIPPS. It was brought by hand just after your lordship went to the Club.

LORD GORING. That will do. *(Exit Phipps.)* Lady Chiltern's handwriting on Lady Chiltern's pink notepaper. That is rather curious. I thought Robert was to write. Wonder what Lady Chiltern has got to say to me? *(Sits at bureau and opens letter, and reads it.)* "I want you. I trust you. I am coming to you. Gertrude." *(Puts down the letter with a puzzled look. Then takes it up, and reads it again slowly.)* "I want you. I trust you. I am coming to you." So she has found out everything! Poor woman! Poor woman! *(Pulls out watch and looks at it.)* But what an hour to call! Ten o'clock! I shall have to give up going to the Berkshires. However, it is always nice to be expected, and not to arrive. I am not expected at the Bachelors' so I shall certainly go there. Well, I will make her stand by her husband. That is the only thing for her to do. That is the only thing for any woman to do. It is the growth of the moral sense in women that makes marriage such a hopeless, one-sided institution. Ten o'clock. She should be here soon. I must tell Phipps I am not in to anyone else.                  *(Goes towards bell.)* *(Enter Phipps.)*

PHIPPS. Lord Caversham.

LORD GORING. Oh, why will parents always appear at the wrong time? Some extraordinary mistake in nature, I suppose. *(Enter Lord Caversham.)* Delighted to see you, my dear father. *(Goes to meet him.)*

LORD CAVERSHAM. Take my cloak off.

LORD GORING. Is it worth while, father?

LORD CAVERSHAM. Of course it is worth while, sir. Which is the most comfortable chair?

LORD GORING. This one, father. It is the chair I use myself, when I have visitors.

LORD CAVERSHAM. Thank ye. No draught, I hope, in this room?

LORD GORING. No, father.

LORD CAVERSHAM. *(Sitting down.)* Glad to hear it. Can't stand draughts. No draughts at home.

LORD GORING. Good many breezes, father.

LORD CAVERSHAM. Eh? Eh? Don't understand what you mean. Want to have a serious conversation with you, sir.

LORD GORING. My dear father! At this hour?

LORD CAVERSHAM. Well, sir, it is only ten o'clock. What is your objection to the hour? I think the hour is an admirable hour!

LORD GORING. Well, the fact is, father, this is not my day for talking seriously. I am very sorry, but it is not my day.

LORD CAVERSHAM. What do you mean, sir?

LORD GORING. During the season, father, I only talk seriously on the first Tuesday in every month, from four to seven.

LORD CAVERSHAM. Well, make it Tuesday, sir, make it Tuesday.

LORD GORING. But it is after seven, father, and my doctor says I must not have any serious conversation after seven. It makes me talk in my sleep.

LORD CAVERSHAM. Talk in your sleep, sir? What does that matter? You are not married.

LORD GORING. No, father, I am not married.

LORD CAVERSHAM. Hum! That is what I have come to talk to you about, sir. You have got to get married, and at once. Why, when I was your age, sir, I had been an inconsolable widower for three months, and was already paying my addresses to your admirable mother. Damme, sir, it is your duty to get married. You can't be always living for pleasure. Every man of position is married nowadays. Bachelors are not fashionable any more. They are a damaged lot. Too much is known about them. You must get a wife, sir. Look where your friend Robert Chiltern has got to by probity, hard work, and a sensible marriage with a good woman. Why don't you imitate him, sir? Why don't you take him for your model?

LORD GORING. I think I shall, father.

LORD CAVERSHAM. I wish you would, sir. Then I should be happy. At present I make your mother's life miserable on your account. You are heartless, sir, quite heartless.

LORD GORING. I hope not, father.

LORD CAVERSHAM. And it is high time for you to get married. You are thirty-four years of age, sir.

LORD GORING. Yes, father, but I only admit to thirty-two—thirty-one and a half when I have a really good buttonhole. This buttonhole is not . . . trivial enough.

LORD CAVERSHAM. I tell you you are thirty-four, sir. And there is a draught in your room, besides, which makes your conduct worse.

Why did you tell me there was no draught, sir? I feel a draught, sir, I feel it distinctly.

LORD GORING. So do I, father. It is a dreadful draught. I will come and see you to-morrow, father. We can talk over anything you like. Let me help you on with your cloak, father.

LORD CAVERSHAM. No, sir; I have called this evening for a definite purpose, and I am going to see it through at all costs to my health or yours. Put down my cloak, sir.

LORD GORING. Certainly, father. But let us go into another room. *(Rings bell.)* There is a dreadful draught here. *(Enter Phipps.)* Phipps, is there a good fire in the smoking-room?

PHIPPS. Yes, my lord.

LORD GORING. Come in there, father. Your sneezes are quite heart-rending.

LORD CAVERSHAM. Well, sir, I suppose I have a right to sneeze when I choose?

LORD GORING. *(Apologetically.)* Quite so, father. I was merely expressing sympathy.

LORD CAVERSHAM. Oh, damn sympathy. There is a great deal too much of that sort of thing going on nowadays.

LORD GORING. I quite agree with you, father. If there was less sympathy in the world there would be less trouble in the world.

LORD CAVERSHAM. *(Going towards the smoking-room.)* That is a paradox, sir. I hate paradoxes.

LORD GORING. So do I, father. Everybody one meets is a paradox nowadays. It is a great bore. It makes society so obvious.

LORD CAVERSHAM. *(Turning round, and looking at his son beneath his bushy eyebrows.)* Do you always really understand what you say, sir?

LORD GORING. *(After some hesitation.)* Yes, father, if I listen attentively.

LORD CAVERSHAM. *(Indignantly.)* If you listen attentively! . . . Conceited young puppy!

*(Goes off grumbling into the smoking-room. PHIPPS enters.)*

LORD GORING. Phipps, there is a lady coming to see me this evening on particular business. Show her into the drawing-room when she arrives. You understand?

PHIPPS. Yes, my lord.

LORD GORING. It is a matter of the gravest importance, Phipps.

PHIPPS. I understand, my lord.

LORD GORING. No one else is to be admitted, under any circumstances.

PHIPPS. I understand, my lord. *(Bell rings.)*

LORD GORING. Ah! that is probably the lady. I shall see her myself.

*(Just as he is going towards the door Lord Caversham enters from the smoking-room.)*

LORD CAVERSHAM. Well, sir? am I to wait attendance on you?

LORD GORING. *(Considerably perplexed.)* In a moment, father. Do excuse me. *(Lord Caversham goes back.)* Well, remember my instructions, Phipps—into that room.

PHIPPS. Yes, my lord.

*(Lord Goring goes into the smoking-room. Harold, the footman, shows Mrs. Cheveley in. Lamia-like, she is in green and silver. She has a cloak of black satin, lined with dead rose-leaf silk.)*

HAROLD. What name, madam?

MRS. CHEVELEY. *(To Phipps, who advances towards her.)* Is Lord Goring not here? I was told he was at home?

PHIPPS. His lordship is engaged at present with Lord Caversham, madam.

*(Turns a cold, glassy eye on Harold, who at once retires.)*

MRS. CHEVELEY. *(To herself.)* How very filial!

PHIPPS. His lordship told me to ask you, madam, to be kind enough to wait in the drawing-room for him. His lordship will come to you there.

MRS. CHEVELEY. *(With a look of surprise.)* Lord Goring expects me?

PHIPPS. Yes, madam.

MRS. CHEVELEY. Are you quite sure?

PHIPPS. His lordship told me that if a lady called I was to ask her to wait in the drawing-room. *(Goes to the door of the drawing-room and opens it.)* His lordship's directions on the subject were very precise.

MRS. CHEVELEY. *(To herself.)* How thoughtful of him! To expect the unexpected shows a thoroughly modern intellect. *(Goes towards the drawing-room and looks in.)* Ugh! How dreary a bachelor's drawing-room always looks. I shall have to alter all this. *(Phipps brings the lamp from the writing-table.)* No, I don't care for that lamp. It is far too glaring. Light some candles.

PHIPPS. *(Replaces lamp.)* Certainly, madam.

MRS. CHEVELEY. I hope the candles have very becoming shades.

PHIPPS. We have had no complaints about them, madam, as yet.

*(Passes into the drawing-room and begins to light the candles.)*

MRS. CHEVELEY. *(To herself.)* I wonder what woman he is waiting for to-night. It will be delightful to catch him. Men always look so silly when they are caught. And they are always being caught. *(Looks about room and approaches the writing-table.)* What a very interesting room! What a very interesting picture! Wonder what his correspondence is like. *(Takes up letters.)* Oh, what a very uninteresting correspondence! Bills and cards, debts and dowagers! Who on earth writes to him on pink paper? How silly to write on pink paper! It looks like the beginning of a middle-class romance. Romance should never begin with sentiment. It should begin with science and end with a settlement. *(Puts letter down, then takes it up again.)* I know that handwriting. That is Gertrude Chiltern's. I remember it perfectly. The ten commandments in every stroke of the pen, and the moral law all over the page. Wonder what Gertrude is writing to him about! Something horrid about me, I suppose. How I detest that woman! *(Reads it.)* "I trust you. I want you. I am coming to you. Gertrude." "I trust you. I want you. I am coming to you." *(A look of triumph comes over her face. She is just about to steal the letter, when Phipps comes in.)*

PHIPPS. The candles in the drawing-room are lit, madam, as you directed.

MRS. CHEVELEY. Thank you. *(Rises hastily, and slips the letter under a large silver-cased blotting-book that is lying on the table.)*

PHIPPS. I trust the shades will be to your liking, madam. They are the most becoming we have. They are the same as his lordship uses himself when he is dressing for dinner.

MRS. CHEVELEY. *(With a smile.)* Then I am sure they will be perfectly right.

PHIPPS. *(Gravely.)* Thank you, madam.

*(Mrs. Cheveley goes into the drawing-room. Phipps closes the door and re-tires. The door is then slowly opened, and Mrs. Cheveley comes out and creeps stealthily towards the writing-table. Suddenly voices are heard from the smoking-room. Mrs. Cheveley grows pale, and stops. The voices grow louder, and she goes back into the drawing-room, biting her lip.)*

*(Enter Lord Goring and Lord Caversham.)*

LORD GORING. *(Expostulating.)* My dear father, if I am to get married, surely you will allow me to choose the time, place, and person? Particularly the person.

LORD CAVERSHAM. *(Testily.)* That is a matter for me, sir. You would probably make a very poor choice. It is I who should be consulted, not you. There is property at stake. It is not a matter for affection. Affection comes later on in married life.

LORD GORING. Yes. In married life affection comes when people thoroughly dislike each other, father, doesn't it? *(Puts on Lord Caversham's cloak for him.)*

LORD CAVERSHAM. Certainly, sir. I mean certainly not, sir. You are talking very foolishly to-night. What I say is that marriage is a matter for common sense.

LORD GORING. But women who have common sense are so curiously plain, father, aren't they? Of course I only speak from hearsay.

LORD CAVERSHAM. No woman, plain or pretty, has any common sense at all, sir. Common sense is the privilege of our sex.

LORD GORING. Quite so. And we men are so self-sacrificing that we never use it, do we, father?

LORD CAVERSHAM. I use it, sir. I use nothing else.

LORD GORING. So my mother tells me.

LORD CAVERSHAM. It is the secret of your mother's happiness. You are very heartless, sir, very heartless.

LORD GORING. I hope not, father.

*(Goes out for a moment. Then returns, looking rather put out, with Sir Robert Chiltern.)*

SIR ROBERT CHILTERN. My dear Arthur, what a piece of good luck meeting you on the doorstep! Your servant had just told me you were not at home. How extraordinary!

LORD GORING. The fact is, I am horribly busy to-night, Robert, and I gave orders I was not at home to anyone. Even my father had a comparatively cold reception. He complained of a draught the whole time.

SIR ROBERT CHILTERN. Ah! you must be at home to me, Arthur. You are my best friend. Perhaps by to-morrow you will be my only friend. My wife has discovered everything.

LORD GORING. Ah! I guessed as much!

SIR ROBERT CHILTERN. *(Looking at him.)* Really! How?

LORD GORING. *(After some hesitation.)* Oh, merely by something in the expression of your face as you came in. Who told her?

SIR ROBERT CHILTERN. Mrs. Cheveley herself. And the woman I love knows that I began my career with an act of low dishonesty, that I built up my life upon sands of shame—that I sold, like a common huckster, the secret that had been intrusted to me as a man of honour. I thank heaven poor Lord Radley died without knowing that I betrayed him. I would to God I had died before I had been so horribly tempted, or had fallen so low.

*(Burying his face in his hands.)*

LORD GORING. *(After a pause.)* You have heard nothing from Vienna yet, in answer to your wire?

SIR ROBERT CHILTERN. *(Looking up.)* Yes; I got a telegram from the first secretary at eight o'clock to-night.

LORD GORING. Well?

SIR ROBERT CHILTERN. Nothing is absolutely known against her. On the contrary, she occupies a rather high position in society. It is a sort of open secret that Baron Arnheim left her the greater portion of his immense fortune. Beyond that I can learn nothing.

LORD GORING. She doesn't turn out to be a spy, then?

SIR ROBERT CHILTERN. Oh! spies are of no use nowadays. Their profession is over. The newspapers do their work instead.

LORD GORING. And thunderingly well they do it.

SIR ROBERT CHILTERN. Arthur, I am parched with thirst. May I ring for something? Some hock and seltzer?

LORD GORING. Certainly. Let me. *(Rings the bell.)*

SIR ROBERT CHILTERN. Thanks! I don't know what to do, Arthur, I don't know what to do, and you are my only friend. But what a friend you are—the one friend I can trust. I can trust you absolutely, can't I?

*(Enter Phipps.)*

LORD GORING. My dear Robert, of course. Oh! *(To Phipps.)* Bring some hock and seltzer.

PHIPPS. Yes, my lord.

LORD GORING. And Phipps!

PHIPPS. Yes, my lord.

LORD GORING. Will you excuse me for a moment, Robert? I want to give some directions to my servant.

SIR ROBERT CHILTERN. Certainly.

LORD GORING. When that lady calls, tell her that I am not expected home this evening. Tell her that I have been suddenly called out of town. You understand?

PHIPPS. The lady is in that room, my lord. You told me to show her into that room, my lord.

LORD GORING. You did perfectly right. *(Exit Phipps.)* What a mess I am in. No; I think I shall get through it. I'll give her a lecture through the door. Awkward thing to manage, though.

SIR ROBERT CHILTERN. Arthur, tell me what I should do. My life seems to have crumbled about me. I am a ship without a rudder in a night without a star.

LORD GORING. Robert, you love your wife, don't you?

SIR ROBERT CHILTERN. I love her more than anything in the world. I used to think ambition the great thing. It is not. Love is the great thing in the world. There is nothing but love, and I love her. But I am defamed in her eyes. I am ignoble in her eyes. There is a wide gulf between us now. She has found me out, Arthur, she has found me out.

LORD GORING. Has she never in her life done some folly—some indiscretion—that she should not forgive your sin?

SIR ROBERT CHILTERN. My wife! Never! She does not know what

weakness or temptation is. I am of clay like other men. She stands apart as good women do—pitiless in her perfection—cold and stern and without mercy. But I love her, Arthur. We are childless, and I have no one else to love, no one else to love me. Perhaps if God had sent us children she might have been kinder to me. But God has given us a lonely house. And she has cut my heart in two. Don't let us talk of it. I was brutal to her this evening. But I suppose when sinners talk to saints they are brutal always. I said to her things that were hideously true, on my side, from my standpoint, from the standpoint of men. But don't let us talk of that.

LORD GORING. Your wife will forgive you. Perhaps at this moment she is forgiving you. She loves you, Robert. Why should she not forgive?

SIR ROBERT CHILTERN. God grant it! God grant it! *(Buries his face in his hands.)* But there is something more I have to tell you, Arthur. *(Enter Phipps with drinks.)*

PHIPPS. *(Hands hock and seltzer to Sir Robert Chiltern.)* Hock and seltzer, sir.

SIR ROBERT CHILTERN. Thank you.

LORD GORING. Is your carriage here, Robert?

SIR ROBERT CHILTERN. No; I walked from the club.

LORD GORING. Sir Robert will take my cab, Phipps.

PHIPPS. Yes, my lord. *(Exit.)*

LORD GORING. Robert, you don't mind my sending you away?

SIR ROBERT CHILTERN. Arthur, you must let me stay for five minutes. I have made up my mind what I am going to do to-night in the House. The debate on the Argentine Canal is to begin at eleven. *(A chair falls in the drawing-room.)* What is that?

LORD GORING. Nothing.

SIR ROBERT CHILTERN. I heard a chair fall in the next room. Some one has been listening.

LORD GORING. No, no; there is no one there.

SIR ROBERT CHILTERN. There is some one. There are lights in the room, and the door is ajar. Some one has been listening to every secret of my life. Arthur, what does this mean?

LORD GORING. Robert, you are excited, unnerved. I tell you there is no one in that room. Sit down, Robert.

SIR ROBERT CHILTERN. Do you give me your word that there is no one there?

LORD GORING. Yes.

SIR ROBERT CHILTERN. Your word of honour? *(Sits down.)*

LORD GORING. Yes.

SIR ROBERT CHILTERN. *(Rises.)* Arthur, let me see for myself.

LORD GORING. No, no.

SIR ROBERT CHILTERN. If there is no one there why should I not look in that room? Arthur, you must let me go into that room and satisfy myself. Let me know that no eavesdropper has heard my life's secret. Arthur, you don't realize what I am going through.

LORD GORING. Robert, this must stop. I have told you that there is no one in that room—that is enough.

SIR ROBERT CHILTERN. *(Rushes to the door of the room.)* It is not enough. I insist on going into this room. You have told me there is no one there, so what reason can you have for refusing me?

LORD GORING. For God's sake, don't! There is some one there. Some one whom you must not see.

SIR ROBERT CHILTERN. Ah, I thought so!

LORD GORING. I forbid you to enter that room.

SIR ROBERT CHILTERN. Stand back. My life is at stake. And I don't care who is there. I will know who it is to whom I have told my secret and my shame. *(Enters room.)*

LORD GORING. Great Heavens! his own wife!

*(Sir Robert Chiltern comes back, with a look of scorn and anger on his face.)*

SIR ROBERT CHILTERN. What explanation have you to give me for the presence of that woman here?

LORD GORING. Robert, I swear to you on my honour that that lady is stainless and guiltless of all offence towards you.

SIR ROBERT CHILTERN. She is a vile, an infamous thing!

LORD GORING. Don't say that Robert! It was for your sake she came here. It was to try and save you she came here. She loves you and no one else.

SIR ROBERT CHILTERN. You are mad. What have I to do with her intrigues with you? Let her remain your mistress! You are well suited to each other. She, corrupt and shameful—you, false as a friend, treacherous as an enemy even——

LORD GORING. It is not true, Robert. Before heaven, it is not true. In her presence and in yours I will explain all.

SIR ROBERT CHILTERN. Let me pass, sir. You have lied enough upon your word of honour.

*(Sir Robert Chiltern goes out. Lord Goring rushes to the door of the drawing-room, when Mrs. Cheveley comes out, looking radiant and much amused.)*

MRS. CHEVELEY. *(With a mock curtsey.)* Good evening, Lord Goring!

LORD GORING. Mrs. Cheveley! Great Heavens! . . . May I ask what you were doing in my drawing-room?

MRS. CHEVELEY. Merely listening. I have a perfect passion for listening through keyholes. One always hears such wonderful things through them.

LORD GORING. Doesn't that sound rather like tempting Providence?

MRS. CHEVELEY. Oh! surely Providence can resist temptation by this time. *(Makes a sign to him to take her cloak off, which he does.)*

LORD GORING. I am glad you have called. I am going to give you some good advice.

MRS. CHEVELEY. Oh! pray don't. One should never give a woman anything that she can't wear in the evening.

LORD GORING. I see you are quite as wilful as you used to be.

MRS. CHEVELEY. Far more! I have greatly improved. I have had more experience.

LORD GORING. Too much experience is a dangerous thing. Pray have a cigarette. Half the pretty women in London smoke cigarettes. Personally I prefer the other half.

MRS. CHEVELEY. Thanks. I never smoke. My dressmaker wouldn't like it, and a woman's first duty in life is to her dressmaker, isn't it? What the second duty is, no one has as yet discovered.

LORD GORING. You have come here to sell me Robert Chiltern's letter, haven't you?

MRS. CHEVELEY. To offer it to you on conditions. How did you guess that?

LORD GORING. Because you haven't mentioned the subject. Have you got it with you?

MRS. CHEVELEY. *(Sitting down.)* Oh, no! A well-made dress has no pockets.

LORD GORING. What is your price for it?

MRS. CHEVELEY. How absurdly English you are! The English think that a cheque-book can solve every problem in life. Why, my dear Arthur, I have very much more money than you have, and quite as much as Robert Chiltern has got hold of. Money is not what I want.

LORD GORING. What do you want then, Mrs. Cheveley?

MRS. CHEVELEY. Why don't you call me Laura?

LORD GORING. I don't like the name.

MRS. CHEVELEY. You used to adore it.

LORD GORING. Yes: that's why. *(Mrs. Cheveley motions to him to sit down beside her. He smiles, and does so.)*

MRS. CHEVELEY. Arthur, you loved me once.

LORD GORING. Yes.

MRS. CHEVELEY. And you asked me to be your wife.

LORD GORING. That was the natural result of my loving you.

MRS. CHEVELEY. And you threw me over because you saw, or said you saw, poor old Lord Mortlake trying to have a violent flirtation with me in the conservatory at Tenby.

LORD GORING. I am under the impression that my lawyer settled that matter with you on certain terms . . . dictated by yourself.

MRS. CHEVELEY. At that time I was poor; you were rich.

LORD GORING. Quite so. That is why you pretended to love me.

MRS. CHEVELEY. *(Shrugging her shoulders.)* Poor old Lord Mortlake, who had only two topics of conversation, his gout and his wife! I never could quite make out which of the two he was talking about. He used the most horrible language about them both. Well, you were silly, Arthur. Why, Lord Mortlake was never anything more to me than an amusement. One of those utterly tedious amusements one only finds at an English country house on an English country Sunday. I don't think anyone at all morally responsible for what he or she does at an English country house.

LORD GORING. Yes. I know lots of people think that.

MRS. CHEVELEY. I loved you, Arthur.

LORD GORING. My dear Mrs. Cheveley, you have always been far too clever to know anything about love.

MRS. CHEVELEY. I did love you. And you loved me. You know you loved me; and love is a very wonderful thing. I suppose that when a man has once loved a woman, he will do anything for her, except continue to love her? *(Puts her hand on his.)*

LORD GORING. *(Taking his hand away quietly.)* Yes: except that.

MRS. CHEVELEY. *(After a pause.)* I am tired of living abroad. I want to come back to London. I want to have a charming house here. I want to have a salon. If one could only teach the English how to talk, and the Irish how to listen, society here would be quite civilized. Besides, I have arrived at the romantic stage. When I saw you last night at the Chilterns', I knew you were the only person I had ever cared for, if I ever have cared for anybody, Arthur. And so, on the morning of the day you marry me, I will give you Robert Chiltern's letter. That is my offer. I will give it to you now, if you promise to marry me.

LORD GORING. Now?

MRS. CHEVELEY. *(Smiling.)* To-morrow.

LORD GORING. Are you really serious?

MRS. CHEVELEY. Yes, quite serious.

LORD GORING. I should make you a very bad husband.

MRS. CHEVELEY. I don't mind bad husbands. I have had two. They amused me immensely.

LORD GORING. You mean that you amused yourself immensely, don't you?

MRS. CHEVELEY. What do you know about my married life?

LORD GORING. Nothing: but I can read it like a book.

MRS. CHEVELEY. What book?

LORD GORING. *(Rising.)* The Book of Numbers.

MRS. CHEVELEY. Do you think it quite charming of you to be so rude to a woman in your own house?

LORD GORING. In the case of very fascinating women, sex is a challenge, not a defence.

MRS. CHEVELEY. I suppose that is meant for a compliment. My dear Arthur, women are never disarmed by compliments. Men always are. That is the difference between the two sexes.

LORD GORING. Women are never disarmed by anything, as far as I know them.

MRS. CHEVELEY. *(After a pause.)* Then you are going to allow your greatest friend, Robert Chiltern, to be ruined, rather than marry some one who really has considerable attractions left. I thought you would have risen to some great height of self-sacrifice, Arthur. I think you should. And the rest of your life you could spend in contemplating your own perfections.

LORD GORING. Oh! I do that as it is. And self-sacrifice is a thing that should be put down by law. It is so demoralizing to the people for whom one sacrifices oneself. They always go to the bad.

MRS. CHEVELEY. As if anything could demoralize Robert Chiltern! You seem to forget that I know his real character.

LORD GORING. What you know about him is not his real character. It was an act of folly done in his youth, dishonourable, I admit, shameful, I admit, unworthy of him, I admit, and therefore . . . not his true character.

MRS. CHEVELEY. How you men stand up for each other!

LORD GORING. How you women war against each other!

MRS. CHEVELEY. *(Bitterly.)* I only war against one woman, against Gertrude Chiltern. I hate her. I hate her now more than ever.

LORD GORING. Because you have brought a real tragedy into her life, I suppose.

MRS. CHEVELEY. *(With a sneer.)* Oh, there is only one real tragedy in a woman's life. The fact that her past is always her lover, and her future invariably her husband.

LORD GORING. Lady Chiltern knows nothing of the kind of life to which you are alluding.

MRS. CHEVELEY. A woman whose size in gloves is seven and three-quarters never knows much about anything. You know Gertrude has always worn seven and three-quarters? That is one of the reasons why there was never any moral sympathy between us. . . . Well, Arthur, I suppose this romantic interview may be regarded as at an end. You admit it was romantic, don't you? For the privilege of being your wife I was ready to surrender a great prize, the climax of my diplomatic career. You decline. Very well. If Sir Robert doesn't uphold my Argentine scheme, I expose him. *Voilà tout.*

LORD GORING. You mustn't do that. It would be vile, horrible, infamous.

MRS. CHEVELEY. *(Shrugging her shoulders.)* Oh! don't use big words. They mean so little. It is a commercial transaction. That is all. There is no good mixing up sentimentality in it. I offered to sell Robert Chiltern a certain thing. If he won't pay me my price, he will have to pay the world a greater price. There is no more to be said. I must go. Good-bye. Won't you shake hands?

LORD GORING. With you? No. Your transaction with Robert Chiltern may pass as a loathsome commercial transaction of a loathsome commercial age; but you seem to have forgotten that you who came here to-night to talk of love, you whose lips desecrated the word love, you to whom the thing is a book closely sealed, went this afternoon to the house of one of the most noble and gentle women in the world to degrade her husband in her eyes, to try and kill her love for him, to put poison in her heart, and bitterness in her life, to break her idol and, it may be, spoil her soul. That I cannot forgive you. That was horrible. For that there can be no forgiveness.

MRS. CHEVELEY. Arthur, you are unjust to me. Believe me, you are quite unjust to me. I didn't go to taunt Gertrude at all. I had no idea of doing anything of the kind when I entered. I called with Lady Markby simply to ask whether an ornament, a jewel, that I lost somewhere last night, had been found at the Chilterns'. If you don't believe me, you can ask Lady Markby. She will tell you it is true. The scene that occurred happened after Lady Markby had left, and was really forced on me by Gertrude's rudeness and sneers. I called, oh!—a little out of malice if you like—but really to ask if a diamond brooch of mine had been found. That was the origin of the whole thing.

LORD GORING. A diamond snake-brooch with a ruby?

MRS. CHEVELEY. Yes. How do you know?

LORD GORING. Because it is found. In point of fact, I found it myself, and stupidly forgot to tell the butler anything about it as I was leaving. *(Goes over to the writing-table and pulls out the drawers.)* It is in this drawer. No, that one. This is the brooch, isn't it? *(Holds up the brooch.)*

MRS. CHEVELEY. Yes. I am so glad to get it back. It was . . . a present.

LORD GORING. Won't you wear it?

MRS. CHEVELEY. Certainly, if you pin it in. *(Lord Goring suddenly clasps it on her arm.)* Why do you put it on as a bracelet? I never knew it could be worn as a bracelet.

LORD GORING. Really?

MRS. CHEVELEY. *(Holding out her handsome arm.)* No; but it looks very well on me as a bracelet, doesn't it?

LORD GORING. Yes; much better than when I saw it last.

MRS. CHEVELEY. When did you see it last?

LORD GORING. *(Calmly.)* Oh, ten years ago, on Lady Berkshire, from whom you stole it.

MRS. CHEVELEY. *(Starting.)* What do you mean?

LORD GORING. I mean that you stole that ornament from my cousin, Mary Berkshire, to whom I gave it when she was married. Suspicion fell on a wretched servant, who was sent away in disgrace. I recognized it last night. I determined to say nothing about it till I had found the thief. I have found the thief now, and I have heard her own confession.

MRS. CHEVELEY. *(Tossing her head.)* It is not true.

LORD GORING. You know it is true. Why, thief is written across your face at this moment.

MRS. CHEVELEY. I will deny the whole affair from beginning to end. I will say that I have never seen this wretched thing, that it was never in my possession.

*(Mrs. Cheveley tries to get the bracelet off her arm, but fails. Lord Goring looks on amused. Her thin fingers tear at the jewel to no purpose. A curse breaks from her.)*

LORD GORING. The drawback of stealing a thing, Mrs. Cheveley, is that one never knows how wonderful the thing that one steals is. You can't get that bracelet off, unless you know where the spring is. And I see you don't know where the spring is. It is rather difficult to find.

MRS. CHEVELEY. You brute! You coward! *(She tries again to unclasp the bracelet, but fails.)*

LORD GORING. Oh! don't use big words. They mean so little.

MRS. CHEVELEY. *(Again tears at the bracelet in a paroxysm of rage, with inarticulate sounds. Then stops, and looks at Lord Goring.)* What are you going to do?

LORD GORING. I am going to ring for my servant. He is an admirable servant. Always comes in the moment one rings for him. When he comes I will tell him to fetch the police.

MRS. CHEVELEY. *(Trembling.)* The police? What for?

LORD GORING. To-morrow the Berkshires will prosecute you. That is what the police are for.

MRS. CHEVELEY. *(Is now in an agony of physical terror. Her face is distorted. Her mouth awry. A mask has fallen from her. She is, for the moment, dreadful to look at.)* Don't do that. I will do anything you want. Anything in the world you want.

LORD GORING. Give me Robert Chiltern's letter.

MRS. CHEVELEY. Stop! Stop! Let me have time to think.

LORD GORING. Give me Robert Chiltern's letter.

MRS. CHEVELEY. I have not got it with me. I will give it to you to-morrow.

LORD GORING. You know you are lying. Give it to me at once. *(Mrs. Cheveley pulls the letter out, and hands it to him. She is horribly pale.)* This is it?

MRS. CHEVELEY. *(In a hoarse voice.)* Yes.

LORD GORING. *(Takes the letter, examines it, sighs, and burns it over the lamp.)* For so well-dressed a woman, Mrs. Cheveley, you have moments of admirable common sense. I congratulate you.

MRS. CHEVELEY. *(Catches sight of Lady Chiltern's letter, the cover of which is just showing from under the blotting-book.)* Please get me a glass of water.

LORD GORING. Certainly.

*(Goes to the corner of the room and pours out a glass of water. While his back is turned Mrs. Cheveley steals Lady Chiltern's letter. When Lord Goring returns with the glass she refuses it with a gesture.)*

MRS. CHEVELEY. Thank you. Will you help me on with my cloak?

LORD GORING. With pleasure.

*(Puts her cloak on.)*

MRS. CHEVELEY. Thanks. I am never going to try to harm Robert Chiltern again.

LORD GORING. Fortunately you have not the chance, Mrs. Cheveley.

MRS. CHEVELEY. Well, if even I had the chance, I wouldn't. On the contrary, I am going to render him a great service.

LORD GORING. I am charmed to hear it. It is a reformation.

MRS. CHEVELEY. Yes. I can't bear so upright a gentleman, so honourable an English gentleman, being so shamefully deceived, and so——

LORD GORING. Well?

MRS. CHEVELEY. I find that somehow Gertrude Chiltern's dying speech and confession has strayed into my pocket.

LORD GORING. What do you mean?

MRS. CHEVELEY. *(With a bitter note of triumph in her voice.)* I mean that I am going to send Robert Chiltern the love letter his wife wrote to you to-night.

LORD GORING. Love letter?

MRS. CHEVELEY. *(Laughing.)* "I want you. I trust you. I am coming to you. Gertrude."

*(Lord Goring rushes to the bureau and takes the envelope, finds it empty, and turns round.)*

LORD GORING. You wretched woman, must you always be thieving? Give me back that letter. I'll take it from you by force. You shall not leave my room till I have got it.

*(He rushes towards her, but Mrs. Cheveley at once puts her hand on the*

*electric bell that is on the table. The bell sounds with shrill reverberations, and Phipps enters.)*

MRS. CHEVELEY. *(After a pause.)* Lord Goring merely rang that you should show me out. Good-night, Lord Goring!

*(Goes out, followed by Phipps. Her face is illumined with evil triumph. There is joy in her eyes. Youth seems to have come back to her. Her last glance is like a swift arrow. Lord Goring bites his lip, and lights a cigarette.)*

ACT-DROP

# FOURTH ACT

SCENE—*Same as Act II.*

*(Lord Goring is standing by the fireplace with his hands in his pockets. He is looking rather bored.)*

LORD GORING. *(Pulls out his watch, inspects it, and rings the bell.)* It is a great nuisance. I can't find anyone in this house to talk to. And I am full of interesting information. I feel like the latest edition of something or other.

*(Enter Servant.)*

JAMES. Sir Robert is still at the Foreign Office, my lord.

LORD GORING. Lady Chiltern not down yet?

JAMES. Her ladyship has not yet left her room. Miss Chiltern has just come in from riding.

LORD GORING. *(To himself.)* Ah! that is something.

JAMES. Lord Caversham has been waiting some time in the library for Sir Robert. I told him your lordship was here.

LORD GORING. Thank you. Would you kindly tell him I've gone?

JAMES. *(Bowing.)* I shall do so, my lord.

*(Exit Servant.)*

LORD GORING. Really, I don't want to meet my father three days running. It is a great deal too much excitement for any son. I hope to goodness he won't come up. Fathers should be neither seen nor heard. That is the only proper basis for family life. Mothers are different. Mothers are darlings. *(Throws himself down into a chair, picks up a paper and begins to read it.)*

*(Enter Lord Caversham.)*

LORD CAVERSHAM. Well, sir, what are you doing here? Wasting your time as usual, I suppose?

LORD GORING. *(Throws down paper and rises.)* My dear father, when one pays a visit it is for the purpose of wasting other people's time, not one's own.

LORD CAVERSHAM. Have you been thinking over what I spoke to you about last night?

LORD GORING. I have been thinking about nothing else.

LORD CAVERSHAM. Engaged to be married yet?

LORD GORING. *(Genially.)* Not yet: but I hope to be before lunchtime.

LORD CAVERSHAM. *(Caustically.)* You can have till dinner-time if it would be of any convenience to you.

LORD GORING. Thanks awfully, but I think I'd sooner be engaged before lunch.

LORD CAVERSHAM. Humph! Never know when you are serious or not.

LORD GORING. Neither do I, father.

*(A pause.)*

LORD CAVERSHAM. I suppose you have read "The Times" this morning?

LORD GORING. *(Airily.)* "The Times"? Certainly not. I only read "The Morning Post." All that one should know about modern life is where the Duchesses are; anything else is quite demoralizing.

LORD CAVERSHAM. Do you mean to say you have not read "The Times" leading article on Robert Chiltern's career?

LORD GORING. Good heavens! No. What does it say?

LORD CAVERSHAM. What should it say, sir? Everything complimentary, of course. Chiltern's speech last night on this Argentine Canal Scheme was one of the finest pieces of oratory ever delivered in the House since Canning.

LORD GORING. Ah! Never heard of Canning. Never wanted to. And did . . . did Chiltern uphold the scheme?

LORD CAVERSHAM. Uphold it, sir? How little you know him! Why, he denounced it roundly, and the whole system of modern political finance. This speech is the turning-point in his career, as "The Times" points out. You should read this article, sir. *(Opens*

*"The Times."*) "Sir Robert Chiltern . . . most rising of all our young statesmen . . . Brilliant orator . . . Unblemished career . . . Well-known integrity of character . . . Represents what is best in English public life . . . Noble contrast to the lax morality so common among foreign politicians." They will never say that of you, sir.

LORD GORING. I sincerely hope not, father. However, I am delighted at what you tell me about Robert, thoroughly delighted. It shows he has got pluck.

LORD CAVERSHAM. He has got more than pluck, sir, he has got genius.

LORD GORING. Ah! I prefer pluck. It is not so common, nowadays, as genius is.

LORD CAVERSHAM. I wish you would go into Parliament?

LORD GORING. My dear father, only people who look dull ever get into the House of Commons, and only people who are dull ever succeed there.

LORD CAVERSHAM. Why don't you try to do something useful in life?

LORD GORING. I am far too young.

LORD CAVERSHAM. *(Testily.)* I hate this affectation of youth, sir. It is a great deal too prevalent nowadays.

LORD GORING. Youth isn't an affectation. Youth is an art.

LORD CAVERSHAM. Why don't you propose to that pretty Miss Chiltern?

LORD GORING. I am of a very nervous disposition, especially in the morning.

LORD CAVERSHAM. I don't suppose there is the smallest chance of her accepting you.

LORD GORING. I don't know how the betting stands to-day.

LORD CAVERSHAM. If she did accept you she would be the prettiest fool in England.

LORD GORING. That is just what I should like to marry. A thoroughly sensible wife would reduce me to a condition of absolute idiocy in less than six months.

LORD CAVERSHAM. You don't deserve her, sir.

LORD GORING. My dear father, if we men married the women we deserved, we should have a very bad time of it.

*(Enter Mabel Chiltern.)*

MABEL CHILTERN. Oh! ... How do you do, Lord Caversham? I hope Lady Caversham is quite well?

LORD CAVERSHAM. Lady Caversham is as usual, as usual.

LORD GORING. Good morning, Miss Mabel!

MABEL CHILTERN. *(Taking no notice at all of Lord Goring, and addressing herself exclusively to Lord Caversham.)* And Lady Caversham's bonnets ... are they at all better?

LORD CAVERSHAM. They have had a serious relapse, I am sorry to say.

LORD GORING. Good morning, Miss Mabel!

MABEL CHILTERN. *(To Lord Caversham.)* I hope an operation will not be necessary.

LORD CAVERSHAM. *(Smiling at her pertness.)* If it is we shall have to give Lady Caversham a narcotic. Otherwise she would never consent to have a feather touched.

LORD GORING. *(With increased emphasis.)* Good morning, Miss Mabel!

MABEL CHILTERN. *(Turning round with feigned surprise.)* Oh, are you here? Of course you understand that after your breaking your appointment I am never going to speak to you again.

LORD GORING. Oh, please don't say such a thing. You are the one person in London I really like to have to listen to me.

MABEL CHILTERN. Lord Goring, I never believe a single word that either you or I say to each other.

LORD CAVERSHAM. You are quite right, my dear, quite right ... as far as he is concerned, I mean.

MABEL CHILTERN. Do you think you could possibly make your son behave a little better occasionally? Just as a change.

LORD CAVERSHAM. I regret to say, Miss Chiltern, that I have no influence at all over my son. I wish I had. If I had, I know what I would make him do.

MABEL CHILTERN. I am afraid that he has one of those terribly weak natures that are not susceptible to influence.

LORD CAVERSHAM. He is very heartless, very heartless.

LORD GORING. It seems to me that I am a little in the way here.

MABEL CHILTERN. It is very good for you to be in the way, and to know what people say of you behind your back.

LORD GORING. I don't at all like knowing what people say of me behind my back. It makes me far too conceited.

LORD CAVERSHAM. After that, my dear, I really must bid you good morning.

MABEL CHILTERN. Oh! I hope you are not going to leave me all alone with Lord Goring? Especially at such an early hour in the day.

LORD CAVERSHAM. I am afraid I can't take him with me to Downing Street. It is not the Prime Minister's day for seeing the unemployed.

*(Shakes hands with Mabel Chiltern, takes up his hat and stick, and goes out, with a parting glare of indignation at Lord Goring.)*

MABEL CHILTERN. *(Takes up roses and begins to arrange them in a bowl on the table.)* People who don't keep their appointments in the Park are horrid.

LORD GORING. Detestable.

MABEL CHILTERN. I am glad you admit it. But I wish you wouldn't look so pleased about it.

LORD GORING. I can't help it. I always look pleased when I am with you.

MABEL CHILTERN. *(Sadly.)* Then I suppose it is my duty to remain with you?

LORD GORING. Of course it is.

MABEL CHILTERN. Well, my duty is a thing I never do, on principle. It always depresses me. So I am afraid I must leave you.

LORD GORING. Please don't, Miss Mabel. I have something very particular to say to you.

MABEL CHILTERN. *(Rapturously.)* Oh! is it a proposal?

LORD GORING. *(Somewhat taken aback.)* Well, yes, it is—I am bound to say it is.

MABEL CHILTERN. *(With a sigh of pleasure.)* I am so glad. That makes the second to-day.

LORD GORING. *(Indignantly.)* The second to-day? What conceited ass has been impertinent enough to dare to propose to you before I had proposed to you?

MABEL CHILTERN. Tommy Trafford, of course. It is one of Tommy's days for proposing. He always proposes on Tuesdays and Thursdays, during the season.

LORD GORING. You didn't accept him, I hope?

MABEL CHILTERN. I make it a rule never to accept Tommy. That is why he goes on proposing. Of course, as you didn't turn up this morning, I very nearly said yes. It would have been an excellent lesson both for him and for you if I had. It would have taught you both better manners.

LORD GORING. Oh! bother Tommy Trafford. Tommy is a silly little ass. I love you.

MABEL CHILTERN. I know. And I think you might have mentioned it before. I am sure I have given you heaps of opportunities.

LORD GORING. Mabel, do be serious. Please be serious.

MABEL CHILTERN. Ah! that is the sort of thing a man always says to a girl before he has been married to her. He never says it afterwards.

LORD GORING. *(Taking hold of her hand.)* Mabel, I have told you that I love you. Can't you love me a little in return?

MABEL CHILTERN. You silly Arthur! If you knew anything about . . . anything, which you don't, you would know that I adore you. Everyone in London knows it except you. It is a public scandal the way I adore you. I have been going about for the last six months telling the whole of society that I adore you. I wonder you consent to have anything to say to me. I have no character left at all. At least, I feel so happy that I am quite sure I have no character left at all.

LORD GORING. *(Catches her in his arms and kisses her. Then there is a pause of bliss.)* Dear! Do you know I was awfully afraid of being refused!

MABEL CHILTERN. *(Looking up at him.)* But you never have been refused yet by anybody, have you, Arthur? I can't imagine anyone refusing you.

LORD GORING. *(After kissing her again.)* Of course I'm not nearly good enough for you, Mabel.

MABEL CHILTERN. *(Nestling close to him.)* I am so glad, darling. I was afraid you were.

LORD GORING. *(After some hesitation.)* And I'm . . . I'm a little over thirty.

MABEL CHILTERN. Dear, you look weeks younger than that.

LORD GORING. *(Enthusiastically.)* How sweet of you to say so! . . . And it is only fair to tell you frankly that I am fearfully extravagant.

MABEL CHILTERN. But so am I, Arthur. So we're sure to agree. And now I must go and see Gertrude.

LORD GORING. Must you really? *(Kisses her.)*

MABEL CHILTERN. Yes.

LORD GORING. Then do tell her I want to talk to her particularly. I have been waiting here all the morning to see either her or Robert.

MABEL CHILTERN. Do you mean to say you didn't come here expressly to propose to me?

LORD GORING. *(Triumphantly.)* No; that was a flash of genius.

MABEL CHILTERN. Your first.

LORD GORING. *(With determination.)* My last.

MABEL CHILTERN. I am delighted to hear it. Now don't stir. I'll be back in five minutes. And don't fall into any temptations while I am away.

LORD GORING. Dear Mabel, while you are away, there are none. It makes me horribly dependent on you.

*(Enter Lady Chiltern.)*

LADY CHILTERN. Good morning, dear! How pretty you are looking!

MABEL CHILTERN. How pale you are looking, Gertrude! It is most becoming!

LADY CHILTERN. Good morning, Lord Goring!

LORD GORING. *(Bowing.)* Good morning, Lady Chiltern!

MABEL CHILTERN. *(Aside to Lord Goring.)* I shall be in the conservatory, under the second palm tree on the left.

LORD GORING. Second on the left?

MABEL CHILTERN. *(With a look of mock surprise.)* Yes; the usual palm tree.

*(Blows a kiss to him, unobserved by Lady Chiltern, and goes out.)*

LORD GORING. Lady Chiltern, I have a certain amount of very good news to tell you. Mrs. Cheveley gave me up Robert's letter last night, and I burned it. Robert is safe.

LADY CHILTERN. *(Sinking on the sofa.)* Safe! Oh! I am so glad of that. What a good friend you are to him—to us!

LORD GORING. There is only one person now that could be said to be in any danger.

LADY CHILTERN. Who is that?

LORD GORING. *(Sitting down beside her.)* Yourself.

LADY CHILTERN. I! In danger? What do you mean?

LORD GORING. Danger is too great a word. It is a word I should not have used. But I admit I have something to tell you that may distress you, that terribly distresses me. Yesterday evening you wrote me a very beautiful, womanly letter, asking me for my help. You wrote to me as one of your oldest friends, one of your husband's oldest friends. Mrs. Cheveley stole that letter from my rooms.

LADY CHILTERN. Well, what use is it to her? Why should she not have it?

LORD GORING. *(Rising.)* Lady Chiltern, I will be quite frank with you. Mrs. Cheveley puts a certain construction on that letter and proposes to send it to your husband.

LADY CHILTERN. But what construction could she put on it? . . . Oh! not that! not that! If I in—in trouble, and wanting your help, trusting you, propose to come to you . . . that you may advise me . . . assist me . . . Oh! are there women so horrible as that . . . ? And she proposes to send it to my husband? Tell me what happened. Tell me all that happened.

LORD GORING. Mrs. Cheveley was concealed in a room adjoining my library, without my knowledge. I thought that the person who was waiting in that room to see me was yourself. Robert came in unexpectedly. A chair or something fell in the room. He forced his way in, and he discovered her. We had a terrible scene.

I still thought it was you. He left me in anger. At the end of everything Mrs. Cheveley got possession of your letter—she stole it, when or how, I don't know.

LADY CHILTERN. At what hour did this happen?

LORD GORING. At half-past ten. And now I propose that we tell Robert the whole thing at once.

LADY CHILTERN. *(Looking at him with amazement that is almost terror.)* You want me to tell Robert that the woman you expected was not Mrs. Cheveley, but myself? That it was I whom you thought was concealed in a room in your house, at half-past ten o'clock at night? You want me to tell him that?

LORD GORING. I think it is better that he should know the exact truth.

LADY CHILTERN. *(Rising.)* Oh, I couldn't, I couldn't!

LORD GORING. May I do it?

LADY CHILTERN. No.

LORD GORING. *(Gravely.)* You are wrong, Lady Chiltern.

LADY CHILTERN. No. The letter must be intercepted. That is all. But how can I do it? Letters arrive for him every moment of the day. His secretaries open them and hand them to him. I dare not ask the servants to bring me his letters. It would be impossible. Oh! why don't you tell me what to do?

LORD GORING. Pray be calm, Lady Chiltern, and answer the questions I am going to put to you. You said his secretaries open his letters.

LADY CHILTERN. Yes.

LORD GORING. Who is with him to-day? Mr. Trafford, isn't it?

LADY CHILTERN. No. Mr. Montfort, I think.

LORD GORING. You can trust him?

LADY CHILTERN. *(With a gesture of despair.)* Oh! how do I know?

LORD GORING. He would do what you asked him, wouldn't he?

LADY CHILTERN. I think so.

LORD GORING. Your letter was on pink paper. He could recognize it without reading it, couldn't he? By the colour?

LADY CHILTERN. I suppose so.

LORD GORING. Is he in the house now?

LADY CHILTERN. Yes.

LORD GORING. Then I will go and see him myself, and tell him that a certain letter, written on pink paper, is to be forwarded to Robert to-day, and that at all costs it must not reach him. *(Goes to the door, and opens it.)* Oh! Robert is coming upstairs with the letter in his hand. It has reached him already.

LADY CHILTERN. *(With a cry of pain.)* Oh! you have saved his life; what have you done with mine!

*(Enter Sir Robert Chiltern. He has the letter in his hand, and is reading it. He comes towards his wife, not noticing Lord Goring's presence.)*

SIR ROBERT CHILTERN. "I want you. I trust you. I am coming to you. Gertrude." Oh, my love! Is this true? Do you indeed trust me, and want me? If so, it was for me to come to you, not for you to write of coming to me. This letter of yours, Gertrude, makes me feel that nothing that the world may do can hurt me now. You want me, Gertrude?

*(Lord Goring, unseen by Sir Robert Chiltern, makes an imploring sign to Lady Chiltern to accept the situation and Sir Robert's error.)*

LADY CHILTERN. Yes.

SIR ROBERT CHILTERN. You trust me, Gertrude?

LADY CHILTERN. Yes.

SIR ROBERT CHILTERN. Ah! why did you not add you loved me?

LADY CHILTERN. *(Taking his hand.)* Because I loved you.

*(Lord Goring passes into the conservatory.)*

SIR ROBERT CHILTERN. *(Kisses her.)* Gertrude, you don't know what I feel. When Montfort passed me your letter across the table— he had opened it by mistake, I suppose, without looking at the handwriting on the envelope—and I read it—oh! I did not care what disgrace or punishment was in store for me, I only thought you loved me still.

LADY CHILTERN. There is no disgrace in store for you, nor any public shame. Mrs. Cheveley has handed over to Lord Goring the document that was in her possession, and he has destroyed it.

SIR ROBERT CHILTERN. Are you sure of this, Gertrude?

LADY CHILTERN. Yes; Lord Goring has just told me.

SIR ROBERT CHILTERN. Then I am safe! Oh! what a wonderful thing to be safe! For two days I have been in terror. I am safe now. How did Arthur destroy my letter? Tell me.

LADY CHILTERN. He burned it.

SIR ROBERT CHILTERN. I wish I had seen that one sin of my youth burning to ashes. How many men there are in modern life who would like to see their past burning to white ashes before them! Is Arthur still here?

LADY CHILTERN. Yes; he is in the conservatory.

SIR ROBERT CHILTERN. I am so glad now I made that speech last night in the House, so glad. I made it thinking that public disgrace might be the result. But it has not been so.

LADY CHILTERN. Public honour has been the result.

SIR ROBERT CHILTERN. I think so. I fear so, almost. For although I am safe from detection, although every proof against me is destroyed, I suppose, Gertrude . . . I suppose I should retire from public life? *(He looks anxiously at his wife.)*

LADY CHILTERN. *(Eagerly.)* Oh yes, Robert, you should do that. It is your duty to do that.

SIR ROBERT CHILTERN. It is much to surrender.

LADY CHILTERN. No; it will be much to gain.

*(Sir Robert Chiltern walks up and down the room with a troubled expression. Then comes over to his wife, and puts his hand on her shoulder.)*

SIR ROBERT CHILTERN. And you would be happy living somewhere alone with me, abroad perhaps, or in the country away from London, away from public life? You would have no regrets?

LADY CHILTERN. Oh! none, Robert.

SIR ROBERT CHILTERN. *(Sadly.)* And your ambition for me? You used to be ambitious for me.

LADY CHILTERN. Oh, my ambition! I have none now, but that we two may love each other. It was your ambition that led you astray. Let us not talk about ambition.

*(Lord Goring returns from the conservatory, looking very pleased with himself, and with an entirely new buttonhole that some one has made for him.)*

SIR ROBERT CHILTERN. *(Going towards him.)* Arthur, I have to thank you for what you have done for me. I don't know how I can repay you. *(Shakes hands with him.)*

LORD GORING. My dear fellow, I'll tell you at once. At the present moment, under the usual palm tree ... I mean in the conservatory ...

*(Enter Mason.)*

MASON. Lord Caversham.

LORD GORING. That admirable father of mine really makes a habit of turning up at the wrong moment. It is very heartless of him, very heartless indeed.

*(Enter Lord Caversham. Mason goes out.)*

LORD CAVERSHAM. Good morning, Lady Chiltern! Warmest congratulations to you, Chiltern, on your brilliant speech last night. I have just left the Prime Minister, and you are to have the vacant seat in the Cabinet.

SIR ROBERT CHILTERN. *(With a look of joy and triumph.)* A seat in the Cabinet?

LORD CAVERSHAM. Yes; here is the Prime Minister's letter. *(Hands letter.)*

SIR ROBERT CHILTERN. *(Takes letter and reads it.)* A seat in the Cabinet!

LORD CAVERSHAM. Certainly, and you well deserve it too. You have got what we want so much in political life nowadays—high character, high moral tone, high principles. *(To Lord Goring.)* Everything that you have not got, sir, and never will have.

LORD GORING. I don't like principles, father. I prefer prejudices.

*(Sir Robert Chiltern is on the brink of accepting the Prime Minister's offer, when he sees his wife looking at him with her clear, candid eyes. He then realizes that it is impossible.)*

SIR ROBERT CHILTERN. I cannot accept this offer, Lord Caversham. I have made up my mind to decline it.

LORD CAVERSHAM. Decline it, sir!

SIR ROBERT CHILTERN. My intention is to retire at once from public life.

LORD CAVERSHAM. *(Angrily.)* Decline a seat in the Cabinet, and retire from public life? Never heard such damned nonsense in the whole course of my existence. I beg your pardon, Lady Chiltern.

Chiltern, I beg your pardon. *(To Lord Goring.)* Don't grin like that, sir.

LORD GORING. No, father.

LORD CAVERSHAM. Lady Chiltern, you are a sensible woman, the most sensible woman in London, the most sensible woman I know. Will you kindly prevent your husband from making such a ... from talking such ... Will you kindly do that, Lady Chiltern?

LADY CHILTERN. I think my husband is right in his determination, Lord Caversham. I approve of it.

LORD CAVERSHAM. You approve of it? Good Heavens!

LADY CHILTERN. *(Taking her husband's hand.)* I admire him for it. I admire him immensely for it. I have never admired him so much before. He is finer than even I thought him. *(To Sir Robert Chiltern.)* You will go and write your letter to the Prime Minister now, won't you? Don't hesitate about it, Robert.

SIR ROBERT CHILTERN. *(With a touch of bitterness.)* I suppose I had better write it at once. Such offers are not repeated. I will ask you to excuse me for a moment, Lord Caversham.

LADY CHILTERN. I may come with you, Robert, may I not?

SIR ROBERT CHILTERN. Yes, Gertrude.

*(Lady Chiltern goes out with him.)*

LORD CAVERSHAM. What is the matter with this family? Something wrong here, eh? *(Tapping his forehead.)* Idiocy? Hereditary, I suppose. Both of them, too. Wife as well as husband. Very sad. Very sad indeed! And they are not an old family. Can't understand it.

LORD GORING. It is not idiocy, father, I assure you.

LORD CAVERSHAM. What is it then, sir?

LORD GORING. *(After some hesitation.)* Well, it is what is called nowadays a high moral tone, father. That is all.

LORD CAVERSHAM. Hate these new-fangled names. Same thing as we used to call idiocy fifty years ago. Shan't stay in this house any longer.

LORD GORING. *(Taking his arm.)* Oh! just go in here for a moment, father. Third palm tree to the left, the usual palm tree.

LORD CAVERSHAM. What, sir?

LORD GORING. I beg your pardon, father, I forgot. The conservatory, father, the conservatory—there is some one there I want you to talk to.

LORD CAVERSHAM. What about, sir?

LORD GORING. About me, father.

LORD CAVERSHAM. *(Grimly.)* Not a subject on which much eloquence is possible.

LORD GORING. No, father; but the lady is like me. She doesn't care much for eloquence in others. She thinks it a little loud.

*(Lord Caversham goes into the conservatory. Lady Chiltern enters.)*

LORD GORING. Lady Chiltern, why are you playing Mrs. Cheveley's cards?

LADY CHILTERN. *(Startled.)* I don't understand you.

LORD GORING. Mrs. Cheveley made an attempt to ruin your husband. Either to drive him from public life, or to make him adopt a dishonourable position. From the latter tragedy you saved him. The former you are now thrusting on him. Why should you do him the wrong Mrs. Cheveley tried to do and failed?

LADY CHILTERN. Lord Goring?

LORD GORING. *(Pulling himself together for a great effort, and showing the philosopher that underlies the dandy.)* Lady Chiltern, allow me. You wrote me a letter last night in which you said you trusted me and wanted my help. Now is the moment when you really want my help, now is the time when you have got to trust me, to trust in my counsel and judgment. You love Robert. Do you want to kill his love for you? What sort of existence will he have if you rob him of the fruits of his ambition, if you take him from the splendour of a great political career, if you close the doors of public life against him, if you condemn him to sterile failure, he who was made for triumph and success? Women are not meant to judge us, but to forgive us when we need forgiveness. Pardon, not punishment, is their mission. Why should you scourge him with rods for a sin done in his youth, before he knew you, before he knew himself? A man's life is of more value than a woman's. It has larger issues, wider scope, greater ambitions. A woman's life revolves in curves of emotions. It is upon lines of intellect that a man's life progresses. Don't make any terrible mistake, Lady Chiltern. A woman who can keep a man's love, and love him in return, has done all the world wants of women, or should want of them.

LADY CHILTERN. *(Troubled and hesitating.)* But it is my husband himself who wishes to retire from public life. He feels it is his duty. It was he who first said so.

LORD GORING. Rather than lose your love, Robert would do anything, wreck his whole career, as he is on the brink of doing now. He is making for you a terrible sacrifice. Take my advice, Lady Chiltern, and do not accept a sacrifice so great. If you do, you will live to repent it bitterly. We men and women are not made to accept such sacrifices from each other. We are not worthy of them. Besides, Robert has been punished enough.

LADY CHILTERN. We have both been punished. I set him up too high.

LORD GORING. *(With deep feeling in his voice.)* Do not for that reason set him down now too low. If he has fallen from his altar, do not thrust him into the mire. Failure to Robert would be the very mire of shame. Power is his passion. He would lose everything, even his power to feel love. Your husband's life is at this moment in your hands, your husband's love is in your hands. Don't mar both for him.

*(Enter Sir Robert Chiltern.)*

SIR ROBERT CHILTERN. Gertrude, here is the draft of my letter. Shall I read it to you?

LADY CHILTERN. Let me see it.

*(Sir Robert hands her the letter. She reads it, and then, with a gesture of passion, tears it up.)*

SIR ROBERT CHILTERN. What are you doing?

LADY CHILTERN. A man's life is of more value than a woman's. It has larger issues, wider scope, greater ambitions. Our lives revolve in curves of emotions. It is upon lines of intellect that a man's life progresses. I have just learnt this, and much else with it, from Lord Goring. And I will not spoil your life for you, nor see you spoil it as a sacrifice to me, a useless sacrifice!

SIR ROBERT CHILTERN. Gertrude! Gertrude!

LADY CHILTERN. You can forget. Men easily forget. And I forgive. That is how women help the world. I see that now.

SIR ROBERT CHILTERN. *(Deeply overcome by emotion, embraces her.)* My wife! my wife! *(To Lord Goring.)* Arthur, it seems that I am always to be in your debt.

LORD GORING. Oh dear no, Robert. Your debt is to Lady Chiltern, not to me!

SIR ROBERT CHILTERN. I owe you much. And now tell me what you were going to ask me just now as Lord Caversham came in.

LORD GORING. Robert, you are your sister's guardian, and I want your consent to my marriage with her. That is all.

LADY CHILTERN. Oh, I am so glad! I am so glad! *(Shakes hands with Lord Goring.)*

LORD GORING. Thank you, Lady Chiltern.

SIR ROBERT CHILTERN. *(With a troubled look.)* My sister to be your wife?

LORD GORING. Yes.

SIR ROBERT CHILTERN. *(Speaking with great firmness.)* Arthur, I am very sorry, but the thing is quite out of the question. I have to think of Mabel's future happiness. And I don't think her happiness would be safe in your hands. And I cannot have her sacrificed!

LORD GORING. Sacrificed!

SIR ROBERT CHILTERN. Yes, utterly sacrificed. Loveless marriages are horrible. But there is one thing worse than an absolutely loveless marriage. A marriage in which there is love, but on one side only; faith, but on one side only; devotion, but on one side only, and in which of the two hearts one is sure to be broken.

LORD GORING. But I love Mabel. No other woman has any place in my life.

LADY CHILTERN. Robert, if they love each other, why should they not be married?

SIR ROBERT CHILTERN. Arthur cannot bring Mabel the love that she deserves.

LORD GORING. What reason have you for saying that?

SIR ROBERT CHILTERN. *(After a pause.)* Do you really require me to tell you?

LORD GORING. Certainly I do.

SIR ROBERT CHILTERN. As you choose. When I called on you yesterday evening I found Mrs. Cheveley concealed in your rooms. It was between ten and eleven o'clock at night. I do not wish to say anything more. Your relations with Mrs. Cheveley have, as I said to you last night, nothing whatsoever to do with me. I know you were engaged to be married to her once. The fascination she exercised over you then seems to have returned. You spoke to me last night of her as of a woman pure and stainless, a woman whom you respected and honoured. That may be so. But I cannot give my sister's life into your hands. It would be wrong of me. It would be unjust, infamously unjust to her.

LORD GORING. I have nothing more to say.

LADY CHILTERN. Robert, it was not Mrs. Cheveley whom Lord Goring expected last night.

SIR ROBERT CHILTERN. Not Mrs. Cheveley! Who was it then?

LORD GORING. Lady Chiltern!

LADY CHILTERN. It was your own wife. Robert, yesterday afternoon Lord Goring told me that if ever I was in trouble I could come to him for help, as he was our oldest and best friend. Later on, after that terrible scene in this room, I wrote to him telling him that I trusted him, that I had need of him, that I was coming to him for help and advice. *(Sir Robert Chiltern takes the letter out of his pocket.)* Yes, that letter. I didn't go to Lord Goring's, after all. I felt that it is from ourselves alone that help can come. Pride made me think that. Mrs. Cheveley went. She stole my letter and sent it anonymously to you this morning, that you should think . . . Oh! Robert, I cannot tell you what she wished you to think. . . .

SIR ROBERT CHILTERN. What! Had I fallen so low in your eyes that you thought that even for a moment I could have doubted your goodness? Gertrude, Gertrude, you are to me the white image of all good things, and sin can never touch you. Arthur, you can go to Mabel, and you have my best wishes! Oh! stop a moment. There is no name at the beginning of this letter. The brilliant

Mrs. Cheveley does not seem to have noticed that. There should be a name.

LADY CHILTERN. Let me write yours. It is you I trust and need. You and none else.

LORD GORING. Well, really, Lady Chiltern, I think I should have back my own letter.

LADY CHILTERN. *(Smiling.)* No; you shall have Mabel. *(Takes the letter and writes her husband's name on it.)*

LORD GORING. Well, I hope she hasn't changed her mind. It's nearly twenty minutes since I saw her last.

*(Enter Mabel Chiltern and Lord Caversham.)*

MABEL CHILTERN. Lord Goring, I think your father's conversation much more improving than yours. I am only going to talk to Lord Caversham in the future, and always under the usual palm tree.

LORD GORING. Darling! *(Kisses her.)*

LORD CAVERSHAM. *(Considerably taken aback.)* What does this mean, sir? You don't mean to say that this charming, clever young lady, has been so foolish as to accept you?

LORD GORING. Certainly, father! And Chiltern's been wise enough to accept the seat in the Cabinet.

LORD CAVERSHAM. I am very glad to hear that, Chiltern . . . I congratulate you, sir. If the country doesn't go to the dogs or the Radicals, we shall have you Prime Minister, some day.

*(Enter Mason.)*

MASON. Luncheon is on the table, my Lady!

*(Mason goes out.)*

LADY CHILTERN. You'll stop to luncheon, Lord Caversham, won't you?

LORD CAVERSHAM. With pleasure, and I'll drive you down to Downing Street afterwards, Chiltern. You have a great future before you, a great future. Wish I could say the same for you, sir. *(To Lord Goring.)* But your career will have to be entirely domestic.

LORD GORING. Yes, father, I prefer it domestic.

LORD CAVERSHAM. And if you don't make this young lady an ideal husband, I'll cut you off with a shilling.

MABEL CHILTERN. An ideal husband! Oh, I don't think I should like that. It sounds like something in the next world.

LORD CAVERSHAM. What do you want him to be then, dear?

MABEL CHILTERN. He can be what he chooses. All I want is to be ... to be ... oh! a real wife to him.

LORD CAVERSHAM. Upon my word, there is a good deal of common sense in that, Lady Chiltern.

*(They all go out except Sir Robert Chiltern. He sinks into a chair, wrapt in thought. After a little time Lady Chiltern returns to look for him.)*

LADY CHILTERN. *(Leaning over the back of the chair.)* Aren't you coming in, Robert?

SIR ROBERT CHILTERN. *(Taking her hand.)* Gertrude, is it love you feel for me, or is it pity merely?

LADY CHILTERN. *(Kisses him.)* It is love, Robert. Love, and only love. For both of us a new life is beginning.

CURTAIN

# THE IMPORTANCE OF
# BEING EARNEST

# THE PERSONS OF THE PLAY

JOHN WORTHING, J. P.
ALGERNON MONCRIEFF
REV. CANON CHASUBLE, D.D.
MERRIMAN, Butler
LANE, Manservant

LADY BRACKNELL
HON. GWENDOLEN FAIRFAX
CECILY CARDEW
MISS PRISM, Governess

# THE SCENES OF THE PLAY

ACT I    *Algernon Moncrieff's Flat in Half-Moon Street, W.*
ACT II   *The Garden at the Manor House, Woolton.*
ACT III *Drawing-Room at the Manor House, Woolton.*

*Time .... The Present*

# LONDON: ST. JAMES'S THEATRE

*Lessee and Manager: Mr. George Alexander*
*February 14th, 1895*

JOHN WORTHING, J. P.   *Mr. George Alexander*
ALGERNON MONCRIEFF   *Mr. Allen Aynesworth*
REV. CANON CHASUBLE, D.D.   *Mr. H. H. Vincent*
MERRIMAN (*Butler*)   *Mr. Frank Dyall*
LANE (*Manservant*)   *Mr. F. Kinsey Peile*
LADY BRACKNELL   *Miss Rose Leclercq*
HON. GWENDOLEN FAIRFAX   *Miss Irene Vanbrugh*
CECILY CARDEW   *Miss Evelyn Millard*
MISS PRISM (*Governess*)   *Mrs. George Canninge*

# First Act

SCENE—*Morning-room in Algernon's flat in Half-Moon Street. The room is luxuriously and artistically furnished. The sound of a piano is heard in the adjoining room.*

*(Lane is arranging afternoon tea on the table, and after the music has ceased, Algernon enters.)*

ALGERNON. Did you hear what I was playing, Lane?

LANE. I didn't think it polite to listen, sir.

ALGERNON. I'm sorry for that, for your sake. I don't play accurately—anyone can play accurately—but I play with wonderful expression. As far as the piano is concerned, sentiment is my forte. I keep science for Life.

LANE. Yes, sir.

ALGERNON. And, speaking of the science of Life, have you got the cucumber sandwiches cut for Lady Bracknell?

LANE. Yes, sir. *(Hands them on a salver.)*

ALGERNON. *(Inspects them, takes two, and sits down on the sofa.)* Oh! . . . by the way, Lane, I see from your book that on Thursday night, when Lord Shoreman and Mr. Worthing were dining with me, eight bottles of champagne are entered as having been consumed.

LANE. Yes, sir; eight bottles and a pint.

ALGERNON. Why is it that at a bachelor's establishment the servants invariably drink the champagne? I ask merely for information.

LANE. I attribute it to the superior quality of the wine, sir. I have often observed that in married households the champagne is rarely of a first-rate brand.

ALGERNON. Good Heavens! Is marriage so demoralizing as that?

LANE. I believe it *is* a very pleasant state, sir. I have had very little experience of it myself up to the present. I have only been married once. That was in consequence of a misunderstanding between myself and a young person.

ALGERNON. *(Languidly.)* I don't know that I am much interested in your family life, Lane.

LANE. No, sir; it is not a very interesting subject. I never think of it myself.

ALGERNON. Very natural, I am sure. That will do, Lane, thank you.

LANE. Thank you, sir.

*(Lane goes out.*

ALGERNON. Lane's views on marriage seem somewhat lax. Really, if the lower orders don't set us a good example, what on earth is the use of them? They seem, as a class, to have absolutely no sense of moral responsibility.

*(Enter Lane.)*

LANE. Mr. Ernest Worthing.

*(Enter Jack.)*                                          *( Lane goes out.)*

ALGERNON. How are you, my dear Ernest? What brings you up to town?

JACK. Oh, pleasure, pleasure! What else should bring one anywhere? Eating as usual, I see, Algy!

ALGERNON. *(Stiffly.)* I believe it is customary in good society to take some slight refreshment at five o'clock. Where have you been since last Thursday?

JACK. *(Sitting down on the sofa.)* In the country.

ALGERNON. What on earth do you do there?

JACK. *(Pulling off his gloves.)* When one is in town one amuses oneself. When one is in the country one amuses other people. It is excessively boring.

ALGERNON. And who are the people you amuse?

JACK. *(Airily.)* Oh, neighbours, neighbours.

ALGERNON. Got nice neighbours in your part of Shropshire?

JACK. Perfectly horrid! Never speak to one of them.

ALGERNON. How immensely you must amuse them! *(Goes over and takes sandwich.)* By the way, Shropshire is your county, is it not?

JACK. Eh? Shropshire? Yes, of course. Hallo! Why all these cups?

Why cucumber sandwiches? Why such reckless extravagance in
one so young? Who is coming to tea?

ALGERNON. Oh! merely Aunt Augusta and Gwendolen.

JACK. How perfectly delightful!

ALGERNON. Yes, that is all very well; but I am afraid Aunt Augusta
won't quite approve of your being here.

JACK. May I ask why?

ALGERNON. My dear fellow, the way you flirt with Gwendolen is
perfectly disgraceful. It is almost as bad as the way Gwendolen
flirts with you.

JACK. I am in love with Gwendolen. I have come up to town expressly to propose to her.

ALGERNON. I thought you had come up for pleasure? . . . I call that
business.

JACK. How utterly unromantic you are!

ALGERNON. I really don't see anything romantic in proposing. It is
very romantic to be in love. But there is nothing romantic about
a definite proposal. Why, one may be accepted. One usually is, I
believe. Then the excitement is all over. The very essence of romance is uncertainty. If ever I get married, I'll certainly try to
forget the fact.

JACK. I have no doubt about that, dear Algy. The Divorce Court was
specially invented for people whose memories are so curiously
constituted.

ALGERNON. Oh! there is no use speculating on that subject. Di-
vorces are made in Heaven—— *(Jack puts out his hand to take a
sandwich. ALGERNON at once interferes.)* Please don't touch the cucumber sandwiches. They are ordered specially for Aunt Augusta. *(Takes one and eats it.)*

JACK. Well, you have been eating them all the time.

ALGERNON. That is quite a different matter. She is my aunt. *(Takes
plate from below.)* Have some bread and butter. The bread and butter is for Gwendolen. Gwendolen is devoted to bread and butter.

JACK. *(Advancing to table and helping himself.)* And very good bread and
butter it is too.

ALGERNON. Well, my dear fellow, you need not eat as if you were going to eat it all. You behave as if you were married to her already. You are not married to her already, and I don't think you ever will be.

JACK. Why on earth do you say that?

ALGERNON. Well, in the first place girls never marry the men they flirt with. Girls don't think it right.

JACK. Oh, that is nonsense!

ALGERNON. It isn't. It is a great truth. It accounts for the extraordinary number of bachelors that one sees all over the place. In the second place, I don't give my consent.

JACK. Your consent!

ALGERNON. My dear fellow, Gwendolen is my first cousin. And before I allow you to marry her, you will have to clear up the whole question of Cecily. *(Rings bell.)*

JACK. Cecily! What on earth do you mean? What do you mean, Algy, by Cecily? I don't know anyone of the name of Cecily.

*(Enter Lane.)*

ALGERNON. Bring me that cigarette case Mr. Worthing left in the smoking-room the last time he dined here.

LANE. Yes, sir.

*(Lane goes out.)*

JACK. Do you mean to say you have had my cigarette case all this time? I wish to goodness you had let me know. I have been writing frantic letters to Scotland Yard about it. I was very nearly offering a large reward.

ALGERNON. Well, I wish you would offer one. I happen to be more than usually hard up.

JACK. There is no good offering a large reward now that the thing is found.

*(Enter Lane with the cigarette case on a salver. Algernon takes it at once. Lane goes out.)*

ALGERNON. I think that is rather mean of you, Ernest, I must say. *(Opens case and examines it.)* However, it makes no matter, for, now that I look at the inscription inside, I find that the thing isn't yours after all.

JACK. Of course it's mine. *(Moving to him.)* You have seen me with it a hundred times, and you have no right whatsoever to read what is written inside. It is a very ungentlemanly thing to read a private cigarette case.

ALGERNON. Oh! it is absurd to have a hard-and-fast rule about what one should read and what one shouldn't. More than half of modern culture depends on what one shouldn't read.

JACK. I am quite aware of the fact, and I don't propose to discuss modern culture. It isn't the sort of thing one should talk of in private. I simply want my cigarette case back.

ALGERNON. Yes; but this isn't your cigarette case. This cigarette case is a present from someone of the name of Cecily, and you said you didn't know anyone of that name.

JACK. Well, if you want to know, Cecily happens to be my aunt.

ALGERNON. Your aunt!

JACK. Yes. Charming old lady she is too. Lives at Tunbridge Wells. Just give it back to me, Algy.

ALGERNON. *(Retreating to back of sofa.)* But why does she call herself little Cecily if she is your aunt and lives at Tunbridge Wells? *(Reading.)* "From little Cecily with her fondest love."

JACK. *(Moving to sofa and kneeling upon it.)* My dear fellow, what on earth is there in that? Some aunts are tall, some aunts are not tall. That is a matter that surely an aunt may be allowed to decide for herself. You seem to think that every aunt should be exactly like your aunt! That is absurd! For Heaven's sake give me back my cigarette case. *(Follows Algernon round the room.)*

ALGERNON. Yes. But why does your aunt call you her uncle? "From little Cecily, with her fondest love to her dear Uncle Jack." There is no objection, I admit, to an aunt being a small aunt, but why an aunt, no matter what her size may be, should call her own nephew her uncle, I can't quite make out. Besides, your name isn't Jack at all; it is Ernest.

JACK. It isn't Ernest; it's Jack.

ALGERNON. You have always told me it was Ernest. I have introduced you to everyone as Ernest. You answer to the name of Ernest. You look as if your name was Ernest. You are the most earnest looking person I ever saw in my life. It is perfectly absurd your saying that your name isn't Ernest. It's on your cards. Here is one of them. *(Taking it from case.)* "Mr. Ernest Worthing, B. 4, The Albany." I'll keep this as a proof that your name is Ernest if ever you attempt to deny it to me, or to Gwendolen, or to anyone else. *(Puts the card in his pocket.)*

JACK. Well, my name is Ernest in town and Jack in the country, and the cigarette case was given to me in the country.

ALGERNON. Yes, but that does not account for the fact that your small Aunt Cecily, who lives at Tunbridge Wells, calls you her dear uncle. Come, old boy, you had much better have the thing out at once.

JACK. My dear Algy, you talk exactly as if you were a dentist. It is very vulgar to talk like a dentist when one isn't a dentist. It produces a false impression.

ALGERNON. Well, that is exactly what dentists always do. Now go on! Tell me the whole thing. I may mention that I have always suspected you of being a confirmed and secret Bunburyist; and I am quite sure of it now.

JACK. Bunburyist? What on earth do you mean by a Bunburyist?

ALGERNON. I'll reveal to you the meaning of that incomparable expression as soon as you are kind enough to inform me why you are Ernest in town and Jack in the country.

JACK. Well, produce my cigarette case first.

ALGERNON. Here it is. *(Hands cigarette case.)* Now produce your explanation, and pray make it improbable. *(Sits on sofa.)*

JACK. My dear fellow, there is nothing improbable about my explanation at all. In fact it's perfectly ordinary. Old Mr. Thomas Cardew, who adopted me when I was a little boy, made me in his will guardian to his grand-daughter, Miss Cecily Cardew. Cecily, who addresses me as her uncle from motives of respect that you could not possibly appreciate, lives at my place in the country under the charge of her admirable governess, Miss Prism.

ALGERNON. Where is that place in the country, by the way?

JACK. That is nothing to you, dear boy. You are not going to be invited. . . . I may tell you candidly that the place is not in Shropshire.

ALGERNON. I suspected that, my dear fellow! I have Bunburyed all over Shropshire on two separate occasions. Now, go on. Why are you Ernest in town and Jack in the country?

JACK. My dear Algy, I don't know whether you will be able to understand my real motives. You are hardly serious enough. When one is placed in the position of guardian, one has to adopt a very high moral tone on all subjects. It's one's duty to do so. And as a high moral tone can hardly be said to conduce very much to either one's health or one's happiness, in order to get up to town I have always pretended to have a younger brother of the name of Ernest, who lives in the Albany, and gets into the most dreadful scrapes. That, my dear Algy, is the whole truth pure and simple.

ALGERNON. The truth is rarely pure and never simple. Modern life would be very tedious if it were either, and modern literature a complete impossibility!

JACK. That wouldn't be at all a bad thing.

ALGERNON. Literary criticism is not your forte, my dear fellow. Don't try it. You should leave that to people who haven't been at a University. They do it so well in the daily papers. What you really are is a Bunburyist. I was quite right in saying you were a Bunburyist. You are one of the most advanced Bunburyists I know.

JACK. What on earth do you mean?

ALGERNON. You have invented a very useful younger brother called Ernest, in order that you may be able to come up to town as often as you like. I have invented an invaluable permanent invalid called Bunbury, in order that I may be able to go down into the country whenever I choose. Bunbury is perfectly invaluable. If it wasn't for Bunbury's extraordinary bad health, for instance, I wouldn't be able to dine with you at Willis's to-night, for I have been really engaged to Aunt Augusta for more than a week.

JACK. I haven't asked you to dine with me anywhere to-night.

ALGERNON. I know. You are absurdly careless about sending out invitations. It is very foolish of you. Nothing annoys people so much as not receiving invitations.

JACK. You had much better dine with your Aunt Augusta.

ALGERNON. I haven't the smallest intention of doing anything of the kind. To begin with, I dined there on Monday, and once a week is quite enough to dine with one's own relations. In the second place, whenever I do dine there I am always treated as a member of the family, and sent down with either no woman at all, or two. In the third place, I know perfectly well whom she will place me next to, to-night. She will place me next Mary Farquhar, who always flirts with her own husband across the dinner-table. That is not very pleasant. Indeed, it is not even decent . . . and that sort of thing is enormously on the increase. The amount of women in London who flirt with their own husbands is perfectly scandalous. It looks so bad. It is simply washing one's clean linen in public. Besides, now that I know you to be a confirmed Bunburyist I naturally want to talk to you about Bunburying. I want to tell you the rules.

JACK. I'm not a Bunburyist at all. If Gwendolen accepts me, I am going to kill my brother, indeed I think I'll kill him in any case. Cecily is a little too much interested in him. It is rather a bore. So I am going to get rid of Ernest. And I strongly advise you to do the same with Mr. . . . with your invalid friend who has the absurd name.

ALGERNON. Nothing will induce me to part with Bunbury, and if you ever get married, which seems to me extremely problematic, you will be very glad to know Bunbury. A man who marries without knowing Bunbury has a very tedious time of it.

JACK. That is nonsense. If I marry a charming girl like Gwendolen, and she is the only girl I ever saw in my life that I would marry, I certainly won't want to know Bunbury.

ALGERNON. Then your wife will. You don't seem to realize, that in married life three is company and two is none.

JACK. *(Sententiously.)* That, my dear young friend, is the theory that the corrupt French Drama has been propounding for the last fifty years.

ALGERNON. Yes; and that the happy English home has proved in half the time.

JACK. For heaven's sake, don't try to be cynical. It's perfectly easy to be cynical.

ALGERNON. My dear fellow, it isn't easy to be anything now-a-days. There's such a lot of beastly competition about. *(The sound of an electric bell is heard.)* Ah! that must be Aunt Augusta. Only relatives, or creditors, ever ring in that Wagnerian manner. Now, if I get her out of the way for ten minutes, so that you can have an opportunity for proposing to Gwendolen, may I dine with you to-night at Willis's?

JACK. I suppose so, if you want to.

ALGERNON. Yes, but you must be serious about it. I hate people who are not serious about meals. It is so shallow of them.

*(Enter Lane.)*

LANE. Lady Bracknell and Miss Fairfax.

*(Algernon goes forward to meet them. Enter Lady Bracknell and Gwendolen.)*

LADY BRACKNELL. Good afternoon, dear Algernon, I hope you are behaving very well.

ALGERNON. I'm feeling very well, Aunt Augusta.

LADY BRACKNELL. That's not quite the same thing. In fact the two things rarely go together. *(Sees Jack and bows to him with icy coldness.)*

ALGERNON. *(To Gwendolen.)* Dear me, you are smart!

GWENDOLEN. I am always smart! Aren't I, Mr. Worthing?

JACK. You're quite perfect, Miss Fairfax.

GWENDOLEN. Oh! I hope I am not that. It would leave no room for developments, and I intend to develop in many directions. *(Gwendolen and Jack sit down together in the corner.)*

LADY BRACKNELL. I'm sorry if we are a little late, Algernon, but I was obliged to call on dear Lady Harbury. I hadn't been there since her poor husband's death. I never saw a woman so altered; she looks quite twenty years younger. And now I'll have a cup of tea, and one of those nice cucumber sandwiches you promised me.

ALGERNON. Certainly, Aunt Augusta. *(Goes over to tea-table.)*

LADY BRACKNELL. Won't you come and sit here, Gwendolen?

GWENDOLEN. Thanks, mamma, I'm quite comfortable where I am.

ALGERNON. *(Picking up empty plate in horror.)* Good heavens! Lane! Why are there no cucumber sandwiches? I ordered them specially.

LANE. *(Gravely.)* There were no cucumbers in the market this morning, sir. I went down twice.

ALGERNON. No cucumbers!

LANE. No, sir. Not even for ready money.

ALGERNON. That will do, Lane, thank you.

LANE. Thank you, sir.

*(Goes out.)*

ALGERNON. I am greatly distressed, Aunt Augusta, about there being no cucumbers, not even for ready money.

LADY BRACKNELL. It really makes no matter, Algernon. I had some crumpets with Lady Harbury, who seems to me to be living entirely for pleasure now.

ALGERNON. I hear her hair has turned quite gold from grief.

LADY BRACKNELL. It certainly has changed its colour. From what cause I, of course, cannot say. *(Algernon crosses and hands tea.)* Thank you. I've quite a treat for you to-night, Algernon. I am going to send you down with Mary Farquhar. She is such a nice woman, and so attentive to her husband. It's delightful to watch them.

ALGERNON. I am afraid, Aunt Augusta, I shall have to give up the pleasure of dining with you to-night after all.

LADY BRACKNELL. *(Frowning.)* I hope not, Algernon. It would put my table completely out. Your uncle would have to dine upstairs. Fortunately he is accustomed to that.

ALGERNON. It is a great bore, and, I need hardly say, a terrible disappointment to me, but the fact is I have just had a telegram to say that my poor friend Bunbury is very ill again. *(Exchanges glances with Jack.)* They seem to think I should be with him.

LADY BRACKNELL. It is very strange. This Mr. Bunbury seems to suffer from curiously bad health.

ALGERNON. Yes; poor Bunbury is a dreadful invalid.

LADY BRACKNELL. Well, I must say, Algernon, that I think it is high time that Mr. Bunbury made up his mind whether he was going to live or to die. This shilly-shallying with the question is absurd. Nor do I in any way approve of the modern sympathy with invalids. I consider it morbid. Illness of any kind is hardly a thing to be encouraged in others. Health is the primary duty of life. I am always telling that to your poor uncle, but he never seems to take much notice . . . as far as any improvement in his ailments goes. I should be much obliged if you would ask Mr. Bunbury, from me, to be kind enough not to have a relapse on Saturday, for I rely on you to arrange my music for me. It is my last reception, and one wants something that will encourage conversation, particularly at the end of the season when everyone has practically said whatever they had to say, which, in most cases, was probably not much.

ALGERNON. I'll speak to Bunbury, Aunt Augusta, if he is still conscious, and I think I can promise you he'll be all right by Saturday. Of course the music is a great difficulty. You see, if one plays good music, people don't listen, and if one plays bad music people don't talk. But I'll run over the programme I've drawn out, if you will kindly come into the next room for a moment.

LADY BRACKNELL. Thank you, Algernon. It is very thoughtful of you. *(Rising, and following Algernon.)* I'm sure the programme will be delightful, after a few expurgations. French songs I cannot possibly allow. People always seem to think that they are improper, and either look shocked, which is vulgar, or laugh, which is worse. But German sounds a thoroughly respectable language and indeed, I believe is so. Gwendolen, you will accompany me.

GWENDOLEN. Certainly, mamma.

*(Lady Bracknell and Algernon go into the music-room, Gwendolen remains behind.)*

JACK. Charming day it has been, Miss Fairfax.

GWENDOLEN. Pray don't talk to me about the weather, Mr. Worthing. Whenever people talk to me about the weather, I always feel quite certain that they mean something else. And that makes me so nervous.

JACK. I do mean something else.

GWENDOLEN. I thought so. In fact, I am never wrong.

JACK. And I would like to be allowed to take advantage of Lady Bracknell's temporary absence . . .

GWENDOLEN. I would certainly advise you to do so. Mamma has a way of coming back suddenly into a room that I have often had to speak to her about.

JACK. *(Nervously.)* Miss Fairfax, ever since I met you I have admired you more than any girl . . . I have ever met since . . . I met you.

GWENDOLEN. Yes, I am quite aware of the fact. And I often wish that in public, at any rate, you had been more demonstrative. For me you have always had an irresistible fascination. Even before I met you I was far from indifferent to you. *(Jack looks at her in amazement.)* We live, as I hope you know, Mr. Worthing, in an age of ideals. The fact is constantly mentioned in the more expensive monthly magazines, and has reached the provincial pulpits I am told: and my ideal has always been to love some one of the name of Ernest. There is something in that name that inspires absolute confidence. The moment Algernon first mentioned to me that he had a friend called Ernest, I knew I was destined to love you.

JACK. You really love me, Gwendolen?

GWENDOLEN. Passionately!

JACK. Darling! You don't know how happy you've made me.

GWENDOLEN. My own Ernest!

JACK. But you don't really mean to say that you couldn't love me if my name wasn't Ernest?

GWENDOLEN. But your name is Ernest.

JACK. Yes, I know it is. But supposing it was something else? Do you mean to say you couldn't love me then?

GWENDOLEN. *(Glibly.)* Ah! that is clearly a metaphysical speculation, and like most metaphysical speculations has very little reference at all to the actual facts of real life, as we know them.

JACK. Personally, darling, to speak quite candidly, I don't much care about the name of Ernest . . . I don't think the name suits me at all.

GWENDOLEN. It suits you perfectly. It is a divine name. It has a music of its own. It produces vibrations.

JACK. Well, really, Gwendolen, I must say that I think there are lots of other much nicer names. I think Jack, for instance, a charming name.

GWENDOLEN. Jack? . . . No, there is very little music in the name Jack, if any at all, indeed. It does not thrill. It produces absolutely no vibrations. . . . I have known several Jacks, and they all, without exception, were more than usually plain. Besides, Jack is a notorious domesticity for John! And I pity any woman who is married to a man called John. She would probably never be allowed to know the entrancing pleasure of a single moment's solitude. The only really safe name is Ernest.

JACK. Gwendolen, I must get christened at once—I mean we must get married at once. There is no time to be lost.

GWENDOLEN. Married, Mr. Worthing?

JACK. *(Astounded.)* Well . . . surely. You know that I love you, and you led me to believe, Miss Fairfax, that you were not absolutely indifferent to me.

GWENDOLEN. I adore you. But you haven't proposed to me yet. Nothing has been said at all about marriage. The subject has not even been touched on.

JACK. Well . . . may I propose to you now?

GWENDOLEN. I think it would be an admirable opportunity. And to spare you any possible disappointment, Mr. Worthing, I think it only fair to tell you quite frankly beforehand that I am fully determined to accept you.

JACK. Gwendolen!

GWENDOLEN. Yes, Mr. Worthing, what have you got to say to me?

JACK. You know what I have got to say to you.

GWENDOLEN. Yes, but you don't say it.

JACK. Gwendolen, will you marry me? *(Goes on his knees.)*

GWENDOLEN. Of course I will, darling. How long you have been about it! I am afraid you have had very little experience in how to propose.

JACK. My own one, I have never loved anyone in the world but you.

GWENDOLEN. Yes, but men often propose for practice. I know my brother Gerald does. All my girl-friends tell me so. What wonderfully blue eyes you have, Ernest! They are quite, quite, blue. I hope you will always look at me just like that, especially when there are other people present.

*(Enter Lady Bracknell.)*

LADY BRACKNELL. Mr. Worthing! Rise, sir, from this semi-recumbent posture. It is most indecorous.

GWENDOLEN. Mamma! *(He tries to rise; she restrains him.)* I must beg you to retire. This is no place for you. Besides, Mr. Worthing has not quite finished yet.

LADY BRACKNELL. Finished what, may I ask?

GWENDOLEN. I am engaged to Mr. Worthing, mamma. *(They rise together.)*

LADY BRACKNELL. Pardon me, you are not engaged to anyone. When you do become engaged to some one, I, or your father, should his health permit him, will inform you of the fact. An engagement should come on a young girl as a surprise, pleasant or unpleasant, as the case may be. It is hardly a matter that she could be allowed to arrange for herself. . . . And now I have a few questions to put to you, Mr. Worthing. While I am making these inquiries, you, Gwendolen, will wait for me below in the carriage.

GWENDOLEN. *(Reproachfully.)* Mamma!

LADY BRACKNELL. In the carriage, Gwendolen! *(Gwendolen goes to the door. She and Jack blow kisses to each other behind Lady Bracknell's back. Lady Bracknell looks vaguely about as if she could not understand what the noise was. Finally turns round.)* Gwendolen, the carriage!

GWENDOLEN. Yes, mamma.           *(Goes out, looking back at Jack.)*

LADY BRACKNELL. *(Sitting down.)* You can take a seat, Mr. Worthing. *(Looks in her pocket for note-book and pencil.)*

JACK. Thank you, Lady Bracknell, I prefer standing.

LADY BRACKNELL. *(Pencil and note-book in hand.)* I feel bound to tell you that you are not down on my list of eligible young men, although I have the same list as the dear Duchess of Bolton has. We work together, in fact. However, I am quite ready to enter your name, should your answers be what a really affectionate mother requires. Do you smoke?

JACK. Well, yes, I must admit I smoke.

LADY BRACKNELL. I am glad to hear it. A man should always have an occupation of some kind. There are far too many idle men in London as it is. How old are you?

JACK. Twenty-nine.

LADY BRACKNELL. A very good age to be married at. I have always been of opinion that a man who desires to get married should know either everything or nothing. Which do you know?

JACK. *(After some hesitation.)* I know nothing, Lady Bracknell.

LADY BRACKNELL. I am pleased to hear it. I do not approve of anything that tampers with natural ignorance. Ignorance is like a delicate exotic fruit; touch it and the bloom is gone. The whole theory of modern education is radically unsound. Fortunately in England, at any rate, education produces no effect whatsoever. If it did, it would prove a serious danger to the upper classes, and probably lead to acts of violence in Grosvenor Square. What is your income?

JACK. Between seven and eight thousand a year.

LADY BRACKNELL. *(Makes a note in her book.)* In land, or in investments?

JACK. In investments, chiefly.

LADY BRACKNELL. That is satisfactory. What between the duties expected of one during one's lifetime, and the duties exacted from one after one's death, land has ceased to be either a profit or a pleasure. It gives one position, and prevents one from keeping it up. That's all that can be said about land.

JACK. I have a country house with some land, of course, attached to it, about fifteen hundred acres, I believe; but I don't depend on that for my real income. In fact, as far as I can make out, the poachers are the only people who make anything out of it.

LADY BRACKNELL. A country house! How many bedrooms? Well, that point can be cleared up afterwards. You have a town house, I hope? A girl with a simple, unspoiled nature, like Gwendolen, could hardly be expected to reside in the country.

JACK. Well, I own a house in Belgrave Square, but it is let by the year to Lady Bloxham. Of course, I can get it back whenever I like, at six months' notice.

LADY BRACKNELL. Lady Bloxham? I don't know her.

JACK. Oh, she goes about very little. She is a lady considerably advanced in years.

LADY BRACKNELL. Ah, now-a-days that is no guarantee of respectability of character. What number in Belgrave Square?

JACK. 149.

LADY BRACKNELL. *(Shaking her head.)* The unfashionable side. I thought there was something. However, that could easily be altered.

JACK. Do you mean the fashion, or the side?

LADY BRACKNELL. *(Sternly.)* Both, if necessary, I presume. What are your politics?

JACK. Well, I am afraid I really have none. I am a Liberal Unionist.

LADY BRACKNELL. Oh, they count as Tories. They dine with us. Or come in the evening, at any rate. Now to minor matters. Are your parents living?

JACK. I have lost both my parents.

LADY BRACKNELL. Both? . . . That seems like carelessness. Who was your father? He was evidently a man of some wealth. Was he born in what the Radical papers call the purple of commerce, or did he rise from the ranks of the aristocracy?

JACK. I am afraid I really don't know. The fact is, Lady Bracknell, I said I had lost my parents. It would be nearer the truth to say that my parents seem to have lost me . . . I don't actually know who I am by birth. I was . . . well, I was found.

LADY BRACKNELL. Found!

JACK. The late Mr. Thomas Cardew, an old gentleman of a very charitable and kindly disposition, found me, and gave me the name of Worthing, because he happened to have a first-class ticket for Worthing in his pocket at the time. Worthing is a place in Sussex. It is a seaside resort.

LADY BRACKNELL. Where did the charitable gentleman who had a first-class ticket for this seaside resort find you?

JACK. *(Gravely.)* In a hand-bag.

LADY BRACKNELL. A hand-bag?

JACK. *(Very seriously.)* Yes, Lady Bracknell. I was in a hand-bag—

a somewhat large, black leather hand-bag, with handles to it—an ordinary hand-bag in fact.

LADY BRACKNELL. In what locality did this Mr. James, or Thomas, Cardew come across this ordinary hand-bag?

JACK. In the cloak-room at Victoria Station. It was given to him in mistake for his own.

LADY BRACKNELL. The cloak-room at Victoria Station?

JACK. Yes. The Brighton line.

LADY BRACKNELL. The line is immaterial. Mr. Worthing, I confess I feel somewhat bewildered by what you have just told me. To be born, or at any rate bred, in a hand-bag, whether it had handles or not, seems to me to display a contempt for the ordinary decencies of family life that remind one of the worst excesses of the French Revolution. And I presume you know what that unfortunate movement led to? As for the particular locality in which the hand-bag was found, a cloak-room at a railway station might serve to conceal a social indiscretion—has probably, indeed, been used for that purpose before now—but it could hardly be regarded as an assured basis for a recognized position in good society.

JACK. May I ask you then what you would advise me to do? I need hardly say I would do anything in the world to ensure Gwendolen's happiness.

LADY BRACKNELL. I would strongly advise you, Mr. Worthing, to try and acquire some relations as soon as possible, and to make a definite effort to produce at any rate one parent, of either sex, before the season is quite over.

JACK. Well, I don't see how I could possibly manage to do that. I can produce the hand-bag at any moment. It is in my dressing-room at home. I really think that should satisfy you, Lady Bracknell.

LADY BRACKNELL. Me, sir! What has it to do with me? You can hardly imagine that I and Lord Bracknell would dream of allowing our only daughter—a girl brought up with the utmost care—to marry into a cloak-room, and form an alliance with a parcel? Good morning, Mr. Worthing!

*(Lady Bracknell sweeps out in majestic indignation.)*

JACK. Good morning! *(Algernon, from the other room, strikes up the Wedding March. Jack looks perfectly furious, and goes to the door.)* For goodness' sake don't play that ghastly tune, Algy! How idiotic you are!

*(The music stops, and Algernon enters cheerily.)*

ALGERNON. Didn't it go off all right, old boy? You don't mean to say Gwendolen refused you? I know it is a way she has. She is always refusing people, I think it is most ill-natured of her.

JACK. Oh, Gwendolen is as right as a trivet. As far as she is concerned, we are engaged. Her mother is perfectly unbearable. Never met such a Gorgon . . . I don't really know what a Gorgon is like, but I am quite sure that Lady Bracknell is one. In any case, she is a monster, without being a myth, which is rather unfair . . . I beg your pardon, Algy, I suppose I shouldn't talk about your own aunt in that way before you.

ALGERNON. My dear boy, I love hearing my relations abused. It is the only thing that makes me put up with them at all. Relations are simply a tedious pack of people, who haven't got the remotest knowledge of how to live, nor the smallest instinct about when to die.

JACK. Oh, that is nonsense!

ALGERNON. It isn't!

JACK. Well, I won't argue about the matter. You always want to argue about things.

ALGERNON. That is exactly what things were originally made for.

JACK. Upon my word, if I thought that, I'd shoot myself . . . *(A pause.)* You don't think there is any chance of Gwendolen becoming like her mother in about a hundred and fifty years, do you Algy?

ALGERNON. All women become like their mothers. That is their tragedy. No man does. That's his.

JACK. Is that clever?

ALGERNON. It is perfectly phrased! and quite as true as any observation in civilized life should be.

JACK. I am sick to death of cleverness. Everybody is clever now-a-days. You can't go anywhere without meeting clever people.

The thing has become an absolute public nuisance. I wish to goodness we had a few fools left.

ALGERNON. We have.

JACK. I should extremely like to meet them. What do they talk about?

ALGERNON. The fools? Oh! about the clever people, of course.

JACK. What fools!

ALGERNON. By the way, did you tell Gwendolen the truth about your being Ernest in town, and Jack in the country?

JACK. *(In a very patronising manner.)* My dear fellow, the truth isn't quite the sort of thing one tells to a nice sweet refined girl. What extraordinary ideas you have about the way to behave to a woman!

ALGERNON. The only way to behave to a woman is to make love to her, if she is pretty, and to someone else if she is plain.

JACK. Oh, that is nonsense.

ALGERNON. What about your brother? What about the profligate Ernest?

JACK. Oh, before the end of the week, I shall have got rid of him. I'll say he died in Paris of apoplexy. Lots of people die of apoplexy, quite suddenly, don't they?

ALGERNON. Yes, but it's hereditary, my dear fellow. It's a sort of thing that runs in families. You had much better say a severe chill.

JACK. You are sure a severe chill isn't hereditary, or anything of that kind?

ALGERNON. Of course it isn't!

JACK. Very well, then. My poor brother Ernest is carried off suddenly in Paris, by a severe chill. That gets rid of him.

ALGERNON. But I thought you said that . . . Miss Cardew was a little too much interested in your poor brother Ernest? Won't she feel his loss a good deal?

JACK. Oh, that is all right. Cecily is not a silly romantic girl, I am glad to say. She has got a capital appetite, goes long walks, and pays no attention at all to her lessons.

ALGERNON. I would rather like to see Cecily.

JACK. I will take very good care you never do. She is excessively pretty, and she is only just eighteen.

ALGERNON. Have you told Gwendolen yet that you have an excessively pretty ward who is only just eighteen?

JACK. Oh! one doesn't blurt these things out to people. Cecily and Gwendolen are perfectly certain to be extremely great friends. I'll bet you anything you like that half an hour after they have met, they will be calling each other sister.

ALGERNON. Women only do that when they have called each other a lot of other things first. Now, my dear boy, if we want to get a good table at Willis's, we really must go and dress. Do you know it is nearly seven?

JACK. *(Irritably.)* Oh! it always is nearly seven.

ALGERNON. Well, I'm hungry.

JACK. I never knew you when you weren't. . . .

ALGERNON. What shall we do after dinner? Go to a theatre?

JACK. Oh no! I loathe listening.

ALGERNON. Well, let us go to the Club?

JACK. Oh, no! I hate talking.

ALGERNON. Well, we might trot round to the Empire at ten?

JACK. Oh no! I can't bear looking at things. It is so silly.

ALGERNON. Well, what shall we do?

JACK. Nothing!

ALGERNON. It is awfully hard work doing nothing. However, I don't mind hard work where there is no definite object of any kind.

*(Enter Lane.)*

LANE. Miss Fairfax.

*(Enter Gwendolen. Lane goes out.)*

ALGERNON. Gwendolen, upon my word!

GWENDOLEN. Algy, kindly turn your back. I have something very particular to say to Mr. Worthing.

ALGERNON. Really, Gwendolen, I don't think I can allow this at all.

GWENDOLEN. Algy, you always adopt a strictly immoral attitude towards life. You are not quite old enough to do that. *(Algernon retires to the fireplace.)*

JACK. My own darling!

GWENDOLEN. Ernest, we may never be married. From the expression on mamma's face I fear we never shall. Few parents now-a-days pay any regard to what their children say to them. The old-fashioned respect for the young is fast dying out. Whatever influence I ever had over mamma, I lost at the age of three. But although she may prevent us from becoming man and wife, and I may marry someone else, and marry often, nothing that she can possibly do can alter my eternal devotion to you.

JACK. Dear Gwendolen!

GWENDOLEN. The story of your romantic origin, as related to me by mamma, with unpleasing comments, has naturally stirred the deeper fibres of my nature. Your Christian name has an irresistible fascination. The simplicity of your character makes you exquisitely incomprehensible to me. Your town address at the Albany I have. What is your address in the country?

JACK. The Manor House, Woolton, Hertfordshire.

*(Algernon, who has been carefully listening, smiles to himself, and writes the address on his shirt-cuff. Then picks up the Railway Guide.)*

GWENDOLEN. There is a good postal service, I suppose? It may be necessary to do something desperate. That of course will require serious consideration. I will communicate with you daily.

JACK. My own one!

GWENDOLEN. How long do you remain in town?

JACK. Till Monday.

GWENDOLEN. Good! Algy, you may turn round now.

ALGERNON. Thanks, I've turned round already.

GWENDOLEN. You may also ring the bell.

JACK. You will let me see you to your carriage, my own darling?

GWENDOLEN. Certainly.

JACK. *(To Lane, who now enters.)* I will see Miss Fairfax out.

LANE. Yes, sir.

*(Jack and Gwendolen go off.)*

*(Lane presents several letters on a salver to Algernon. It is to be surmised that they are bills, as Algernon after looking at the envelopes, tears them up.)*

ALGERNON. A glass of sherry, Lane.

LANE. Yes, sir.

ALGERNON. To-morrow, Lane, I'm going Bunburying.

LANE. Yes, sir.

ALGERNON. I shall probably not be back till Monday. You can put up my dress clothes, my smoking jacket, and all the Bunbury suits . . .

LANE. Yes, sir. *(Handing sherry.)*

ALGERNON. I hope to-morrow will be a fine day, Lane.

LANE. It never is, sir.

ALGERNON. Lane, you're a perfect pessimist.

LANE. I do my best to give satisfaction, sir.

*(Enter Jack. Lane goes off.)*

JACK. There's a sensible, intellectual girl! the only girl I ever cared for in my life. *(Algernon is laughing immoderately.)* What on earth are you so amused at?

ALGERNON. Oh, I'm a little anxious about poor Bunbury, that is all.

JACK. If you don't take care, your friend Bunbury will get you into a serious scrape some day.

ALGERNON. I love scrapes. They are the only things that are never serious.

JACK. Oh, that's nonsense, Algy. You never talk anything but non-sense.

ALGERNON. Nobody ever does.

*(Jack looks indignantly at him, and leaves the room. ALGERNON lights a cigarette, reads his shirt-cuff, and smiles.)*

## ACT-DROP

# SECOND ACT

*SCENE—Garden at the Manor House. A flight of gray stone steps leads up to the house. The garden, an old-fashioned one, full of roses. Time of year, July. Basket chairs, and a table covered with books, are set under a large yew tree.*

*(Miss Prism discovered seated at the table. Cecily is at the back watering flowers.)*

MISS PRISM. *(Calling.)* Cecily, Cecily! Surely such a utilitarian occupation as the watering of flowers is rather Moulton's duty than yours? Especially at a moment when intellectual pleasures await you. Your German grammar is on the table. Pray open it at page fifteen. We will repeat yesterday's lesson.

CECILY. *(Coming over very slowly.)* But I don't like German. It isn't at all a becoming language. I know perfectly well that I look quite plain after my German lesson.

MISS PRISM. Child, you know how anxious your guardian is that you should improve yourself in every way. He laid particular stress on your German, as he was leaving for town yesterday. Indeed, he always lays stress on your German when he is leaving for town.

CECILY. Dear Uncle Jack is so very serious! Sometimes he is so serious that I think he cannot be quite well.

MISS PRISM. *(Drawing herself up.)* Your guardian enjoys the best of health, and his gravity of demeanour is especially to be commended in one so comparatively young as he is. I know no one who has a higher sense of duty and responsibility.

CECILY. I suppose that is why he often looks a little bored when we three are together.

MISS PRISM. Cecily! I am surprised at you. Mr. Worthing has many troubles in his life. Idle merriment and triviality would be out of place in his conversation. You must remember his constant anxiety about that unfortunate young man his brother.

CECILY. I wish Uncle Jack would allow that unfortunate young man, his brother, to come down here sometimes. We might have a good influence over him, Miss Prism. I am sure you certainly would. You know German, and geology, and things of that kind influence a man very much.

*(Cecily begins to write in her diary.)*

MISS PRISM. *(Shaking her head.)* I do not think that even I could produce any effect on a character that according to his own brother's admission is irretrievably weak and vacillating. Indeed I am not sure that I would desire to reclaim him. I am not in favour of this modern mania for turning bad people into good people at a moment's notice. As a man sows so let him reap. You must put away your diary, Cecily. I really don't see why you should keep a diary at all.

CECILY. I keep a diary in order to enter the wonderful secrets of my life. If I didn't write them down I should probably forget all about them.

MISS PRISM. Memory, my dear Cecily, is the diary that we all carry about with us.

CECILY. Yes, but it usually chronicles the things that have never happened, and couldn't possibly have happened. I believe that Memory is responsible for nearly all the three-volume novels that Mudie sends us.

MISS PRISM. Do not speak slightingly of the three-volume novel, Cecily. I wrote one myself in earlier days.

CECILY. Did you really, Miss Prism? How wonderfully clever you are! I hope it did not end happily? I don't like novels that end happily. They depress me so much.

MISS PRISM. The good ended happily, and the bad unhappily. That is what Fiction means.

CECILY. I suppose so. But it seems very unfair. And was your novel ever published?

MISS PRISM. Alas! no. The manuscript unfortunately was abandoned. I use the word in the sense of lost or mislaid. To your work, child, these speculations are profitless.

CECILY. *(Smiling.)* But I see dear Dr. Chasuble coming up through the garden.

MISS PRISM. *(Rising and advancing.)* Dr. Chasuble! This is indeed a pleasure.

*(Enter Canon Chasuble.)*

CHASUBLE. And how are we this morning? Miss Prism, you are, I trust, well?

CECILY. Miss Prism has just been complaining of a slight headache. I think it would do her so much good to have a short stroll with you in the Park, Dr. Chasuble.

MISS PRISM. Cecily, I have not mentioned anything about a headache.

CECILY. No, dear Miss Prism, I know that, but I felt instinctively that you had a headache. Indeed I was thinking about that, and not about my German lesson, when the Rector came in.

CHASUBLE. I hope, Cecily, you are not inattentive.

CECILY. Oh, I am afraid I am.

CHASUBLE. That is strange. Were I fortunate enough to be Miss Prism's pupil, I would hang upon her lips. *(Miss Prism glares.)* I spoke metaphorically.—My metaphor was drawn from bees. Ahem! Mr. Worthing I suppose, has not returned from town yet?

MISS PRISM. We do not expect him till Monday afternoon.

CHASUBLE. Ah yes, he usually likes to spend his Sunday in London. He is not one of those whose sole aim is enjoyment, as, by all accounts, that unfortunate young man his brother seems to be. But I must not disturb Egeria and her pupil any longer.

MISS PRISM. Egeria? My name is Lætitia, Doctor.

CHASUBLE *(Bowing.)* A classical allusion merely, drawn from the Pagan authors. I shall see you both no doubt at Evensong?

MISS PRISM. I think, dear Doctor, I will have a stroll with you. I find I have a headache after all, and a walk might do it good.

CHASUBLE. With pleasure, Miss Prism, with pleasure. We might go as far as the schools and back.

MISS PRISM. That would be delightful. Cecily, you will read your Political Economy in my absence. The chapter on the Fall of the Rupee you may omit. It is somewhat too sensational. Even these metallic problems have their melodramatic side.

*(Goes down the garden with Dr. Chasuble.)*

CECILY. *(Picks up books and throws them back on table.)* Horrid Political Economy! Horrid Geography! Horrid, horrid German!

*(Enter Merriman with a card on a salver.)*

MERRIMAN. Mr. Ernest Worthing has just driven over from the station. He has brought his luggage with him.

CECILY. *(Takes the card and reads it.)* "Mr. Ernest Worthing, B. 4 The Albany, W." Uncle Jack's brother! Did you tell him Mr. Worthing was in town?

MERRIMAN. Yes, Miss. He seemed very much disappointed. I mentioned that you and Miss Prism were in the garden. He said he was anxious to speak to you privately for a moment.

CECILY. Ask Mr. Ernest Worthing to come here. I suppose you had better talk to the housekeeper about a room for him.

MERRIMAN. Yes, Miss.                    *(MERRIMAN goes off.)*

CECILY. I have never met any really wicked person before. I feel rather frightened. I am so afraid he will look just like everyone else.

*(Enter Algernon, very gay and debonnair.)*

He does!

ALGERNON. *(Raising his hat.)* You are my little cousin Cecily, I'm sure.

CECILY. You are under some strange mistake. I am not little. In fact, I believe I am more than usually tall for my age. *(Algernon is rather taken aback.)* But I am your cousin Cecily. You, I see from your card, are Uncle Jack's brother, my cousin Ernest, my wicked cousin Ernest.

ALGERNON. Oh! I am not really wicked at all, cousin Cecily. You mustn't think that I am wicked.

CECILY. If you are not, then you have certainly been deceiving us all in a very inexcusable manner. I hope you have not been leading a double life, pretending to be wicked and being really good all the time. That would be hypocrisy.

ALGERNON. *(Looks at her in amazement.)* Oh! Of course I have been rather reckless.

CECILY. I am glad to hear it.

ALGERNON. In fact, now you mention the subject, I have been very bad in my own small way.

CECILY. I don't think you should be so proud of that, though I am sure it must have been very pleasant.

ALGERNON. It is much pleasanter being here with you.

CECILY. I can't understand how you are here at all. Uncle Jack won't be back till Monday afternoon.

ALGERNON. That is a great disappointment. I am obliged to go up by the first train on Monday morning. I have a business appointment that I am anxious . . . to miss.

CECILY. Couldn't you miss it anywhere but in London?

ALGERNON. No: the appointment is in London.

CECILY. Well, I know, of course, how important it is not to keep a business engagement, if one wants to retain any sense of the beauty of life, but still I think you had better wait till Uncle Jack arrives. I know he wants to speak to you about your emigrating.

ALGERNON. About my what?

CECILY. Your emigrating. He has gone up to buy your outfit.

ALGERNON. I certainly wouldn't let Jack buy my outfit. He has no taste in neckties at all.

CECILY. I don't think you will require neckties. Uncle Jack is sending you to Australia.

ALGERNON. Australia! I'd sooner die.

CECILY. Well, he said at dinner on Wednesday night, that you would have to choose between this world, the next world, and Australia.

ALGERNON. Oh, well! The accounts I have received of Australia and the next world, are not particularly encouraging. This world is good enough for me, cousin Cecily.

CECILY. Yes, but are you good enough for it?

ALGERNON. I'm afraid I'm not that. That is why I want you to reform me. You might make that your mission, if you don't mind, cousin Cecily.

CECILY. I'm afraid I've no time, this afternoon.

ALGERNON. Well, would you mind my reforming myself this afternoon?

CECILY. It is rather Quixotic of you. But I think you should try.

ALGERNON. I will. I feel better already.

CECILY. You are looking a little worse.

ALGERNON. That is because I am hungry.

CECILY. How thoughtless of me. I should have remembered that when one is going to lead an entirely new life, one requires regular and wholesome meals. Won't you come in?

ALGERNON. Thank you. Might I have a button-hole first? I never have any appetite unless I have a button-hole first.

CECILY. A Maréchale Niel? *(Picks up scissors.)*

ALGERNON. No, I'd sooner have a pink rose.

CECILY. Why? *(Cuts a flower.)*

ALGERNON. Because you are like a pink rose, Cousin Cecily.

CECILY. I don't think it can be right for you to talk to me like that. Miss Prism never says such things to me.

ALGERNON. Then Miss Prism is a short-sighted old lady. *(Cecily puts the rose in his button-hole.)* You are the prettiest girl I ever saw.

CECILY. Miss Prism says that all good looks are a snare.

ALGERNON. They are a snare that every sensible man would like to be caught in.

CECILY. Oh! I don't think I would care to catch a sensible man. I shouldn't know what to talk to him about.

*(They pass into the house. Miss Prism and Dr. Chasuble return.)*

MISS PRISM. You are too much alone, dear Dr. Chasuble. You should get married. A misanthrope I can understand—a womanthrope, never!

CHASUBLE. *(With a scholar's shudder.)* Believe me, I do not deserve so neologistic a phrase. The precept as well as the practice of the Primitive Church was distinctly against matrimony.

MISS PRISM. *(Sententiously.)* That is obviously the reason why the

Primitive Church has not lasted up to the present day. And you do not seem to realize, dear Doctor, that by persistently remaining single, a man converts himself into a permanent public temptation. Men should be more careful; this very celibacy leads weaker vessels astray.

CHASUBLE. But is a man not equally attractive when married?

MISS PRISM. No married man is ever attractive except to his wife.

CHASUBLE. And often, I've been told, not even to her.

MISS PRISM. That depends on the intellectual sympathies of the woman. Maturity can always be depended on. Ripeness can be trusted. Young women are green. *(Dr. Chasuble starts.)* I spoke horticulturally. My metaphor was drawn from fruits. But where is Cecily?

CHASUBLE. Perhaps she followed us to the schools.

*(Enter Jack slowly from the back of the garden. He is dressed in the deepest mourning, with crape hat-band and black gloves.)*

MISS PRISM. Mr. Worthing!

CHASUBLE. Mr. Worthing?

MISS PRISM. This is indeed a surprise. We did not look for you till Monday afternoon.

JACK. *(Shakes Miss Prism's hand in a tragic manner.)* I have returned sooner than I expected. Dr. Chasuble, I hope you are well?

CHASUBLE. Dear Mr. Worthing, I trust this garb of woe does not betoken some terrible calamity?

JACK. My brother.

MISS PRISM. More shameful debts and extravagance?

CHASUBLE. Still leading his life of pleasure?

JACK. *(Shaking his head.)* Dead!

CHASUBLE. Your brother Ernest dead?

JACK. Quite dead.

MISS PRISM. What a lesson for him! I trust he will profit by it.

CHASUBLE. Mr. Worthing, I offer you my sincere condolence. You have at least the consolation of knowing that you were always the most generous and forgiving of brothers.

JACK. Poor Ernest! He had many faults, but it is a sad, sad blow.

CHASUBLE. Very sad indeed. Were you with him at the end?

JACK. No. He died abroad; in Paris, in fact. I had a telegram last night from the manager of the Grand Hotel.

CHASUBLE. Was the cause of death mentioned?

JACK. A severe chill, it seems.

MISS PRISM. As a man sows, so shall he reap.

CHASUBLE. *(Raising his hand.)* Charity, dear Miss Prism, charity! None of us are perfect. I myself am peculiarly susceptible to draughts. Will the interment take place here?

JACK. No. He seemed to have expressed a desire to be buried in Paris.

CHASUBLE. In Paris! *(Shakes his head.)* I fear that hardly points to any very serious state of mind at the last. You would no doubt wish me to make some slight allusion to this tragic domestic affliction next Sunday. *(Jack presses his hand convulsively.)* My sermon on the meaning of the manna in the wilderness can be adapted to almost any occasion, joyful, or, as in the present case, distressing. *(All sigh.)* I have preached it at harvest celebrations, christenings, confirmations, on days of humiliation and festal days. The last time I delivered it was in the Cathedral, as a charity sermon on behalf of the Society for the Prevention of Discontent among the Upper Orders. The Bishop, who was present, was much struck by some of the analogies I drew.

JACK. Ah! that reminds me, you mentioned christenings I think, Dr. Chasuble? I suppose you know how to christen all right? *(Dr. Chasuble looks astounded.)* I mean, of course, you are continually christening, aren't you?

MISS PRISM. It is, I regret to say, one of the Rector's most constant duties in this parish. I have often spoken to the poorer classes on the subject. But they don't seem to know what thrift is.

CHASUBLE. But is there any particular infant in whom you are interested, Mr. Worthing? Your brother was, I believe, unmarried, was he not?

JACK. Oh yes.

MISS PRISM. *(Bitterly.)* People who live entirely for pleasure usually are.

JACK. But it is not for any child, dear Doctor. I am very fond of children. No! the fact is, I would like to be christened myself, this afternoon, if you have nothing better to do.

CHASUBLE. But surely, Mr. Worthing, you have been christened already?

JACK. I don't remember anything about it.

CHASUBLE. But have you any grave doubts on the subject?

JACK. I certainly intend to have. Of course I don't know if the thing would bother you in any way, or if you think I am a little too old now.

CHASUBLE. Not at all. The sprinkling, and, indeed, the immersion of adults is a perfectly canonical practice.

JACK. Immersion!

CHASUBLE. You need have no apprehensions. Sprinkling is all that is necessary, or indeed I think advisable. Our weather is so changeable. At what hour would you wish the ceremony performed?

JACK. Oh, I might trot round about five if that would suit you.

CHASUBLE. Perfectly, perfectly! In fact I have two similar ceremonies to perform at that time. A case of twins that occurred recently in one of the outlying cottages on your own estate. Poor Jenkins the carter, a most hard-working man.

JACK. Oh! I don't see much fun in being christened along with other babies. It would be childish. Would half-past five do?

CHASUBLE. Admirably! Admirably! *(Takes out watch.)* And now, dear Mr. Worthing, I will not intrude any longer into a house of sorrow. I would merely beg you not to be too much bowed down by grief. What seem to us bitter trials are often blessings in disguise.

MISS PRISM. This seems to me a blessing of an extremely obvious kind.

*(Enter Cecily from the house.)*

CECILY. Uncle Jack! Oh, I am pleased to see you back. But what horrid clothes you have got on! Do go and change them.

MISS PRISM. Cecily!

CHASUBLE. My child! my child! *(Cecily goes towards Jack; he kisses her brow in a melancholy manner.)*

CECILY. What is the matter, Uncle Jack? Do look happy! You look as if you had toothache, and I have got such a surprise for you. Who do you think is in the dining-room? Your brother!

JACK. Who?

CECILY. Your brother Ernest. He arrived about half an hour ago.

JACK. What nonsense! I haven't got a brother.

CECILY. Oh, don't say that. However badly he may have behaved to you in the past he is still your brother. You couldn't be so heartless as to disown him. I'll tell him to come out. And you will shake hands with him, won't you, Uncle Jack? *(Runs back into the house.)*

CHASUBLE. These are very joyful tidings.

MISS PRISM. After we had all been resigned to his loss, his sudden return seems to me peculiarly distressing.

JACK. My brother is in the dining-room? I don't know what it all means. I think it is perfectly absurd.

*(Enter Algernon and Cecily hand in hand. They come slowly up to JACK.)*

JACK. Good heavens! *(Motions Algernon away.)*

ALGERNON. Brother John, I have come down from town to tell you that I am very sorry for all the trouble I have given you, and that I intend to lead a better life in the future. *(Jack glares at him and does not take his hand.)*

CECILY. Uncle Jack, you are not going to refuse your own brother's hand?

JACK. Nothing will induce me to take his hand. I think his coming down here disgraceful. He knows perfectly well why.

CECILY. Uncle Jack, do be nice. There is some good in everyone. Ernest has just been telling me about his poor invalid friend Mr. Bunbury whom he goes to visit so often. And surely there must be much good in one who is kind to an invalid, and leaves the pleasures of London to sit by a bed of pain.

JACK. Oh! he has been talking about Bunbury has he?

CECILY. Yes, he has told me all about poor Mr. Bunbury, and his terrible state of health.

JACK. Bunbury! Well, I won't have him talk to you about Bunbury or about anything else. It is enough to drive one perfectly frantic.

ALGERNON. Of course I admit that the faults were all on my side.

But I must say that I think that Brother John's coldness to me is peculiarly painful. I expected a more enthusiastic welcome, especially considering it is the first time I have come here.

CECILY. Uncle Jack, if you don't shake hands with Ernest I will never forgive you.

JACK. Never forgive me?

CECILY. Never, never, never!

JACK. Well, this is the last time I shall ever do it. *(Shakes hands with Algernon and glares.)*

CHASUBLE. It's pleasant, is it not, to see so perfect a reconciliation? I think we might leave the two brothers together.

MISS PRISM. Cecily, you will come with us.

CECILY. Certainly, Miss Prism. My little task of reconciliation is over.

CHASUBLE. You have done a beautiful action to-day, dear child.

MISS PRISM. We must not be premature in our judgments.

CECILY. I feel very happy. *(They all go off.)*

JACK. You young scoundrel, Algy, you must get out of this place as soon as possible. I don't allow any Bunburying here.
*(Enter Merriman.)*

MERRIMAN. I have put Mr. Ernest's things in the room next to yours, sir. I suppose that is all right?

JACK. What?

MERRIMAN. Mr. Ernest's luggage, sir. I have unpacked it and put it in the room next to your own.

JACK. His luggage?

MERRIMAN. Yes, sir. Three portmanteaus, a dressing-case, two hat-boxes, and a large luncheon-basket.

ALGERNON. I am afraid I can't stay more than a week this time.

JACK. Merriman, order the dog-cart at once. Mr. Ernest has been suddenly called back to town.

MERRIMAN. Yes, sir. *(Goes back into the house.)*

ALGERNON. What a fearful liar you are, Jack. I have not been called back to town at all.

JACK. Yes, you have.

ALGERNON. I haven't heard anyone call me.

JACK. Your duty as a gentleman calls you back.

ALGERNON. My duty as a gentleman has never interfered with my pleasures in the smallest degree.

JACK. I can quite understand that.

ALGERNON. Well, Cecily is a darling.

JACK. You are not to talk of Miss Cardew like that. I don't like it.

ALGERNON. Well, I don't like your clothes. You look perfectly ridiculous in them. Why on earth don't you go up and change? It is perfectly childish to be in deep mourning for a man who is actually staying for a whole week with you in your house as a guest. I call it grotesque.

JACK. You are certainly not staying with me for a whole week as a guest or anything else. You have got to leave . . . by the four-five train.

ALGERNON. I certainly won't leave you so long as you are in mourning. It would be most unfriendly. If I were in mourning you would stay with me, I suppose. I should think it very unkind if you didn't.

JACK. Well, will you go if I change my clothes?

ALGERNON. Yes, if you are not too long. I never saw anybody take so long to dress, and with such little result.

JACK. Well, at any rate, that is better than being always over-dressed as you are.

ALGERNON. If I am occasionally a little over-dressed, I make up for it by being always immensely over-educated.

JACK. Your vanity is ridiculous, your conduct an outrage, and your presence in my garden utterly absurd. However, you have got to catch the four-five, and I hope you will have a pleasant journey back to town. This Bunburying, as you call it, has not been a great success for you.

*(Goes into the house.)*

ALGERNON. I think it has been a great success. I'm in love with Cecily, and that is everything.

*(Enter Cecily at the back of the garden. She picks up the can and begins to water the flowers.)*

But I must see her before I go, and make arrangements for another Bunbury. Ah, there she is.

CECILY. Oh, I merely came back to water the roses. I thought you were with Uncle Jack.

ALGERNON. He's gone to order the dog-cart for me.

CECILY. Oh, is he going to take you for a nice drive?

ALGERNON. He's going to send me away.

CECILY. Then have we got to part?

ALGERNON. I am afraid so. It's a very painful parting.

CECILY. It is always painful to part from people whom one has known for a very brief space of time. The absence of old friends one can endure with equanimity. But even a momentary separation from anyone to whom one has just been introduced is almost unbearable.

ALGERNON. Thank you.

*(Enter Merriman.)*

MERRIMAN. The dog-cart is at the door, sir. *(Algernon looks appealingly at Cecily.)*

CECILY. It can wait, Merriman . . . for . . . five minutes.

MERRIMAN. Yes, Miss.                                     *(Exit Merriman.)*

ALGERNON. I hope, Cecily, I shall not offend you if I state quite frankly and openly that you seem to me to be in every way the visible personification of absolute perfection.

CECILY. I think your frankness does you great credit, Ernest. If you will allow me I will copy your remarks into my diary. *(Goes over to table and begins writing in diary.)*

ALGERNON. Do you really keep a diary? I'd give anything to look at it. May I?

CECILY. Oh no. *(Puts her hand over it.)* You see, it is simply a very young girl's record of her own thoughts and impressions, and consequently meant for publication. When it appears in volume form I hope you will order a copy. But pray, Ernest, don't stop. I delight in taking down from dictation. I have reached "absolute perfection." You can go on. I am quite ready for more.

ALGERNON. *(Somewhat taken aback.)* Ahem! Ahem!

CECILY. Oh, don't cough, Ernest. When one is dictating one should speak fluently and not cough. Besides, I don't know how to spell a cough. *(Writes as Algernon speaks.)*

ALGERNON. *(Speaking very rapidly.)* Cecily, ever since I first looked upon your wonderful and incomparable beauty, I have dared to love you wildly, passionately, devotedly, hopelessly.

CECILY. I don't think that you should tell me that you love me wildly, passionately, devotedly, hopelessly. Hopelessly doesn't seem to make much sense, does it?

ALGERNON. Cecily!

*(Enter Merriman.)*

MERRIMAN. The dog-cart is waiting, sir.

ALGERNON. Tell it to come round next week, at the same hour.

MERRIMAN. *(Looks at Cecily, who makes no sign.)* Yes, sir.

*(Merriman retires.)*

CECILY. Uncle Jack would be very much annoyed if he knew you were staying on till next week, at the same hour.

ALGERNON. Oh, I don't care about Jack. I don't care for anybody in the whole world but you. I love you, Cecily. You will marry me, won't you?

CECILY. You silly boy! Of course. Why, we have been engaged for the last three months.

ALGERNON. For the last three months?

CECILY. Yes, it will be exactly three months on Thursday.

ALGERNON. But how did we become engaged?

CECILY. Well, ever since dear Uncle Jack first confessed to us that he had a younger brother who was very wicked and bad, you of course have formed the chief topic of conversation between myself and Miss Prism. And of course a man who is much talked about is always very attractive. One feels there must be something in him after all. I daresay it was foolish of me, but I fell in love with you, Ernest.

ALGERNON. Darling! And when was the engagement actually settled?

CECILY. On the 14th of February last. Worn out by your entire ignorance of my existence, I determined to end the matter one way or the other, and after a long struggle with myself I accepted you under this dear old tree here. The next day I bought this little ring in your name, and this is the little bangle with the true lovers' knot I promised you always to wear.

ALGERNON. Did I give you this? It's very pretty, isn't it?

CECILY. Yes, you've wonderfully good taste, Ernest. It's the excuse I've always given for your leading such a bad life. And this is the box in which I keep all your dear letters. *(Kneels at table, opens box, and produces letters tied up with blue ribbon.)*

ALGERNON. My letters! But my own sweet Cecily, I have never written you any letters.

CECILY. You need hardly remind me of that, Ernest. I remember only too well that I was forced to write your letters for you. I wrote always three times a week, and sometimes oftener.

ALGERNON. Oh, do let me read them, Cecily?

CECILY. Oh, I couldn't possibly. They would make you far too conceited. *(Replaces box.)* The three you wrote me after I had broken off the engagement are so beautiful, and so badly spelled, that even now I can hardly read them without crying a little.

ALGERNON. But was our engagement ever broken off?

CECILY. Of course it was. On the 22nd of last March. You can see the entry if you like. *(Shows diary.)* "To-day I broke off my engagement with Ernest. I feel it is better to do so. The weather still continues charming."

ALGERNON. But why on earth did you break it off? What had I done? I had done nothing at all. Cecily, I am very much hurt indeed to hear you broke it off. Particularly when the weather was so charming.

CECILY. It would hardly have been a really serious engagement if it hadn't been broken off at least once. But I forgave you before the week was out.

ALGERNON. *(Crossing to her, and kneeling.)* What a perfect angel you are, Cecily.

CECILY. You dear romantic boy. *(He kisses her, she puts her fingers through his hair.)* I hope your hair curls naturally, does it?

ALGERNON. Yes, darling, with a little help from others.

CECILY. I am so glad.

ALGERNON. You'll never break off our engagement again, Cecily?

CECILY. I don't think I could break it off now that I have actually met you. Besides, of course, there is the question of your name.

ALGERNON. Yes, of course. *(Nervously.)*

CECILY. You must not laugh at me, darling, but it had always been a girlish dream of mine to love some one whose name was Ernest. *(Algernon rises, CECILY also.)* There is something in that name that seems to inspire absolute confidence. I pity any poor married woman whose husband is not called Ernest.

ALGERNON. But, my dear child, do you mean to say you could not love me if I had some other name?

CECILY. But what name?

ALGERNON. Oh, any name you like—Algernon—for instance . . .

CECILY. But I don't like the name of Algernon.

ALGERNON. Well, my own dear, sweet, loving little darling, I really can't see why you should object to the name of Algernon. It is not at all a bad name. In fact, it is rather an aristocratic name. Half of the chaps who get into the Bankruptcy Court are called Algernon. But seriously, Cecily . . . *(Moving to her)* . . . if my name was Algy, couldn't you love me?

CECILY. *(Rising.)* I might respect you, Ernest, I might admire your character, but I fear that I should not be able to give you my undivided attention.

ALGERNON. Ahem! Cecily! *(Picking up hat.)* Your Rector here is, I suppose, thoroughly experienced in the practice of all the rites and ceremonials of the Church?

CECILY. Oh yes. Dr. Chasuble is a most learned man. He had never written a single book, so you can imagine how much he knows.

ALGERNON. I must see him at once on a most important christening—I mean on most important business.

CECILY. Oh!

ALGERNON. I shan't be away more than half an hour.

CECILY. Considering that we have been engaged since February the

14th, and that I only met you to-day for the first time, I think it
is rather hard that you should leave me for so long a period as
half an hour. Couldn't you make it twenty minutes?

ALGERNON. I'll be back in no time.

*(Kisses her and rushes down the garden.)*

CECILY. What an impetuous boy he is! I like his hair so much. I must
enter his proposal in my diary.

*(Enter Merriman.)*

MERRIMAN. A Miss Fairfax has just called to see Mr. Worthing. On
very important business Miss Fairfax states.

CECILY. Isn't Mr. Worthing in his library?

MERRIMAN. Mr. Worthing went over in the direction of the Rectory
some time ago.

CECILY. Pray ask the lady to come out here; Mr. Worthing is sure to
be back soon. And you can bring tea.

MERRIMAN. Yes, Miss. *(Goes out.)*

CECILY. Miss Fairfax! I suppose one of the many good elderly
women who are associated with Uncle Jack in some of his philanthropic work in London. I don't quite like women who are interested in philanthropic work. I think it is so forward of them.

*(Enter Merriman.)*

MERRIMAN. Miss Fairfax.

*(Enter Gwendolen.)* *(Exit Merriman.)*

CECILY. *(Advancing to meet her.)* Pray let me introduce myself to you.
My name is Cecily Cardew.

GWENDOLEN. Cecily Cardew? *(Moving to her and shaking hands.)*
What a very sweet name! Something tells me that we are going
to be great friends. I like you already more than I can say. My
first impressions of people are never wrong.

CECILY. How nice of you to like me so much after we have known
each other such a comparatively short time. Pray sit down.

GWENDOLEN. *(Still standing up.)* I may call you Cecily, may I not?

CECILY. With pleasure!

GWENDOLEN. And you will always call me Gwendolen, won't you.

CECILY. If you wish.

GWENDOLEN. Then that is all quite settled, is it not?

CECILY. I hope so. *(A pause. They both sit down together.)*

GWENDOLEN. Perhaps this might be a favourable opportunity for my mentioning who I am. My father is Lord Bracknell. You have never heard of papa, I suppose?

CECILY. I don't think so.

GWENDOLEN. Outside the family circle, papa, I am glad to say, is entirely unknown. I think that is quite as it should be. The home seems to me to be the proper sphere for the man. And certainly once a man begins to neglect his domestic duties he becomes painfully effeminate, does he not? And I don't like that. It makes men so very attractive. Cecily, mamma, whose views on education are remarkably strict, has brought me up to be extremely short-sighted; it is part of her system; so do you mind my looking at you through my glasses?

CECILY. Oh! not at all, Gwendolen. I am very fond of being looked at.

GWENDOLEN. *(After examining Cecily carefully through a lorgnette.)* You are here on a short visit I suppose.

CECILY. Oh no! I live here.

GWENDOLEN. *(Severely.)* Really? Your mother, no doubt, or some female relative of advanced years, resides here also?

CECILY. Oh no! I have no mother, nor, in fact, any relations.

GWENDOLEN. Indeed?

CECILY. My dear guardian, with the assistance of Miss Prism, has the arduous task of looking after me.

GWENDOLEN. Your guardian?

CECILY. Yes, I am Mr. Worthing's ward.

GWENDOLEN. Oh! It is strange he never mentioned to me that he had a ward. How secretive of him! He grows more interesting hourly. I am not sure, however, that the news inspires me with feelings of unmixed delight. *(Rising and going to her.)* I am very fond of you, Cecily; I have liked you ever since I met you! But I am bound to state that now that I know that you are Mr. Worthing's ward, I cannot help expressing a wish you were—well just a little older than you seem to be—and not quite so very alluring in appearance. In fact, if I may speak candidly——

CECILY. Pray do! I think that whenever one has anything unpleasant to say, one should always be quite candid.

GWENDOLEN. Well, to speak with perfect candour, Cecily, I wish that you were fully forty-two, and more than usually plain for your age. Ernest has a strong upright nature. He is the very soul of truth and honour. Disloyalty would be as impossible to him as deception. But even men of the noblest possible moral character are extremely susceptible to the influence of the physical charms of others. Modern, no less then Ancient History, supplies us with many most painful examples of what I refer to. If it were not so, indeed, History would be quite unreadable.

CECILY. I beg your pardon, Gwendolen, did you say Ernest?

GWENDOLEN. Yes.

CECILY. Oh, but it is not Mr. Ernest Worthing who is my guardian. It is his brother—his elder brother.

GWENDOLEN. *(Sitting down again.)* Ernest never mentioned to me that he had a brother.

CECILY. I am sorry to say they have not been on good terms for a long time.

GWENDOLEN. Ah! that accounts for it. And now that I think of it I have never heard any man mention his brother. The subject seems distasteful to most men. Cecily, you have lifted a load from my mind. I was growing almost anxious. It would have been terrible if any cloud had come across a friendship like ours, would it not? Of course you are quite, quite sure that it is not Mr. Ernest Worthing who is your guardian?

CECILY. Quite sure. *(A pause.)* In fact, I am going to be his.

GWENDOLEN. *(Enquiringly.)* I beg your pardon?

CECILY. *(Rather shy and confidingly.)* Dearest Gwendolen, there is no reason why I should make a secret of it to you. Our little county newspaper is sure to chronicle the fact next week. Mr. Ernest Worthing and I are engaged to be married.

GWENDOLEN. *(Quite politely, rising.)* My darling Cecily, I think there must be some slight error. Mr. Ernest Worthing is engaged to me. The announcement will appear in the "Morning Post" on Saturday at the latest.

CECILY. *(Very politely, rising.)* I am afraid you must be under some misconception. Ernest proposed to me exactly ten minutes ago. *(Shows diary.)*

GWENDOLEN. *(Examines diary through her lorgnette carefully.)* It is certainly very curious, for he asked me to be his wife yesterday afternoon at 5:30. If you would care to verify the incident, pray do so. *(Produces diary of her own.)* I never travel without my diary. One should always have something sensational to read in the train. I am so sorry, dear Cecily, if it is any disappointment to you, but I am afraid *I* have the prior claim.

CECILY. It would distress me more than I can tell you, dear Gwendolen, if it caused you any mental or physical anguish, but I feel bound to point out that since Ernest proposed to you he clearly has changed his mind.

GWENDOLEN. *(Meditatively.)* If the poor fellow has been entrapped into any foolish promise I shall consider it my duty to rescue him at once, and with a firm hand.

CECILY. *(Thoughtfully and sadly.)* Whatever unfortunate entanglement my dear boy may have got into, I will never reproach him with it after we are married.

GWENDOLEN. Do you allude to me, Miss Cardew, as an entanglement? You are presumptuous. On an occasion of this kind it becomes more than a moral duty to speak one's mind. It becomes a pleasure.

CECILY. Do you suggest, Miss Fairfax, that I entrapped Ernest into an engagement? How dare you? This is no time for wearing the shallow mask of manners. When I see a spade I call it a spade.

GWENDOLEN. *(Satirically.)* I am glad to say that I have never seen a spade. It is obvious that our social spheres have been widely different.

*(Enter Merriman, followed by the footman. He carries a salver, table cloth, and plate stand. Cecily is about to retort. The presence of the servants exercises a restraining influence, under which both girls chafe.)*

MERRIMAN. Shall I lay tea here as usual, Miss?

CECILY. *(Sternly, in a calm voice.)* Yes, as usual. *(Merriman begins to clear table and lay cloth. A long pause.* CECILY *and Gwendolen glare at each other.)*

GWENDOLEN. Are there many interesting walks in the vicinity, Miss Cardew?

CECILY. Oh! yes! a great many. From the top of one of the hills quite close one can see five counties.

GWENDOLEN. Five counties! I don't think I should like that. I hate crowds.

CECILY. *(Sweetly.)* I suppose that is why you live in town? *(Gwendolen bites her lip, and beats her foot nervously with her parasol.)*

GWENDOLEN. *(Looking round.)* Quite a well-kept garden this is, Miss Cardew.

CECILY. So glad you like it, Miss Fairfax.

GWENDOLEN. I had no idea there were any flowers in the country.

CECILY. Oh, flowers are as common here, Miss Fairfax, as people are in London.

GWENDOLEN. Personally I cannot understand how anybody manages to exist in the country, if anybody who is anybody does. The country always bores me to death.

CECILY. Ah! This is what the newspapers call agricultural depression, is it not? I believe the aristocracy are suffering very much from it just at present. It is almost an epidemic amongst them, I have been told. May I offer you some tea, Miss Fairfax?

GWENDOLEN. *(With elaborate politeness.)* Thank you. *(Aside.)* Detestable girl! But I require tea!

CECILY. *(Sweetly.)* Sugar?

GWENDOLEN. *(Superciliously.)* No, thank you. Sugar is not fashionable any more. *(Cecily looks angrily at her, takes up the tongs and puts four lumps of sugar into the cup.)*

CECILY. *(Severely.)* Cake or bread and butter?

GWENDOLEN. *(In a bored manner.)* Bread and butter, please. Cake is rarely seen at the best houses now-a-days.

CECILY. *(Cuts a very large slice of cake, and puts it on the tray.)* Hand that to Miss Fairfax.

*(Merriman does so, and goes out with footman. Gwendolen drinks the tea*

*and makes a grimace. Puts down cup at once, reaches out her hand to the bread and butter, looks at it, and finds it is cake. Rises in indignation.)*

GWENDOLEN. You have filled my tea with lumps of sugar, and though I asked most distinctly for bread and butter, you have given me cake. I am known for the gentleness of my disposition, and the extraordinary sweetness of my nature, but I warn you, Miss Cardew, you may go too far.

CECILY. *(Rising.)* To save my poor, innocent, trusting boy from the machinations of any other girl there are no lengths to which I would not go.

GWENDOLEN. From the moment I saw you I distrusted you. I felt that you were false and deceitful. I am never deceived in such matters. My first impressions of people are invariably right.

CECILY. It seems to me, Miss Fairfax, that I am trespassing on your valuable time. No doubt you have many other calls of a similar character to make in the neighbourhood.

*(Enter Jack.)*

GWENDOLEN. *(Catching sight of him.)* Ernest! My own Ernest!

JACK. Gwendolen! Darling! *(Offers to kiss her.)*

GWENDOLEN. *(Drawing back.)* A moment! May I ask if you are engaged to be married to this young lady? *(Points to Cecily.)*

JACK. *(Laughing.)* To dear little Cecily! Of course not! What could have put such an idea into your pretty little head?

GWENDOLEN. Thank you. You may! *(Offers her cheek.)*

CECILY. *(Very sweetly.)* I knew there must be some misunderstanding, Miss Fairfax. The gentleman whose arm is at present round your waist is my dear guardian, Mr. John Worthing.

GWENDOLEN. I beg your pardon?

CECILY. This is Uncle Jack.

GWENDOLEN. *(Receding.)* Jack! Oh!

*(Enter Algernon.)*

CECILY. Here is Ernest.

ALGERNON. *(Goes straight over to Cecily without noticing anyone else.)* My own love! *(Offers to kiss her.)*

CECILY. *(Drawing back.)* A moment, Ernest! May I ask you—are you engaged to be married to this young lady?

ALGERNON. *(Looking round.)* To what young lady? Good heavens! Gwendolen!

CECILY. Yes! to good heavens, Gwendolen, I mean to Gwendolen.

ALGERNON. *(Laughing.)* Of course not! What could have put such an idea into your pretty little head?

CECILY. Thank you. *(Presenting her cheek to be kissed.)* You may. *(Algernon kisses her.)*

GWENDOLEN. I felt there was some slight error, Miss Cardew. The gentleman who is now embracing you is my cousin, Mr. Algernon Moncrieff.

CECILY. *(Breaking away from Algernon.)* Algernon Moncrieff! Oh! *(The two girls move towards each other and put their arms round each other's waists as if for protection.)*

CECILY. Are you called Algernon?

ALGERNON. I cannot deny it.

CECILY. Oh!

GWENDOLEN. Is your name really John?

JACK. *(Standing rather proudly.)* I could deny it if I liked. I could deny anything if I liked. But my name certainly is John. It has been John for years.

CECILY. *(To Gwendolen.)* A gross deception has been practised on both of us.

GWENDOLEN. My poor wounded Cecily!

CECILY. My sweet wronged Gwendolen!

GWENDOLEN. *(Slowly and seriously.)* You will call me sister, will you not? *(They embrace. Jack and Algernon groan and walk up and down.)*

CECILY. *(Rather brightly.)* There is just one question I would like to be allowed to ask my guardian.

GWENDOLEN. An admirable idea! Mr. Worthing, there is just one question I would like to be permitted to put to you. Where is your brother Ernest? We are both engaged to be married to your brother Ernest, so it is a matter of some importance to us to know where your brother Ernest is at present.

JACK. *(Slowly and hesitatingly.)* Gwendolen—Cecily—it is very painful for me to be forced to speak the truth. It is the first time in my life that I have ever been reduced to such a painful position, and

I am really quite inexperienced in doing anything of the kind. However I will tell you quite frankly that I have no brother Ernest. I have no brother at all. I never had a brother in my life, and I certainly have not the smallest intention of ever having one in the future.

CECILY. *(Surprised.)* No brother at all?

JACK. *(Cheerily.)* None!

GWENDOLEN. *(Severely.)* Had you never a brother of any kind?

JACK. *(Pleasantly.)* Never. Not even of any kind.

GWENDOLEN. I am afraid it is quite clear, Cecily, that neither of us is engaged to be married to anyone.

CECILY. It is not a very pleasant position for a young girl suddenly to find herself in. Is it?

GWENDOLEN. Let us go into the house. They will hardly venture to come after us there.

CECILY. No, men are so cowardly, aren't they?

*(They retire into the house with scornful looks.)*

JACK. This ghastly state of things is what you call Bunburying, I suppose?

ALGERNON. Yes, and a perfectly wonderful Bunbury it is. The most wonderful Bunbury I have ever had in my life.

JACK. Well, you've no right whatsoever to Bunbury here.

ALGERNON. That is absurd. One has a right to Bunbury anywhere one chooses. Every serious Bunburyist knows that.

JACK. Serious Bunburyist! Good heavens!

ALGERNON. Well, one must be serious about something, if one wants to have any amusement in life. I happen to be serious about Bunburying. What on earth you are serious about I haven't got the remotest idea. About everything, I should fancy. You have such an absolutely trivial nature.

JACK. Well, the only small satisfaction I have in the whole of this wretched business is that your friend Bunbury is quite exploded. You won't be able to run down to the country quite so often as you used to do, dear Algy. And a very good thing too.

ALGERNON. Your brother is a little off colour, isn't he, dear Jack?

You won't be able to disappear to London quite so frequently as your wicked custom was. And not a bad thing either.

JACK. As for your conduct towards Miss Cardew, I must say that your taking in a sweet, simple, innocent girl like that is quite inexcusable. To say nothing of the fact that she is my ward.

ALGERNON. I can see no possible defence at all for your deceiving a brilliant, clever, thoroughly experienced young lady like Miss Fairfax. To say nothing of the fact that she is my cousin.

JACK. I wanted to be engaged to Gwendolen, that is all. I love her.

ALGERNON. Well, I simply wanted to be engaged to Cecily. I adore her.

JACK. There is certainly no chance of your marrying Miss Cardew.

ALGERNON. I don't think there is much likelihood, Jack, of you and Miss Fairfax being united.

JACK. Well, that is no business of yours.

ALGERNON. If it was my business, I wouldn't talk about it. *(Begins to eat muffins.)* It is very vulgar to talk about one's business. Only people like stockbrokers do that, and then merely at dinner parties.

JACK. How can you sit there, calmly eating muffins when we are in this horrible trouble, I can't make out. You seem to me to be perfectly heartless.

ALGERNON. Well, I can't eat muffins in an agitated manner. The butter would probably get on my cuffs. One should always eat muffins quite calmly. It is the only way to eat them.

JACK. I say it's perfectly heartless your eating muffins at all, under the circumstances.

ALGERNON. When I am in trouble, eating is the only thing that consoles me. Indeed, when I am in really great trouble, as anyone who knows me intimately will tell you, I refuse everything except food and drink. At the present moment I am eating muffins because I am unhappy. Besides, I am particularly fond of muffins. *(Rising.)*

JACK. *(Rising.)* Well, that is no reason why you should eat them all in that greedy way. *(Takes muffins from Algernon.)*

ALGERNON. *(Offering tea-cake.)* I wish you would have tea-cake instead. I don't like tea-cake.

JACK. Good heavens! I suppose a man may eat his own muffins in his own garden.

ALGERNON. But you have just said it was perfectly heartless to eat muffins.

JACK. I said it was perfectly heartless of you, under the circumstances. That is a very different thing.

ALGERNON. That may be. But the muffins are the same. *(He seizes the muffin-dish from Jack.)*

JACK. Algy, I wish to goodness you would go.

ALGERNON. You can't possibly ask me to go without having some dinner. It's absurd. I never go without my dinner. No one ever does, except vegetarians and people like that. Besides I have just made arrangements with Dr. Chasuble to be christened at a quarter to six under the name of Ernest.

JACK. My dear fellow, the sooner you give up that nonsense the better. I made arrangements this morning with Dr. Chasuble to be christened myself at 5:30, and I naturally will take the name of Ernest. Gwendolen would wish it. We can't both be christened Ernest. It's absurd. Besides, I have a perfect right to be christened if I like. There is no evidence at all that I ever have been christened by anybody. I should think it extremely probable I never was, and so does Dr. Chasuble. It is entirely different in your case. You have been christened already.

ALGERNON. Yes, but I have not been christened for years.

JACK. Yes, but you have been christened. That is the important thing.

ALGERNON. Quite so. So I know my constitution can stand it. If you are not quite sure about your ever having been christened, I must say I think it rather dangerous your venturing on it now. It might make you very unwell. You can hardly have forgotten that someone very closely connected with you was very nearly carried off this week in Paris by a severe chill.

JACK. Yes, but you said yourself that a severe chill was not hereditary.

ALGERNON. It usen't to be, I know—but I daresay it is now. Science is always making wonderful improvements in things.

JACK. *(Picking up the muffin-dish.)* Oh, that is nonsense; you are always talking nonsense.

ALGERNON. Jack, you are at the muffins again! I wish you wouldn't. There are only two left. *(Takes them.)* I told you I was particularly fond of muffins.

JACK. But I hate tea-cake.

ALGERNON. Why on earth then do you allow tea-cake to be served up for your guests? What ideas you have of hospitality!

JACK. Algernon! I have already told you to go. I don't want you here. Why don't you go!

ALGERNON. I haven't quite finished my tea yet! and there is still one muffin left.

*(Jack groans, and sinks into a chair. Algernon still continues eating.)*

## ACT-DROP

# Third Act

*(Gwendolen and Cecily are at the window, looking out into the garden.)*

GWENDOLEN. The fact that they did not follow us at once into the house, as anyone else would have done, seems to me to show that they have some sense of shame left.

CECILY. They have been eating muffins. That looks like repentance.

GWENDOLEN. *(After a pause.)* They don't seem to notice us at all. Couldn't you cough?

CECILY. But I haven't got a cough.

GWENDOLEN. They're looking at us. What effrontery!

CECILY. They're approaching. That's very forward of them.

GWENDOLEN. Let us preserve a dignified silence.

CECILY. Certainly. It's the only thing to do now.

*(Enter Jack followed by Algernon. They whistle some dreadful popular air from a British Opera.)*

GWENDOLEN. This dignified silence seems to produce an unpleasant effect.

CECILY. A most distasteful one.

GWENDOLEN. But we will not be the first to speak.

CECILY. Certainly not.

GWENDOLEN. Mr. Worthing, I have something very particular to ask you. Much depends on your reply.

CECILY. Gwendolen, your common sense is invaluable. Mr. Moncrieff, kindly answer me the following question. Why did you pretend to be my guardian's brother?

ALGERNON. In order that I might have an opportunity of meeting you.

CECILY. *(To Gwendolen.)* That certainly seems a satisfactory explanation, does it not?

GWENDOLEN. Yes, dear, if you can believe him.

CECILY. I don't. But that does not affect the wonderful beauty of his answer.

GWENDOLEN. True. In matters of grave importance, style, not sincerity is the vital thing. Mr. Worthing, what explanation can you offer to me for pretending to have a brother? Was it in order that you might have an opportunity of coming up to town to see me as often as possible?

JACK. Can you doubt it, Miss Fairfax?

GWENDOLEN. I have the gravest doubts upon the subject. But I intend to crush them. This is not the moment for German scepticism. *(Moving to Cecily.)* Their explanations appear to be quite satisfactory, especially Mr. Worthing's. That seems to me to have the stamp of truth upon it.

CECILY. I am more than content with what Mr. Moncrieff said. His voice alone inspires one with absolute credulity.

GWENDOLEN. Then you think we should forgive them?

CECILY. Yes. I mean no.

GWENDOLEN. True! I had forgotten. There are principles at stake that one cannot surrender. Which of us should tell them? The task is not a pleasant one.

CECILY. Could we not both speak at the same time?

GWENDOLEN. An excellent idea! I nearly always speak at the same time as other people. Will you take the time from me?

CECILY. Certainly. *(Gwendolen beats time with uplifted finger.)*

GWENDOLEN and CECILY. *(Speaking together.)* Your Christian names are still an insuperable barrier. That is all!

JACK and ALGERNON. *(Speaking together.)* Our Christian names! Is that all? But we are going to be christened this afternoon.

GWENDOLEN. *(To Jack.)* For my sake you are prepared to do this terrible thing?

JACK. I am.

CECILY. *(To Algernon.)* To please me you are ready to face this fearful ordeal?

ALGERNON. I am!

GWENDOLEN. How absurd to talk of the equality of the sexes! Where questions of self-sacrifice are concerned, men are infinitely beyond us.

JACK. We are. *(Clasps hands with Algernon.)*

CECILY. They have moments of physical courage of which we women know absolutely nothing.

GWENDOLEN. *(To Jack.)* Darling!

ALGERNON. *(To Cecily.)* Darling! *(They fall into each other's arms.)*

*(Enter Merriman. When he enters he coughs loudly, seeing the situation.)*

MERRIMAN. Ahem! Ahem! Lady Bracknell!

JACK. Good heavens!

*(Enter Lady Bracknell. The couples separate in alarm. Exit Merriman.)*

LADY BRACKNELL. Gwendolen! What does this mean?

GWENDOLEN. Merely that I am engaged to be married to Mr. Worthing, mamma.

LADY BRACKNELL. Come here. Sit down. Sit down immediately. Hesitation of any kind is a sign of mental decay in the young, of physical weakness in the old. *(Turns to Jack.)* Apprised, sir, of my daughter's sudden flight by her trusty maid, whose confidence I purchased by means of a small coin, I followed her at once by a luggage train. Her unhappy father is, I am glad to say, under the impression that she is attending a more than usually lengthy lecture by the University of Extension Scheme on the Influence of a permanent income on Thought. I do not propose to undeceive him. Indeed I have never undeceived him on any question. I would consider it wrong. But of course, you will clearly understand that all communication between yourself and my daughter must cease immediately from this moment. On this point, as indeed on all points, I am firm.

JACK. I am engaged to be married to Gwendolen, Lady Bracknell!

LADY BRACKNELL. You are nothing of the kind, sir. And now, as regards Algernon! . . . Algernon!

ALGERNON. Yes, Aunt Augusta.

LADY BRACKNELL. May I ask if it is in this house that your invalid friend Mr. Bunbury resides?

ALGERNON. *(Stammering.)* Oh! No! Bunbury doesn't live here. Bunbury is somewhere else at present. In fact, Bunbury is dead.

LADY BRACKNELL. Dead! When did Mr. Bunbury die? His death must have been extremely sudden.

ALGERNON. *(Airily.)* Oh! I killed Bunbury this afternoon. I mean poor Bunbury died this afternoon.

LADY BRACKNELL. What did he die of?

ALGERNON. Bunbury? Oh, he was quite exploded.

LADY BRACKNELL. Exploded! Was he the victim of a revolutionary outrage? I was not aware that Mr. Bunbury was interested in social legislation. If so, he is well punished for his morbidity.

ALGERNON. My dear Aunt Augusta, I mean he was found out! The doctors found out that Bunbury could not live, that is what I mean—so Bunbury died.

LADY BRACKNELL. He seems to have had great confidence in the opinion of his physicians. I am glad, however, that he made up his mind at the last to some definite course of action, and acted under proper medical advice. And now that we have finally got rid of this Mr. Bunbury, may I ask, Mr. Worthing, who is that young person whose hand my nephew Algernon is now holding in what seems to me a peculiarly unnecessary manner?

JACK. That lady is Miss Cecily Cardew, my ward. *(Lady Bracknell bows coldly to Cecily.)*

ALGERNON. I am engaged to be married to Cecily, Aunt Augusta.

LADY BRACKNELL. I beg your pardon?

CECILY. Mr. Moncrieff and I are engaged to be married, Lady Bracknell.

LADY BRACKNELL. *(With a shiver, crossing to the sofa and sitting down.)* I do not know whether there is anything peculiarly exciting in the air of this particular part of Hertfordshire, but the number of engagements that go on seems to me considerably above the proper average that statistics have laid down for our guidance. I think some preliminary enquiry on my part would not be out of place. Mr. Worthing, is Miss Cardew at all connected with any of the larger railway stations in London? I merely desire information. Until yesterday I had no idea that there were any families or persons whose origin was a Terminus. *(Jack looks perfectly furious, but restrains himself.)*

JACK. *(In a clear, cold voice.)* Miss Cardew is the granddaughter of the late Mr. Thomas Cardew of 149, Belgrave Square, S.W.; Gervase Park, Dorking, Surrey; and the Sporran, Fifeshire, N.B.

LADY BRACKNELL. That sounds not unsatisfactory. Three addresses always inspire confidence, even in tradesmen. But what proof have I of their authenticity?

JACK. I have carefully preserved the Court Guides of the period. They are open to your inspection, Lady Bracknell.

LADY BRACKNELL. *(Grimly.)* I have known strange errors in that publication.

JACK. Miss Cardew's family solicitors are Messrs. Markby, Markby, and Markby.

LADY BRACKNELL. Markby, Markby, and Markby? A firm of the very highest position in their profession. Indeed I am told that one of the Mr. Markbys is occasionally to be seen at dinner parties. So far I am satisfied.

JACK. *(Very irritably.)* How extremely kind of you, Lady Bracknell! I have also in my possession, you will be pleased to hear, certificates of Miss Cardew's birth, baptism, whooping cough, registration, vaccination, confirmation, and the measles; both the German and the English variety.

LADY BRACKNELL. Ah! A life crowded with incident, I see; though perhaps somewhat too exciting for a young girl. I am not myself in favour of premature experiences. *(Rises, looks at her watch.)* Gwendolen! the time approaches for our departure. We have not a moment to lose. As a matter of form, Mr. Worthing, I had better ask you if Miss Cardew has any little fortune?

JACK. Oh! about a hundred and thirty thousand pounds in the Funds. That is all. Good-bye, Lady Bracknell. So pleased to have seen you.

LADY BRACKNELL. *(Sitting down again.)* A moment, Mr. Worthing. A hundred and thirty thousand pounds! And in the Funds! Miss Cardew seems to me a most attractive young lady, now that I look at her. Few girls of the present day have any really solid qualities, any of the qualities that last, and improve with time. We live, I regret to say, in an age of surfaces. *(To Cecily.)* Come over here, dear. *(Cecily goes across.)* Pretty child! your dress is sadly simple, and your hair seems almost as Nature might have left it. But we can soon alter all that. A thoroughly experienced French maid produces a really marvellous result in a very brief space of time. I remember recommending one to young Lady Lancing, and after three months her own husband did not know her.

JACK. *(Aside.)* And after six months nobody knew her.

LADY BRACKNELL. *(Glares at Jack for a few moments. Then bends, with a practised smile, to Cecily.)* Kindly turn round, sweet child. *(Cecily turns completely round.)* No, the side view is what I want. *(Cecily presents her profile.)* Yes, quite as I expected. There are distinct social possibilities in your profile. The two weak points in our age are its want of principle and its want of profile. The chin a little higher, dear. Style largely depends on the way the chin is worn. They are worn very high, just at present. Algernon!

ALGERNON. Yes, Aunt Augusta!

LADY BRACKNELL. There are distinct social possibilities in Miss Cardew's profile.

ALGERNON. Cecily is the sweetest, dearest, prettiest girl in the whole world. And I don't care twopence about social possibilities.

LADY BRACKNELL. Never speak disrespectfully of Society, Algernon. Only people who can't get into it do that. *(To Cecily.)* Dear child, of course you know that Algernon has nothing but his debts to depend upon. But I do not approve of mercenary marriages. When I married Lord Bracknell I had no fortune of any kind. But I never dreamed for a moment of allowing that to stand in my way. Well, I suppose I must give my consent.

ALGERNON. Thank you, Aunt Augusta.

LADY BRACKNELL. Cecily, you may kiss me!

CECILY. *(Kisses her.)* Thank you, Lady Bracknell.

LADY BRACKNELL. You may also address me as Aunt Augusta for the future.

CECILY. Thank you, Aunt Augusta.

LADY BRACKNELL. The marriage, I think, had better take place quite soon.

ALGERNON. Thank you, Aunt Augusta.

CECILY. Thank you, Aunt Augusta.

LADY BRACKNELL. To speak frankly, I am not in favour of long engagements. They give people the opportunity of finding out each other's character before marriage, which I think is never advisable.

JACK. I beg your pardon for interrupting you, Lady Bracknell, but this engagement is quite out of the question. I am Miss Cardew's guardian, and she cannot marry without my consent until she comes of age. That consent I absolutely decline to give.

LADY BRACKNELL. Upon what grounds may I ask? Algernon is an extremely, I may almost say an ostentatiously, eligible young man. He has nothing, but he looks everything. What more can one desire?

JACK. It pains me very much to have to speak frankly to you, Lady Bracknell, about your nephew, but the fact is that I do not approve at all of his moral character. I suspect him of being untruthful. (*Algernon and Cecily look at him in indignant amazement.*)

LADY BRACKNELL. Untruthful! My nephew Algernon? Impossible! He is an Oxonian.

JACK. I fear there can be no possible doubt about the matter. This afternoon, during my temporary absence in London on an important question of romance, he obtained admission to my house by means of the false pretence of being my brother. Under an assumed name he drank, I've just been informed by my butler, an entire pint bottle of my Perrier-Jouet, Brut, '89; a wine I was specially reserving for myself. Continuing his disgraceful deception, he succeeded in the course of the afternoon in alienating the affections of my only ward. He subsequently stayed to tea, and devoured every single muffin. And what makes his conduct all the more heartless is, that he was perfectly well aware from the first that I have no brother, that I never had a brother, and that I don't intend to have a brother, not even of any kind. I distinctly told him so myself yesterday afternoon.

LADY BRACKNELL. Ahem! Mr. Worthing, after careful consideration I have decided entirely to overlook my nephew's conduct to you.

JACK. That is very generous of you, Lady Bracknell. My own decision, however, is unalterable. I decline to give my consent.

LADY BRACKNELL. *(To Cecily.)* Come here, sweet child. *(Cecily goes over.)* How old are you, dear?

CECILY. Well, I am really only eighteen, but I always admit to twenty when I go to evening parties.

LADY BRACKNELL. You are perfectly right in making some slight alteration. Indeed, no woman should ever be quite accurate about her age. It looks so calculating. . . . *(In a meditative manner.)* Eighteen, but admitting to twenty at evening parties. Well, it will not be very long before you are of age and free from the restraints of tutelage. So I don't think your guardian's consent is, after all, a matter of any importance.

JACK. Pray excuse me, Lady Bracknell, for interrupting you again, but it is only fair to tell you that according to the terms of her grandfather's will Miss Cardew does not come legally of age till she is thirty-five.

LADY BRACKNELL. That does not seem to me to be a grave objection. Thirty-five is a very attractive age. London society is full of women of the very highest birth who have, of their own free choice, remained thirty-five for years. Lady Dumbleton is an instance in point. To my own knowledge she has been thirty-five ever since she arrived at the age of forty, which was many years ago now. I see no reason why our dear Cecily should not be even still more attractive at the age you mention than she is at present. There will be a large accumulation of property.

CECILY. Algy, could you wait for me till I was thirty-five?

ALGERNON. Of course I could, Cecily. You know I could.

CECILY. Yes, I felt it instinctively, but I couldn't wait all that time. I hate waiting even five minutes for anybody. It always makes me rather cross. I am not punctual myself, I know, but I do like punctuality in others, and waiting, even to be married, is quite out of the question.

ALGERNON. Then what is to be done, Cecily?

CECILY. I don't know, Mr. Moncrieff.

LADY BRACKNELL. My dear Mr. Worthing, as Miss Cardew states positively that she cannot wait till she is thirty-five—a remark which I am bound to say seems to me to show a somewhat impatient nature—I would beg of you to reconsider your decision.

JACK. But, my dear Lady Bracknell, the matter is entirely in your own hands. The moment you consent to my marriage with Gwendolen, I will most gladly allow your nephew to form an alliance with my ward.

LADY BRACKNELL. *(Rising and drawing herself up.)* You must be quite aware that what you propose is out of the question.

JACK. Then a passionate celibacy is all that any of us can look forward to.

LADY BRACKNELL. That is not the destiny I propose for Gwendolen. Algernon, of course, can choose for himself. *(Pulls out her watch.)* Come, dear; *(Gwendolen rises)* we have already missed five, if not six, trains. To miss any more might expose us to comment on the platform.

*(Enter Dr. Chasuble.)*

CHASUBLE. Everything is quite ready for the christenings.

LADY BRACKNELL. The christenings, sir! Is not that somewhat premature?

CHASUBLE. *(Looking rather puzzled, and pointing to Jack and Algernon.)* Both these gentlemen have expressed a desire for immediate baptism.

LADY BRACKNELL. At their age? The idea is grotesque and irreligious! Algernon, I forbid you to be baptised. I will not hear of such excesses. Lord Bracknell would be highly displeased if he learned that that was the way in which you wasted your time and money.

CHASUBLE. Am I to understand that there are to be no christenings at all this afternoon?

JACK. I don't think that, as things are now, it would be of much practical value to either of us, Dr. Chasuble.

CHASUBLE. I am grieved to hear such sentiments from you, Mr. Worthing. They savour of the heretical views of the Anabaptists, views that I have completely refuted in four of my unpublished sermons. However, as your present mood seems to be one peculiarly secular, I will return to the church at once. Indeed, I have just been informed by the pew-opener that for the last hour and a half Miss Prism has been waiting for me in the vestry.

LADY BRACKNELL. *(Starting.)* Miss Prism! Did I hear you mention a Miss Prism?

CHASUBLE. Yes, Lady Bracknell. I am on my way to join her.

LADY BRACKNELL. Pray allow me to detain you for a moment. This matter may prove to be one of vital importance to Lord Bracknell and myself. Is this Miss Prism a female of repellent aspect, remotely connected with education?

CHASUBLE. *(Somewhat indignantly.)* She is the most cultivated of ladies, and the very picture of respectability.

LADY BRACKNELL. It is obviously the same person. May I ask what position she holds in your household?

CHASUBLE. *(Severely.)* I am a celibate, madam.

JACK. *(Interposing.)* Miss Prism, Lady Bracknell, has been for the last three years Miss Cardew's esteemed governess and valued companion.

LADY BRACKNELL. In spite of what I hear of her, I must see her at once. Let her be sent for.

CHASUBLE. *(Looking off.)* She approaches; she is nigh.

*(Enter Miss Prism hurriedly.)*

MISS PRISM. I was told you expected me in the vestry, dear Canon. I have been waiting for you there for an hour and three quarters. *(Catches sight of Lady Bracknell who has fixed her with a stony glare. Miss Prism grows pale and quails. She looks anxiously round as if desirous to escape.)*

LADY BRACKNELL. *(In a severe, judicial voice.)* Prism! *(Miss Prism bows her head in shame.)* Come here, Prism! *(Miss Prism approaches in a humble manner.)* Prism! Where is that baby? *(General consternation. The Canon starts back in horror. Algernon and Jack pretend to be anxious to shield Cecily and Gwendolen from hearing the details of a terrible public scandal.)* Twenty-eight years ago, Prism, you left Lord Bracknell's house, Number 104, Upper Grosvenor Street, in charge of a perambulator that contained a baby, of the male sex. You never returned. A few weeks later, through the elaborate investigations of the Metropolitan police, the perambulator was discovered at midnight, standing by itself in a remote corner of Bayswater. It contained the manuscript of a three-volume novel of more than usually revolting sentimentality. *(Miss Prism starts in involuntary indignation.)* But the baby was not there! *(Everyone looks at Miss Prism.)* Prism! Where is that baby? *(A pause.)*

MISS PRISM. Lady Bracknell, I admit with shame that I do not know. I only wish I did. The plain facts of the case are these. On the morning of the day you mention, a day that is for ever branded on my memory, I prepared as usual to take the baby out in its perambulator. I had also with me a somewhat old, but capacious hand-bag in which I had intended to place the manuscript of a work of fiction that I had written during my few unoccupied hours. In a moment of mental abstraction, for which I never can forgive myself, I deposited the manuscript in the bassinette, and placed the baby in the hand-bag.

JACK. *(Who has been listening attentively.)* But where did you deposit the hand-bag?

MISS PRISM. Do not ask me, Mr. Worthing.

JACK. Miss Prism, this is a matter of no small importance to me. I insist on knowing where you deposited the hand-bag that contained that infant.

MISS PRISM. I left it in the cloak room of one of the larger railway stations in London.

JACK. What railway station?

MISS PRISM. *(Quite crushed.)* Victoria. The Brighton line. *(Sinks into a chair.)*

JACK. I must retire to my room for a moment. Gwendolen, wait here for me.

GWENDOLEN. If you are not too long, I will wait here for you all my life.

*(Exit Jack in great excitement.)*

CHASUBLE. What do you think this means, Lady Bracknell?

LADY BRACKNELL. I dare not even suspect, Dr. Chasuble. I need hardly tell you that in families of high position strange coincidences are not supposed to occur. They are hardly considered the thing.

*(Noises heard overhead as if someone was throwing trunks about. Everyone looks up.)*

CECILY. Uncle Jack seems strangely agitated.

CHASUBLE. Your guardian has a very emotional nature.

LADY BRACKNELL. This noise is extremely unpleasant. It sounds as if he was having an argument. I dislike arguments of any kind. They are always vulgar, and often convincing.

CHASUBLE. *(Looking up.)* It has stopped now. *(The noise is redoubled.)*

LADY BRACKNELL. I wish he would arrive at some conclusion.

GWENDOLEN. This suspense is terrible. I hope it will last.

*(Enter Jack with a hand-bag of black leather in his hand.)*

JACK. *(Rushing over to Miss Prism.)* Is this the hand-bag, Miss Prism? Examine it carefully before you speak. The happiness of more than one life depends on your answer.

MISS PRISM. *(Calmly.)* It seems to be mine. Yes, here is the injury it received through the upsetting of a Gower Street omnibus in younger and happier days. Here is the stain on the lining caused by the explosion of a temperance beverage, an incident that occurred at Leamington. And here, on the lock, are my initials. I had forgotten that in an extravagant mood I had had them placed there. The bag is undoubtedly mine. I am delighted to have it so unexpectedly restored to me. It has been a great inconvenience being without it all these years.

JACK. *(In a pathetic voice.)* Miss Prism, more is restored to you than this hand-bag. I was the baby you placed in it.

MISS PRISM. *(Amazed.)* You?

JACK. *(Embracing her.)* Yes . . . mother!

MISS PRISM. *(Recoiling in indignant astonishment.)* Mr. Worthing! I am unmarried!

JACK. Unmarried! I do not deny that is a serious blow. But after all, who has the right to cast a stone against one who has suffered?

Cannot repentance wipe out an act of folly? Why should there be one law for men, and another for women? Mother, I forgive you. *(Tries to embrace her again.)*

MISS PRISM. *(Still more indignant.)* Mr. Worthing, there is some error. *(Pointing to Lady Bracknell.)* There is the lady who can tell you who you really are.

JACK. *(After a pause.)* Lady Bracknell, I hate to seem inquisitive, but would you kindly inform me who I am?

LADY BRACKNELL. I am afraid that the news I have to give you will not altogether please you. You are the son of my poor sister, Mrs. Moncrieff, and consequently Algernon's elder brother.

JACK. Algy's elder brother! Then I have a brother after all. I knew I had a brother! I always said I had a brother! Cecily,—how could you have ever doubted that I had a brother. *(Seizes hold of Algernon.)* Dr. Chasuble, my unfortunate brother. Miss Prism, my unfortunate brother. Gwendolen, my unfortunate brother. Algy, you young scoundrel, you will have to treat me with more respect in the future. You have never behaved to me like a brother in all your life.

ALGERNON. Well, not till to-day, old boy, I admit. I did my best, however, though I was out of practice. *(Shakes hands.)*

GWENDOLEN. *(To Jack.)* My own! But what own are you? What is your Christian name, now that you have become someone else?

JACK. Good heavens! . . . I had quite forgotten that point. Your decision on the subject of my name is irrevocable, I suppose?

GWENDOLEN. I never change, except in my affections.

CECILY. What a noble nature you have, Gwendolen!

JACK. Then the question had better be cleared up at once. Aunt Augusta, a moment. At the time when Miss Prism left me in the hand-bag, had I been christened already?

LADY BRACKNELL. Every luxury that money could buy, including christening, had been lavished on you by your fond and doting parents.

JACK. Then I was christened! That is settled. Now, what name was I given? Let me know the worst.

LADY BRACKNELL. Being the eldest son you were naturally christened after your father.

JACK. *(Irritably.)* Yes, but what was my father's Christian name?

LADY BRACKNELL. *(Meditatively.)* I cannot at the present moment recall what the General's Christian name was. But I have no doubt he had one. He was eccentric, I admit. But only in later years. And that was the result of the Indian climate, and marriage, and indigestion, and other things of that kind.

JACK. Algy! Can't you recollect what our father's Christian name was?

ALGERNON. My dear boy, we were never even on speaking terms. He died before I was a year old.

JACK. His name would appear in the Army Lists of the period, I suppose, Aunt Augusta?

LADY BRACKNELL. The General was essentially a man of peace, except in his domestic life. But I have no doubt his name would appear in any military directory.

JACK. The Army Lists of the last forty years are here. These delightful records should have been my constant study. *(Rushes to bookcase and tears the books out.)* M. Generals . . . Mallam, Maxbohm, Magley, what ghastly names they have—Markby, Migsby, Mobbs, Moncreiff! Lieutenant 1840, Captain, Lieutenant-Colonel, Colonel, General 1869, Christian names, Ernest John. *(Puts book very quietly down and speaks quite calmly.)* I always told you, Gwendolen, my name was Ernest, didn't I? Well, it is Ernest after all. I mean it naturally is Ernest.

LADY BRACKNELL. Yes, I remember now that the General was called Ernest. I knew I had some particular reason for disliking the name.

GWENDOLEN. Ernest! My own Ernest! I felt from the first that you could have no other name!

JACK. Gwendolen, it is a terrible thing for a man to find out suddenly that all his life he has been speaking nothing but the truth. Can you forgive me?

GWENDOLEN. I can. For I feel that you are sure to change.

JACK. My own one!

CHASUBLE. *(To Miss Prism.)* Lætitia! *(Embraces her.)*

MISS PRISM. *(Enthusiastically.)* Frederick! At last!

ALGERNON. Cecily! *(Embraces her.)* At last!

JACK. Gwendolen! *(Embraces her.)* At last!

LADY BRACKNELL. My nephew, you seem to be displaying signs of triviality.

JACK. On the contrary, Aunt Augusta, I've now realized for the first time in my life the vital Importance of Being Earnest.

### TABLEAU

### CURTAIN

# NOTES

## LADY WINDERMERE'S FAN
### FIRST ACT

P. 9, LL. 1–2. *Carlton House Terrace:* a prestigious London address, like most addresses mentioned in Wilde's society comedies. This one lies in the St. James's district of London, an area associated with politics and elite men's clubs.

L. 22. *Selby:* the Windermeres' country home.

P. 10, L. 2. *"I'm of age to-day":* Lady Windermere is turning twenty-one.

P. 11, L. 29. *Puritan:* Lady Windermere's usage, in keeping with ours today, styles her as moralistic and as averse to worldly pleasures. The term originally indicated a fundamentalist Protestant offshoot from the established Church of England.

P. 15, L. 11. *trick:* a reference to the card game of bridge, then in fashion.

P. 17, L. 26. *Mayfair:* a highly fashionable London district; *ponies in the Park:* Wealthy individuals from elite society rode their horses in London's Hyde Park.

L. 33. *Homburg . . . Aix:* continental resort towns.

P. 18, L. 25. *a character:* a general letter of introduction and recommendation.

P. 19, L. 26. Exeunt: plural of *exit.*

P. 20, L. 5. *£600:* a very substantial amount of money. In 1892, when *Lady Windermere's Fan* premiered, £600 was roughly equivalent to £37,000 today (or approximately $60,000). That figure is according to an Internet-based calculator hosted by Economic History Services:

<http://eh.net/hmit/ppowerbp/pound_question.php>. Note, however, that money values at different times are only roughly comparable, owing to technological developments which bring about changes in "normal" standards of living, and in the relative costs of various categories of goods and services.

## Second Act

P. 25, L. 9. *your card:* a card listing planned dances, according to which an eligible young woman could list the man who would partner her at each dance.

L. 13. *younger sons:* not the most desirable dance partners, because only first sons stood to inherit family wealth.

P. 30, L. 35. *thinks like a Tory and talks like a Radical:* Tories are broadly conservative, associated with traditionalism, nobility, and landed wealth, while Radicals are associated with reform, democratization, and change.

P. 31, LL. 19–20. *an edition de luxe of a wicked French novel:* While British Victorian novelists were constrained in the subject matter that they could represent, French novelists such as Flaubert and Zola routinely ventured into much racier terrain, such as adultery and prostitution.

P. 36, L. 18. *Grosvenor Square:* an elegant address, so much so that the Duchess's characterization of its denizens as "vulgar" actually underscores her extreme haughtiness.

## Third Act

P. 42, LL. 3–4. *syphons:* small-gauge hoses used to decant fine wines without carrying sediment from the original bottle; *Tantalus frame:* a stand on which wine or brandy decanters can be seen plainly but cannot be withdrawn until a locked bar that connects to the stoppers is released, thus "tantalizing" onlookers; *cigar and cigarette box:* like the foregoing items, a standard accessory in a bachelor gentleman's apartment.

P. 49, L. 13. *Wiesbaden:* an elegant spa and casino town in Germany.

LL. 20–22. *threw their caps over the mills . . . raise the wind:* Dumby mixes two colloquial expressions. "Throwing one's cap over a mill" indicates hardworking ambition and sometimes a touch of recklessness, while "raising the wind" means procuring money.

P. 50, L. 28. *Nonconformist:* here, refers to a moralistic refusal of established social norms. More specifically, Nonconformists were Protestants who refused to observe certain ritual practices within the Church of

England and thereby became ineligible for various privileges and governmental careers.

FOURTH ACT

P. 59, L. 33. *Club Train:* a deluxe train to the Continent via ferry over the English Channel.


## AN IDEAL HUSBAND
FIRST ACT

p. 81, L. 1. *Grosvenor Square:* a prestigious address in Mayfair, London.

LL. 7–8: Triumph of Love, from a design by Boucher: François Boucher (1703–70), a French artist who completed his classically inspired *Triumph of Love* (also known as *Triumph of Venus*) in the 1730s.

L. 12. *Louis Seize sofa:* a sofa hearkening back to the reign of Louis XVI, king of France in the period that brought about the French Revolution in 1789. Like the other features of the Sir Robert's house, the decor suggests continental refinement rather than proud English insularity.

L. 13. *Watteau:* Jean-Antoine Watteau (1684–1721), French rococo painter noted for scenes depicting elegantly costumed ladies and gentlemen at play outdoors.

P. 82, LL. 16–17. *star of the Garter:* a noble military badge; *Whig:* an actual political party until the mid-nineteenth century, known as a progressive force of opposition to the conservative Tories. To use the term *Whig* in Wilde's time is to conjure a figure that is progressive but also securely part of the Establishment; *Lawrence:* Sir Thomas Lawrence (1769–1830), an English painter noted for political portraits at a time when the Whig party was in its heyday.

LL. 28–29. *Tanagra statuette:* a small terra-cotta human figure, characteristically associated with fifth to third century B.C. examples found near the Greek city of Tanagra. Typically, the figures are thinly draped female dancers.

L. 32. *the Row:* the so-called "Rotten Row" in Hyde Park, where the fashionable rode their horses.

P. 83, L. 9. *milliner:* a person, generally a woman, who makes fashionable articles of apparel, especially hats.

L. 24. *hair à la marquise:* a woman's hairstyle associated with pre-revolutionary France, hence in keeping with much of the decorative detail in this Act.

L. 29. *heliotrope:* A shade of purple characteristic of the flower by this name.

P. 85, L. 13. *House of Commons:* the lower house of Parliament in Great Britain.

L. 14. *Vandyck:* Sir Anthony Van Dyck (1599–1641), Flemish painter.

P. 86, L. 35. *blue spectacles:* in the Victorian period, the term *blue* had come to include senses such as *sad* and *depressed,* and it seems that Mrs. Cheveley draws on these senses in opposing the pessimist's view to the optimist's broad grin.

P. 88, L. 3. *Our season:* the annual period of London-based society gatherings that gained momentum in December, accelerated after Easter, and wound down in August when wealthy families headed to the countryside for hunting season.

L. 17. *Corots:* Jean-Baptiste-Camille Corot (1796–1875), French landscape painter.

LL. 29–30. *Penelope:* the Greek wife who faithfully waited decades as her husband Odysseus wended his way home from the Trojan War. In styling Penelope as a "disadvantage" to the worldly man, Mrs. Cheveley is directing yet another volley at marriage.

L. 34. *dandy:* a man primarily concerned with manners, elegance, and fashionable attire; a fop; *romantic:* emphasizing authenticity and genuine feeling, thus too artless and direct to suit the dandified Lord Goring.

P. 91, L. 22. *House:* The House of Commons typically convened in the afternoon and often ran until after midnight with speeches.

P. 92, L. 31. *dowdies:* shabbily or drably attired women.

P. 95, L. 13. *Suez Canal:* Linking the Mediterranean and the Red Sea, the Suez Canal was opened in 1869. In 1875, the British acted on economic and political concerns by purchasing a controlling interest in the Canal.

L. 27. *a second Panama:* a reference to the canal project that had recently stalled following revelations of corruption.

P. 98, L. 22. *Puritanism:* smug moralism. *See note for p. 11, l. 29.*

P. 100, L. 1. *Ladies' Gallery:* a viewing area for women observing the proceedings of the House of Commons.

P. 102, LL. 6–7. *Claridge's:* an elegant hotel.

L. 11. en règle: according to the "rule" or norm (French). Mrs. Cheveley understands that ladies abroad can leave their card to a man, but ladies in England would seem forward in doing so.

L. 29. *Royal Academy:* the most prestigious school of art and exhibition gallery in London.

P. 104, L. 10. *mauve Hungarian music:* mauve is a hue of purple associated with 1890s aestheticism and, by many accounts, with a male homosexual subculture at the time. A very frequent color reference in Wilde's writings, this instance plays with the strangeness of attributing color to music. In that respect, Lord Goring recalls the idea of sense-blending, or synesthesia, that English and French writers in the aestheticist mode had played with for decades.

## SECOND ACT

P. 110, L. 36. *twenty-two at the time:* Assuming that the play is set in the mid-1890s, the "present" of its audience, Sir Robert's deal with Baron Arnheim would appear to have been made in the mid-1870s, contemporary with the British purchase into the Suez Canal (*see note for p. 95, l. 13*). Wilde's stage direction in the First Act tells us that Chiltern is now "a man of forty" (p. 85, l. 1).

P. 112, L. 13. *Park Lane:* elegant address in Mayfair.

P. 113, L. 21. *£110,000:* equivalent to about £5 million today, or $8 million in U.S. currency. Regarding such money conversions, however, *see note for p. 20, l. 5.*

P. 116, L. 5. *cipher:* encoded.

P. 117, L. 9. décolleté: indicating a woman's dress cut low over the bosom. Here the figurative sense is one of Continental raciness.

LL. 23–24. *Woman's Liberal Association:* Wilde seems to have in mind an organization founded in the 1880s to offer women a forum for political activity. When Wilde was working up this play, from 1893 to 1895, the organization was very active, though increasingly divided over questions of female suffrage and, soon, the Boer War. By the end of the 1890s, the Women's Liberal Federation and the Women's National Liberal Association named respectively more and less radical wings of the original entity.

L. 36–P. 118, LL. 1–2. *Factory Acts, Female Inspectors, the Eight Hours' Bill, the Parliamentary Franchise:* various contemporary reforms promoted by liberal thinkers and politicians.

P. 118, L. 24. *Bachelors' Ball:* a fixture event in the social season.

P. 120, L. 23. *German philosophy:* Although generally associated by the English with abstruse idealism, the reference here to German philosophy as pessimistic suggests more specifically the views of Arthur Schopenhauer (1788–1860).

P. 121, L. 17. *The Morning Post:* a daily newspaper.

P. 122, L. 27. *bimetallist:* comically, Mabel Chiltern has grasped at a then-current political debate over whether and how to define a monetary standard using both gold and silver. This is the historical period during which a single-metal gold standard was emerging to facilitate international economy.

P. 123, L. 18. *tableaux:* Also called *tableaux vivants* or "living pictures" (French), these entertainments featured people dressing up and holding a group pose in emulation of a painting or a historical scene; *Triumph of something:* The opening stage direction indicated a French tapestry in the Chiltern home depicting the *Triumph of Love* by Boucher. *See note for p. 81, ll. 7–8.*

P. 126, L. 7. *Bath:* spa town in England.

LL. 13–14. *Higher Education of Women:* Since around 1850, women in increasing numbers had been able to attend British colleges and universities, although at traditional institutions women were limited in their ability to earn regular degrees well into the twentieth century.

P. 127, L. 10. *Upper House:* the hereditary House of Lords in Parliament.

L. 21. *Blue Books:* governmental publications.

L. 25. *yellow covers:* Racy continental novels were sold in yellow paper wraps.

THIRD ACT

P. 134, L. 1. *Adams room:* a room in elegant neoclassical style, after Robert Adams (1728–92), a Scottish architect who was also noted for his interiors. A surviving example of his interior work is Kenwood House in Hampstead Heath.

L. 6. *Sphinx:* Both Greek and Egyptian mythologies tell of this creature with the head of a woman and the body of a winged lion. The Greek version dramatized by Sophocles in *Oedipus Rex* tells of a sphinx that destroys all those who fail to answer its riddle. Wilde often referred to sphinxes in his writings and in his private life.

L. 14. *buttonhole:* a flower or small spray of flowers worn by men in a lapel buttonhole.

P. 139, L. 16. *Lamia-like:* Lamia is a fatal sorceress known for sucking the blood of children. The romantic poet John Keats wrote a famous poem by this name in 1819.

P. 142, L. 34. *hock:* a German white wine.

P. 147, L. 31. *gout:* an illness involving painfully swollen joints, associated especially with wealthy individuals because it was understood to be brought about by high levels of meat consumption.

P. 148, L. 35. *Book of Numbers:* In referring to this book of the Old Testament, which is devoted to lineages, Lord Goring has in mind at least the two marriages of Mrs. Cheveley and perhaps insinuates that she has "known" more than two men along the way.

P. 150, LL. 9–10. Voilà tout: "That is all" (French).

FOURTH ACT

P. 156, L. 29. *Canning:* George Canning (1770–1827), notable politician and, in 1827, prime minister.

P. 159, LL. 12–13. *Downing Street:* residence of the prime minister in Westminster, London.

# THE IMPORTANCE OF BEING EARNEST

FIRST ACT

P. 183, L. 1. *Half-Moon Street:* in Mayfair, London, an elegant residential neighborhood.

L. 15. *salver:* A small tray used in wealthy households to present refreshments, letters, cards, and so forth.

P. 184, L. 32. *Shropshire:* a west-midland county of England.

P. 186, L. 24. *Scotland Yard:* headquarters of the Metropolitan Police in London, especially its detective branch.

P. 187, L. 15. *Tunbridge Wells:* here presumably meant to indicate a respectable but unexciting community. It is east of London, in Kent.

P. 188, L. 3. *The Albany:* a bachelor residence near the Royal Academy, a short walk up Piccadilly from Algernon's dwelling on Half-Moon Street.

L. 17. *Bunburyist:* although Bunbury was an actual, if uncommon, surname in Wilde's period, the term operates here as a provocative and playful coinage. Given that bum is low English slang for buttocks, an uncanny valence of male homosexual erotics permeates Algernon's ostensibly innocent term for his double life.

P. 189, L. 31. *Willis's:* an upscale restaurant near the theater district.

P. 192, L. 8. *ready money:* money paid in cash on the spot as opposed to on an account.

P. 193, L. 26. *German sounds a thoroughly respectable language:* German seems here to play the boring cousin to French, which is consistently associated with raciness. *See note for p. 206, l. 6.*

P. 195, L. 8. *domesticity:* a name used about the house, an informality.

P. 197, L. 15. *Grosvenor Square:* a very affluent address in Mayfair, London, and therefore not a place that the mobs would normally find themselves. Lady Bracknell's image is therefore one of anarchy loosed amid the wealthy.

L. 17. *Between seven and eight thousand a year:* Eight thousand pounds in the 1890s was equivalent to approximately £500,000 or $800,000 today. Regarding such money conversions, however, *see note for p. 20, l. 5.*

L. 35. *Belgrave Square:* a very good address in the Belgravia district of London, south of Hyde Park's eastern end—a bit farther away from the Mayfair and theater district addresses than are most of the fashionable residences referenced throughout Wilde's play; *let:* rented out.

P. 198, L. 13. *Liberal Unionist:* in effect, a conservative liberal. A political crisis in the late 1880s turned on whether to grant "Home Rule," or self-government, to Ireland. The Liberal prime minister Gladstone had advocated that step, thus forcing those Liberals who opposed him to define themselves as Unionists, advocating a united rather than a divided Britain.

L. 13. *Tories:* conservatives of the Tory party.

P. 199, L. 5. *Victoria Station:* one of London's major train stations, primarily for trains setting out to southern locations such as Brighton.

L. 14. *contempt for the ordinary decencies of family life . . . worst excesses of the French Revolution:* Throughout the nineteenth century, conservative Britons ritually invoked the French Revolution as a figure for regrettable anarchism, but Lady Bracknell's reference to "family life" is a more specific—and darkly comic—reference to the mob's invasion of the royal family's residence in Paris on October 6, 1789.

P. 200, LL. 1–2. *Wedding March:* In Wilde's time, both Richard Wagner's music from *Lohengrin* (1850) and Felix Mendelssohn's music for *A Midsummer Night's Dream* (1843) were familiar in English wedding contexts, although the protocol of playing Wagner on the way in and Mendelssohn on the way out was perhaps less fixed than it is today, and Algernon might play either here.

L. 11. *Gorgon:* a repulsive woman, very generally, but the term indicates more specifically any of three Greek mythological females with snakes for hair. To look upon a Gorgon would turn the beholder into stone.

P. 201, L. 20. *apoplexy:* generally indicating what we today call a stroke.

P. 202, L. 21. *Empire:* A step down in social manners from the Club, the Empire was a Leicester Square theater that staged mime shows and dances, most deemed unsuitable for women, and the environs of the theater were known for male and female prostitution.

## SECOND ACT

P. 205, L. 6. *utilitarian:* Miss Prism uses the term as a synonym for practical or mundane activity. Wilde himself knew the term's more elaborated social-philosophical usage, in which *utilitarianism* indicates a program of rational analysis aimed at creating social reforms according to their ability to serve the greatest good for the greatest number of people. For literary writers from Charles Dickens to Wilde, utilitarianism was often a byword for excessively arid and analytical perspectives on human and social experience. In this passage as in several others in this Act, Wilde suggests that Miss Prism and Cecily are each a bit out of their depth in their usage of terms. *See also following note.*

P. 206, L. 6. *German, and geology:* Cecily and Miss Prism view these two areas of study variously as innocuous, boring, or morally improving, but Wilde is inviting us to recognize as well two of the most culturally explosive topics of the period. Historical scholarship in German made the first powerful case for the Bible as a piecemeal text brought to its current form by mundane routes of historical transmission rather than by divine inspiration; meanwhile, geological evidence had confronted Victorians with disturbingly concrete evidence that the age of the earth radically exceeded the four thousand years or so that a literalist reading of the Bible suggested.

L. 25. *Mudie:* a famous lending library of the period.

P. 207, L. 28. *Egeria:* a tutelary goddess of Roman mythology.

P. 208, LL. 2–3. *Political Economy:* the study of economy on a scientific basis, incorporating theories of sociality, human nature, and politics; *Fall of the Rupee:* The rupee, the monetary unit of India, had declined steadily after 1875, when British imperial aspirations in India began to be more emphatic and intrusive.

L. 25. *cousin:* In addressing his pretended niece Cecily this way, Algernon calls on a looser sense of *cousin* that includes any collateral relative more distant than a brother or sister.

P. 209, L. 28. *Australia:* Although once a penal colony and place of last resort for Britons at loose ends, Australia was no longer exactly that in

Wilde's time. All the same, literary works could still bank on that history by styling Australia as the ultimate backwater and exile from society.

P. 210, L. 6. *Quixotic:* characterized by striving after a lofty vision, especially if the vision is false or unrealizable; after the protagonist of the novel *Don Quixote* (1605, 1615) by Miguel de Cervantes.

L. 13. *button-hole:* a flower or small spray of flowers worn by men in a lapel buttonhole.

L. 15. *Maréchale Niel:* also Marachel Niel, a variety of rose. This rose is yellow, exquisite, and not very hardy—in keeping with familiar preoccupations of the aesthetically attuned in Wilde's time.

P. 212, L. 16. *manna:* a food miraculously supplied to the Children of Israel during their progress through the wilderness. See Exodus 16.

P. 215, L. 30. *dog-cart:* a fashionable open carriage, evolved from any of several styles that had enclosed spaces in which sportsmen could bring along their hounds.

P. 222, LL. 8–9. *The home . . . proper sphere for the man:* Gwendolen reverses the then-familiar sentiment that women were properly active within the home while men were creatures of public life and money-making.

L. 17. *lorgnette:* a pair of eyeglasses held up by means of a handle, frequently with magnifying lenses for use at the opera or theater.

P. 223, L. 35. *Morning Post:* a daily newspaper that emphasized the doings of the fashionable.

P. 224, L. 31. *footman:* a uniformed servant, especially one who attends carriages.

THIRD ACT

P. 236, L. 1. *Terminus:* in conventional Victorian usage, the end-stop of a train line or tram line. It was not common usage, however, to capitalize the word as Wilde here does. With an eye to the homoerotic subtext of this play, readers can plausibly see an anal imagery in Wilde's subtle highlighting of the term—the rectum understood as "terminus" of the gastrointestinal tract. *See also note for p. 188, l. 17.*

L. 9. *Court Guides:* a list of society individuals who have been presented to the English royalty court.

LL. 30–31. *a hundred and thirty thousand pounds. . . . in the Funds:* The Funds were investment-grade shares in the National Debt, thus a fluid and modern way of holding one's wealth and also congenial to Lady Bracknell, given her earlier declaration to Jack that wealth in land is burdensome by comparison (see p. 197, ll. 23–35). The amount of Cecily's wealth is immense, the equivalent of some £8.5 million or $13 million today. Regarding such money conversions, however, *see note for p. 20, l. 5.*

P. 238, L. 22. *Oxonian:* a graduate of Oxford, from which university Wilde himself had graduated.

P. 239, L. 13. *not be very long before you are of age:* Lady Bracknell is assuming that Cecily will be legally independent at 21 years of age.

P. 240, L. 36. *Anabaptists:* Chasuble's implication is obscure. He draws on the general association of Protestant dissenters with a "heretical" repudiation of Anglican views on the sacraments and holy orders. Anabaptists in particular are named for their practice of supplementary baptism, either as a ritual or as a one-time event aimed at remedying an infantile baptism deemed ineffective because involuntary.

P. 242, L. 2. *perambulator:* a baby carriage.

L. 6. *Bayswater:* a region in west central London, but also quite some way from Victoria Station.

P. 243, L. 20. *Gower Street omnibus:* a horse-drawn public conveyance operating in the area of Gower Street, in a part of London called Bloomsbury which is associated with education and learning.

L. 22. *temperance:* word used by a movement devoted to the elimination of drunkenness.

L. 23. *Leamington:* an English spa town.

## A NOTE ON THE TYPE

The principal text of this Modern Library edition
was set in a digitized version of Janson, a typeface that
dates from about 1690 and was cut by Nicholas Kis,
a Hungarian working in Amsterdam. The original matrices have
survived and are held by the Stempel foundry in Germany.
Hermann Zapf redesigned some of the weights and sizes for
Stempel, basing his revisions on the original design.

OTHER MODERN LIBRARY PAPERBACK CLASSICS
BY OSCAR WILDE

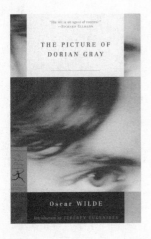

## The Picture of Dorian Gray

INTRODUCTION BY
JEFFREY EUGENIDES

Includes newly commissioned endnotes

*0-375-75151-3; trade paperback; 272 pp.*

## De Profundis

PREFACE BY RICHARD ELLMANN

Includes newly commissioned endnotes

*0-679-78321-0; trade paperback; 160 pp.*

*Available at bookstores everywhere*
www.modernlibrary.com